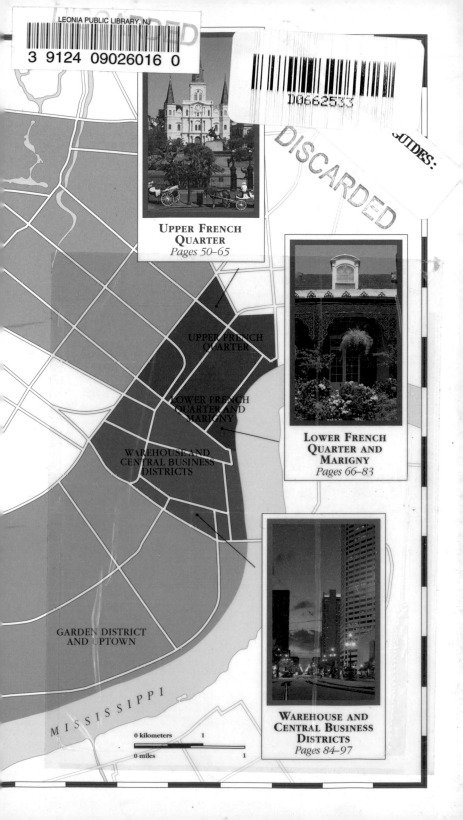

D0662533

GUIDES:

UPPER FRENCH QUARTER
Pages 50–65

LOWER FRENCH QUARTER AND MARIGNY
Pages 66–83

WAREHOUSE AND CENTRAL BUSINESS DISTRICTS
Pages 84–97

UPPER FRENCH QUARTER

LOWER FRENCH QUARTER AND MARIGNY

WAREHOUSE AND CENTRAL BUSINESS DISTRICTS

GARDEN DISTRICT AND UPTOWN

MISSISSIPPI

0 kilometers   1

0 miles   1

EYEWITNESS *TRAVEL GUIDES*

NEW ORLEANS

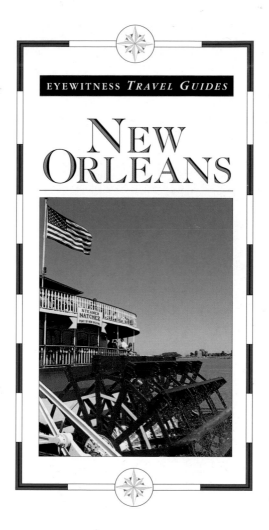

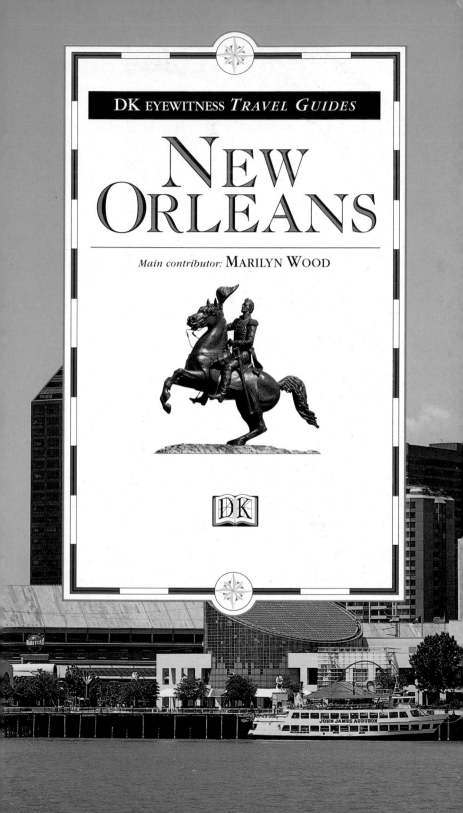

DK EYEWITNESS *TRAVEL GUIDES*

NEW ORLEANS

Main contributor: MARILYN WOOD

DK

LONDON • NEW YORK • MUNICH
MELBOURNE • DELHI

PROJECT EDITOR Alejandro Lajud
PROJECT CO-ORDINATOR Luis Guillermo Coda Garrido
ART EDITOR Victor Hugo Garnica
EDITORS Maria Isabel Amador, Karla Sánchez
DESIGNERS Carlos Muñoz, Alejandro Lajud, Victor Hugo Garnica

Dorling Kindersley Limited
SENIOR PUBLISHING MANAGER Louise Bostock Lang
PUBLISHING MANAGER Kate Poole
DIRECTOR OF PUBLISHING Gillian Allan
EDITORS Stephanie Driver, Mary Sutherland, Andrew Szudek
MAP CO-ORDINATORS David Pugh, Casper Morris
DTP CO-ORDINATORS Jason Little, Conrad van Dyk
PRODUCTION CONTROLLER Joanna Bull

MAIN CONTRIBUTOR
Marilyn Wood

MAPS
Ben Bowles, Rob Clynes and James Macdonald at Mapping Ideas Ltd

PHOTOGRAPHERS
Julio Rochon, Jaime Baldovinos

ILLUSTRATORS
Ricardo Almazan, Ricardo Almazan Jr.

Reproduced by Colourscan, Singapore
Printed and bound by Graphicom, Italy

First American Edition, 2002
02 03 04 05 10 9 8 7 6 5 4 3 2 1

Published in the United States by DK Publishing, Inc.,
375 Hudson Street, New York, New York 10014

Library of Congress Cataloging-in-Publication Data

Wood, Marilyn, 1948
New Orleans / main contributor, Marilyn Wood.
p. cm. -- (Eyewitness travel guides)
Includes index.
1. New Orleans (La.)—Guidebooks. I. Title. II. Series.

F379.N53 W66 2001
917.63'350464—dc21   0789480239

See our complete product line at
www.dk.com

**The information in this
DK Eyewitness Travel Guide is checked continually.**
Every effort has been made to ensure that this book is as up-to-
date as possible at the time of going to press. Some details,
however, such as telephone numbers, opening hours, prices,
gallery hanging arrangements, and travel information are liable to
change. The publishers cannot accept responsibility for any
consequences arising from the use of this book. We value the
views and suggestions of our readers very highly. Please write to:
Publisher, DK Eyewitness Travel Guides, Dorling Kindersley,
80 Strand, London WC2R 0RL, Great Britain.

◁ **View of the Central Business District from the Mississippi River**

CONTENTS

**New Orleans ironwork, Lower
French Quarter**

INTRODUCING
NEW ORLEANS

**The bustling Central
Business District**

Romanesque mansion in the Garden District

Preservation Hall, one of New Orleans' best jazz venues

Crawfish, a popular New Orleans seafood dish

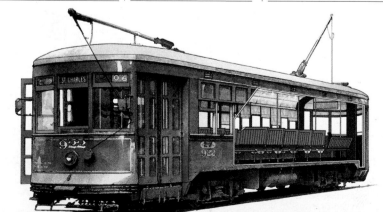

St. Charles Avenue streetcar

HOW TO USE THIS GUIDE

THIS DORLING KINDERSLEY EYEWITNESS travel guide helps you to get the most from your visit to New Orleans. It provides detailed information and expert recommendations.

The chapter titled *Introducing New Orleans* maps the city and the region, and sets it in its historical and cultural context; it also describes the most salient events of the year. *New Orleans at a Glance* is an overview of the city's main attractions. *New Orleans Area by Area* starts on page 44. This is the main

sightseeing section, and it covers all of the important sights, with photographs, maps and illustrations. *Beyond New Orleans* covers nearby Cajun Country, as well as the historic plantations.

Information about hotels, restaurants, shops and markets, entertainment, and sports is found in *Travelers' Needs*. The *Survival Guide* section has advice on everything from using New Orleans' medical services, telephones, banking, and post offices to the public transportation system.

FINDING YOUR WAY AROUND NEW ORLEANS

The city has been divided into five sightseeing areas, each with its own section in the guide. Each section opens with a portrait of the area, summing up its character and history, and listing all the sights to be covered. The sights are

numbered and clearly located on an *Area Map*. After this comes a *Street-by-Street Map* focusing on the most interesting part of the area. Finding your way about the area section is made easy by a numbering system.

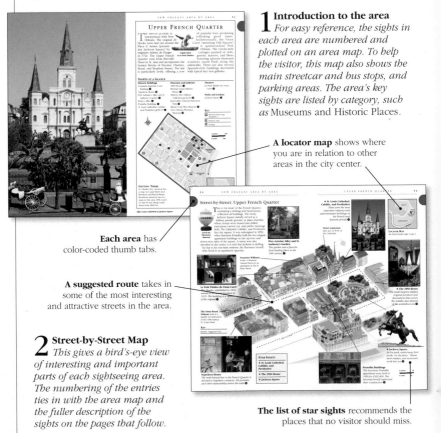

1 Introduction to the area
For easy reference, the sights in each area are numbered and plotted on an area map. To help the visitor, this map also shows the main streetcar and bus stops, and parking areas. The area's key sights are listed by category, such as Museums and Historic Places.

A locator map shows where you are in relation to other areas in the city center.

Each area has color-coded thumb tabs.

A suggested route takes in some of the most interesting and attractive streets in the area.

2 Street-by-Street Map
This gives a bird's-eye view of interesting and important parts of each sightseeing area. The numbering of the entries ties in with the area map and the fuller description of the sights on the pages that follow.

The list of star sights recommends the places that no visitor should miss.

NEW ORLEANS AREA MAP

The colored areas shown on this map *(see inside front cover)* are the five main sightseeing areas used in this guide. Each is covered in a full chapter in *New Orleans Area by Area (see pp44–127)*. They are highlighted on other maps throughout the book. In *New Orleans at a Glance*, for example, they help you locate the top sights *(see pp26–7)*.

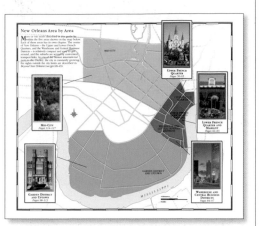

Numbers refer to each sight's position on the area map and its place in the chapter.

Practical information provides everything you need to know to visit each sight. Map references pinpoint the sight's location on the *Street Finder* map *(see pp214–222)*.

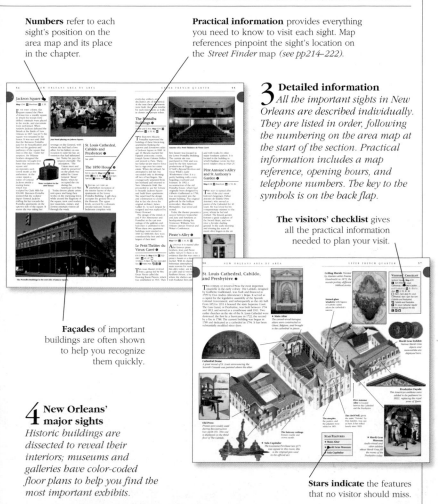

3 Detailed information
All the important sights in New Orleans are described individually. They are listed in order, following the numbering on the area map at the start of the section. Practical information includes a map reference, opening hours, and telephone numbers. The key to the symbols is on the back flap.

The visitors' checklist gives all the practical information needed to plan your visit.

Façades of important buildings are often shown to help you recognize them quickly.

4 New Orleans' major sights
Historic buildings are dissected to reveal their interiors; museums and galleries have color-coded floor plans to help you find the most important exhibits.

Stars indicate the features that no visitor should miss.

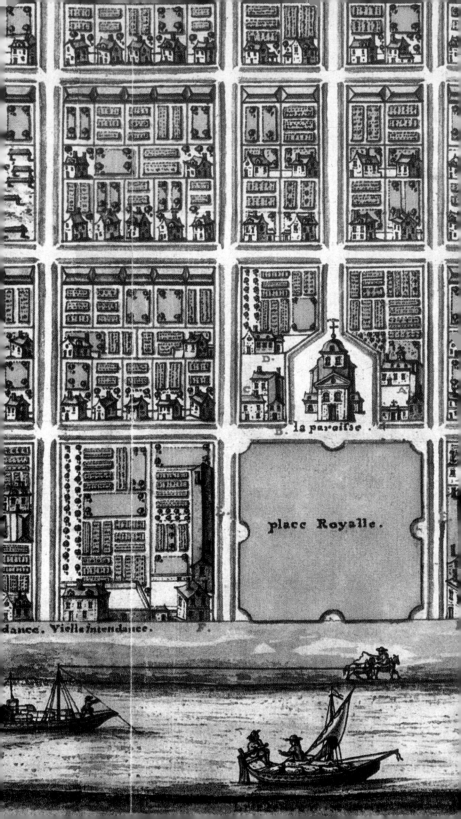

B. la paroisse.

place Royalle.

dance. Vielle Intendance.

INTRODUCING
NEW ORLEANS

fleuve S. lovis
a 400 pieds de profondeur

Putting New Orleans on the Map

NEW ORLEANS has a population of nearly 500,000 residents in an area of 199 sq miles (516 sq km). It is located in southeast Louisiana, between Lake Pontchartrain and the great bend of the Mississippi River. The airport handles international and domestic flights. There are also Interstate highways and rail links connecting the city with the rest of the country.

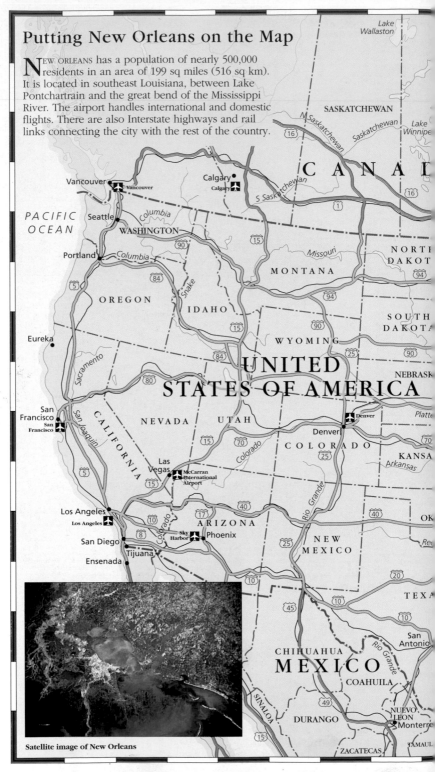

Satellite image of New Orleans

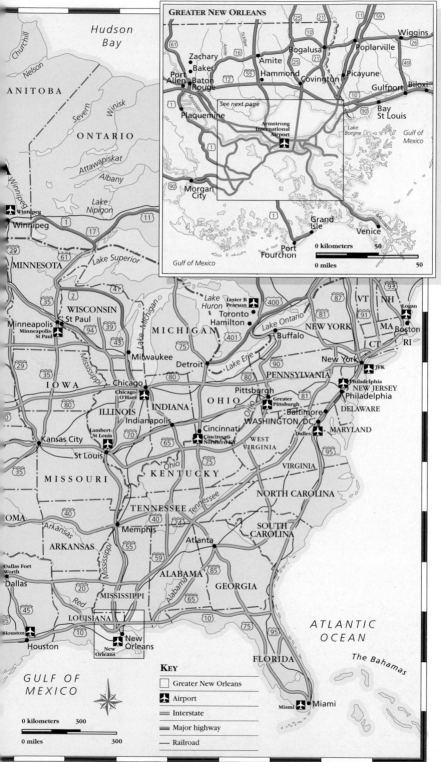

GREATER NEW ORLEANS

KEY

☐ Greater New Orleans

✈ Airport

═ Interstate

═ Major highway

─ Railroad

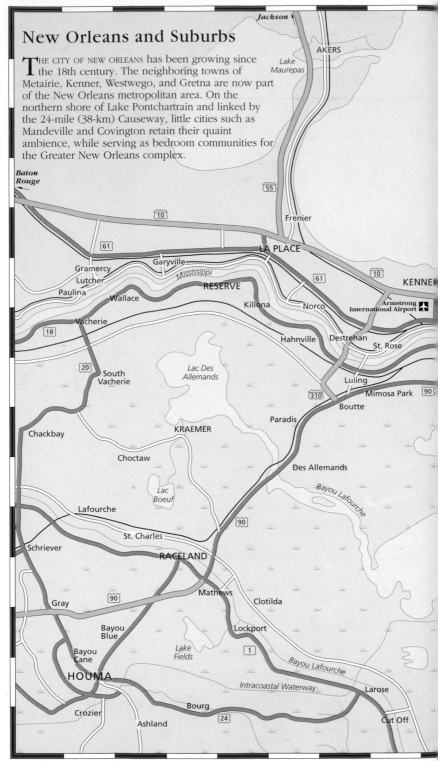

New Orleans and Suburbs

THE CITY OF NEW ORLEANS has been growing since the 18th century. The neighboring towns of Metairie, Kenner, Westwego, and Gretna are now part of the New Orleans metropolitan area. On the northern shore of Lake Pontchartrain and linked by the 24-mile (38-km) Causeway, little cities such as Mandeville and Covington retain their quaint ambience, while serving as bedroom communities for the Greater New Orleans complex.

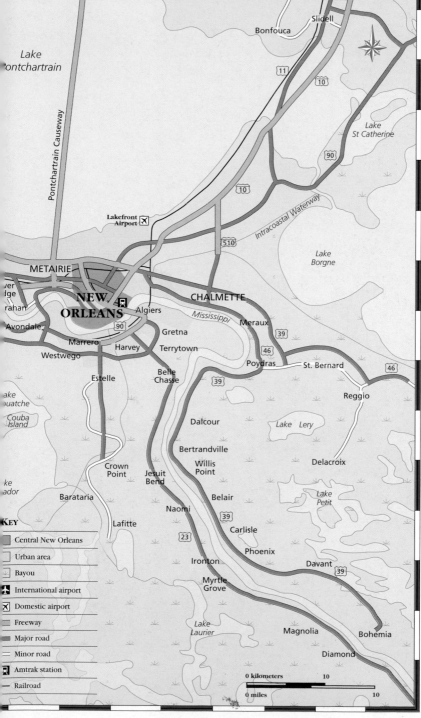

Covington
Oaklawn
12
190
Hattiesburg
10 *Mobile*
Slidell
Bonfouca
11
10
Lake Pontchartrain
Pontchartrain Causeway
Lake St Catherine
90
10
Lakefront Airport
510
Intracoastal Waterway
Lake Borgne
METAIRIE
NEW ORLEANS
Algiers
CHALMETTE
Mississippi
Meraux
39
90
Gretna
39
Avondale
Marrero
Harvey
Terrytown
Poydras
St. Bernard
46
Westwego
46
Estelle
Belle Chasse
39
Reggio
Couba Island
Dalcour
Lake Lery
Bertrandville
Delacroix
Crown Point
Willis Point
Jesuit Bend
Belair
Lake Petit
Barataria
Naomi
39
Lafitte
Carlisle
23
Phoenix
Ironton
Davant
39
Myrtle Grove
Lake Laurier
Magnolia
Bohemia
Diamond

THE HISTORY OF
NEW ORLEANS

I N 1541, SPANISH EXPLORER *Hernando de Soto discovered the Mississippi River, but it was the Frenchman Robert de La Salle who sailed down the river for the first time in 1682 and erected a cross somewhere near the location of modern New Orleans, claiming it and the whole of Louisiana for his king, Louis XIV.*

FRENCH COLONY

The first French settlements were established on the Gulf Coast at Biloxi. It took another 36 years before Jean Baptiste Le Moyne, Sieur de Bienville, established a settlement on the Lower Mississippi at New Orleans in 1718. In 1721, the engineer Adrien de Pauger laid out the French Quarter behind the levees that had been constructed. Two years later the capital of the colony was moved from Biloxi to New Orleans.

Jean Baptiste Le Moyne, founder of New Orleans

However, the colony did not prosper, and the French king turned over control to a private financier and speculator, Scotsman John Law, who floated stock in his Company of the West and promoted Louisiana as a utopia, which it was not. The natives were hostile, the land was a swamp, and the climate pestilential, but, lured by Law's advertisements, thousands of Germans and Swiss left for Louisiana and, if they survived the perilous ocean crossing, settled along the Mississippi. Whenever immigration to the new colony diminished, criminals and prostitutes were deported from France to New Orleans, the first 88 women arriving from La Salpêtrière, a Paris house of correction, in 1721. The first slaves had arrived a year earlier, and in 1727 the Ursuline Sisters arrived and founded their convent. The Company of the West speculative bubble eventually burst and Law's company collapsed. In 1731 the king resumed control and sent Bienville back to govern and to deal with the troublesome Chickasaw and Natchez Indians. Commerce began to grow, despite the restrictions that the French had imposed on trade with England, Spain, Mexico, Florida, and the West Indies. Much of it was illegal. By 1763 river traffic had grown so prodigiously that exports (indigo, sugar, rum, skins, and fur) totaled $304,000.

By that time, the contest for the control of North America had begun in earnest; in 1755 the Seven Years' War had broken out between Britain and France, Spain, and other European powers.

TIMELINE

1682 La Salle explores the Mississippi and claims Louisiana for Louis XIV

1720 The first shipment of slaves arrives on July 7

1727 The Ursuline Sisters arrive in New Orleans

1763 Exports top $300,000

1550   1650   1750

1541 Spanish explorer Hernando de Soto discovers the Mississippi River

1718 Jean-Baptiste Le Moyne, Sieur de Iberville, establishes a settlement

1721 88 women arrive from a house of correction. Adrien de Pauger lays out the Vieux Carré

C. de la Motte, an aristocrat of the French colony

◁ **Americans take control of the city after the Louisiana Purchase**

The Presbytère and Cabildo in Jackson Square, built during Spanish rule

SPANISH CITY

The Seven Years' war ended in 1763, and Louis XV signed the Treaty of Paris, which ended French ambitions in North America. Before signing, however, he had secretly ceded Louisiana to his cousin the Spanish king, Charles III. The French settlers in Louisiana were outraged at the news, and when the Spanish governor Don Antonio de Ulloa arrived in 1766 to take control, they rebelled, driving him back to Havana. Alexander O'Reilly, an Irish-born Spanish general, arrived with 24 warships, 2,000 soldiers, and 50 artillery pieces. He executed six ringleaders of the rebellion at the site of the Old US Mint, on October 25, 1769, and firmly established Spanish power.

During the American Revolution (1775–83), Governor Bernardo de Galvez supported the American colonists and captured Baton Rouge, Natchez, Mobile, and Pensacola for the Spanish king. He also relaxed trade restrictions, allowing citizens

Spanish Governor Bernardo de Galvez (1776–85)

to trade with countries other than Spain. In 1788 a fire on Good Friday, March 21, destroyed 856 buildings. The destruction was so extensive that most of the French-style buildings were lost. After the fire, the Spanish decreed that all buildings of two stories or more were to be constructed of brick, thus giving the rebuilt city a definite Mediterranean look.

In the 1790s, under Baron Carondelet (1792–7), New Orleans thrived. He granted free trade to the Americans on the Mississippi and made New Orleans the port of deposit for three years. The city's first theater and its first newspaper were soon established, gas lamps lit the streets, and a basic police force was recruited. Drainage ditches were dug too, to protect the city against flooding by the Mississippi. Prosperity increased, and the sugar industry was created in 1796, when Jean Etienne Boré first granulated sugar on a commercial scale. The city was home to important

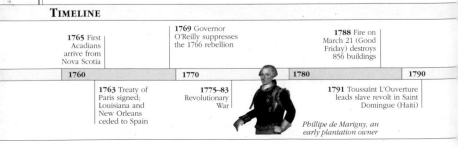

TIMELINE

	1765 First Acadians arrive from Nova Scotia	**1769** Governor O'Reilly suppresses the 1766 rebellion		**1788** Fire on March 21 (Good Friday) destroys 856 buildings	
1760		**1770**		**1780**	**1790**
	1763 Treaty of Paris signed; Louisiana and New Orleans ceded to Spain	**1775–83** Revolutionary War		**1791** Toussaint L'Ouverture leads slave revolt in Saint Domingue (Haiti)	

Phillipe de Marigny, an early plantation owner

plantations like the one owned by Phillipe de Marigny in the Lower French Quarter. New Orleans also received an infusion of talented men from the French colony of Saint Domingue (now Haiti), who had fled the slave uprising there in 1791. By 1804, refugee planters and slaves were pouring into New Orleans. They added a distinct Caribbean cast to the colony, erecting West Indian-style houses. The planters' slaves and free people of color brought the practice of voodoo with them.

Andrew Jackson leading the Battle of New Orleans

THE LOUISIANA PURCHASE AND THE BATTLE OF NEW ORLEANS

Although Spain ceded Louisiana to France in 1800, Napoleon, who was preoccupied in Europe, quickly sold it to the United States for $15,000,000 to help pay for his wars. General James

Representation of the Battle of New Orleans at Chalmette

Wilkinson and William C.C. Claiborne officially ratified the transfer on December 20, 1803, at the Cabildo. On April 30, 1812, Louisiana was admitted to the Union, six weeks before the United States declared war on Great Britain because of restraint of trade and the impressment of Americans into the British navy. In January 1815, despite the Treaty of Ghent, which had theoretically ended the war the month before, British forces launched a fresh attack on New Orleans. Under General Andrew Jackson, a ragtag army of pirates, American frontiersmen, French gentlemen, and free men of color beat back the British, validating the peace treaty and finally ending hostilities.

In 1812 the first steamboat had arrived in New Orleans, and soon after the victory at the Battle of New Orleans waves of newcomers, attracted by rapid commercial growth, drove the population to more than 40,000. Nevertheless, friction between the French Creoles and the Americans gave rise to the creation of two separate districts; the French Quarter and an uptown American section. Canal Street separated the two, and was known as the neutral ground.

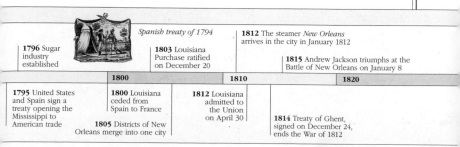

1796 Sugar industry established

Spanish treaty of 1794

1803 Louisiana Purchase ratified on December 20

1812 The steamer *New Orleans* arrives in the city in January 1812

1815 Andrew Jackson triumphs at the Battle of New Orleans on January 8

1800	1810	1820

1795 United States and Spain sign a treaty opening the Mississippi to American trade

1800 Louisiana ceded from Spain to France

1805 Districts of New Orleans merge into one city

1812 Louisiana admitted to the Union on April 30

1814 Treaty of Ghent, signed on December 24, ends the War of 1812

Steamboats, Cotton, and Sugar

The arrival of the first steamboat, in 1812, opened the city's trade to the interior and the upcountry plantations. Before the steamboat, cargo was carried on flatboats, which floated down the Ohio and Mississippi from Louisville, Kentucky, on a journey that took several

The *Robert E. Lee* steamboat on the Mississippi

months. The new steamboats cut the journey to a fraction of that time. Between 1803 and 1833, about 1,000 boats a year docked at the port of New Orleans. By the mid-1830s, the port was shipping half a million bales of cotton, becoming the cotton capital of the world. By 1840 it was the second most important port in the nation, after New York, and the population had passed 80,000. Other commodities that enriched the city were sugar, indigo, coffee, and bananas. As many as 35,000 steamboats docked at the wharves in 1860, clearing $324 million worth of trade.

By this time, New Orleans was the largest city in the South, and, with a population of 168,000, it was the sixth largest city in the nation. The immense wealth that was being generated led to the city's further expansion and cultural development. The city of Lafayette (now the Garden District) was annexed in 1852; the French Opera House was built in 1858; the Mardi Gras festival became more widely celebrated when the first parading krewe, Comus, was found-

1845 portrait of a family

ed in 1857; it also developed a reputation for its courtly life, riverboat gambling, and easy living. The only blights were the frequent epidemics of cholera and yellow fever. Between 1817 and 1860 there were 23 yellow fever epidemics, killing more than 28,000 people. The worst, in 1853, killed 10,300 people.

Civil War and Reconstruction

The Civil War brought this prosperity to an end. In 1861 New Orleans seceded from the Union. In 1862, Union Navy Captain Farragut captured New Orleans, and General Benjamin "Beast" Butler occupied the city on May 1, 1862. Butler hanged William Mumford for tearing the United States flag down from the Mint, confiscated the property of those who refused to sign an oath of allegiance, and passed an ordinance declaring that any woman who insulted a Union soldier would be regarded as a prostitute and locked up. The citizens chafed under his rule and that of his successor, General Nathaniel Banks. After the war, the city struggled to

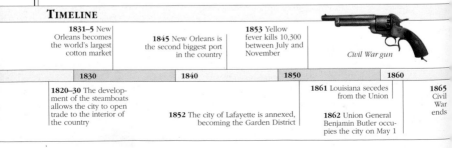

TIMELINE

1831–5 New Orleans becomes the world's largest cotton market

1845 New Orleans is the second biggest port in the country

1853 Yellow fever kills 10,300 between July and November

Civil War gun

	1830	1840	1850	1860

1820–30 The development of the steamboats allows the city to open trade to the interior of the country

1852 The city of Lafayette is annexed, becoming the Garden District

1861 Louisiana secedes from the Union

1862 Union General Benjamin Butler occupies the city on May 1

1865 Civil War ends

recover, but the source of so much of the city's wealth – the upriver plantations – had been destroyed. The "Old South" never recovered; the steamboat era was over, and the economic shift toward the northeast left New Orleans languishing.

Poor race relations troubled the city after the Civil War. In 1865, at the end of the Civil War, slaves were freed but lived in legal limbo. In 1866, a white mob attacked Mechanics Hall in downtown New Orleans, where a group of white and black men were drafting a new state constitution to extend full rights to black men (women would not vote until the 20th century). During the attack, 37 delegates were killed and 136 wounded; the violence of the Mechanics Hall riot was a key element in Congress's decision to organize Reconstruction as a military occupation of the old Confederacy by federal troops.

In 1877 federal troops withdrew, but the legal and social gains made by African Americans during Reconstruction soon began to erode

Slave cabin in a cotton plantation, circa 1860

as old Confederates resumed full political, civil, and economic power. Segregation became entrenched in 1896 when Plessy vs. Ferguson established the so-called "separate but equal" mandates. Segregation was not successfully challenged again for more than 50 years. Racial tensions only worsened as waves of Italians and Irish immigrants arrived in the late 19th century.

Although the 1884 Cotton Centennial Exposition helped boost the city's profile as a major commercial center, crime, prostitution, and corruption remained rampant. In 1897, in an attempt to control the lawlessness that was troubling the city, Alderman Sidney Story sponsored a bill that legalized prostitution in a 38-block area bounded by Iberville, Basin, Robertson, and St. Louis streets. This area, which became known as "Storyville", fostered the beginnings of a new style of improvisational music, called jazz (see pp20–21).

Painting of a fleet of Civil War frigates

History of New Orleans Jazz

Blue Lu Barker

JAZZ IS AMERICA'S original contribution to world culture. It evolved slowly and almost imperceptibly from a number of sources – from the music played at balls, parades, dances, and funerals, and New Orleans' unique blend of cultures. Its musical inspirations included African work chants, black spirituals, and European and American folk influences – the entire mélange of music that was played in 19th-century New Orleans.

Trumpeter Oscar "Papa" Celestin
The founder of the Tuxedo Brass Band in 1911 also composed "Down by the Riverside."

Congo Square
On Sundays, slaves gathered here to celebrate their one day off, playing music and dancing.

Papa Jack's Dixieland Jazz Band
This all-white band, led by Nick LaRocca, made the first jazz recording in 1917.

Louis Armstrong
This world-famous jazz trumpeter began singing on the streets of New Orleans. He played with Kid Ory before leaving the city in 1923 to join King Oliver's band in Chicago.

Bordellos, or "sporting houses," were where jazz gained its popularity.

LEADING JAZZ MUSICIANS

Buddy Bolden (1877–1931), a barber born in New Orleans, played cornet and formed one of the first jazz bands in the 1890s

Joe "King" Oliver (1885–1938) started playing cornet in New Orleans in 1904, but moved to Chicago with his Creole Jazz Band

"King" Oliver

1880	1900	1920

Jelly Roll Morton (1890–1941) began his piano career in the brothels of Storyville. He was the first great jazz composer and pianist

Sidney Bechet (1897–1959) played clarinet and soprano saxophone with early leaders like Freddie Keppard

Riverboat Jazz Bands
After Storyville was closed down in 1917, New Orleans' best musicians moved onto the boats or migrated to northern cities. Pianist Fate Marable's band included Louis Armstrong, who played the cornet.

Kid Ory's Trombone
Edward "Kid" Ory played with King Oliver and Louis Armstrong's famous Hot Five band.

The Boswell Sisters
Connie, Martha, and Vet Boswell sang and recorded in the early 1930s. This was the most popular female jazz group of its time.

Musicians were screened off so that they could not see the patrons.

STORYVILLE JAZZ SALON
Many early jazz artists entertained in Storyville at the bordellos, playing behind screens – Buddy Bolden, King Oliver, Jelly Roll Morton, Sidney Bechet, Kid Ory, Freddy Keppard, and Manuel Perez among them.

Jelly Roll Morton
Ferdinand "Jelly Roll" Morton, who formed the band The Red Hot Peppers, claimed to have invented jazz in 1902.

Louis Armstrong (1901–1971) was the greatest of all jazz musicians. From 1940 to 1960 he played with his All Star Band

Louis Armstrong

Terence Blanchard (1962–), a trumpeter, played with Lionel Hampton and Art Blakey before forming his own quintet. He is famous for composing and playing the music for Spike Lee's films

1940	1960	1980	2000

Danny Barker (1909–1994) played guitar and banjo with the big bands in the 1930s and 1940s before returning to New Orleans

Pete Fountain (1930–) is considered one of the best clarinetists in the world

Harry Connick, Jr. (1967–) played in New Orleans clubs as a teenager, later becoming a major jazz-pop music star and arranging the score for *When Harry Met Sally*

A World War II Higgins boat

20TH-CENTURY NEW ORLEANS – FROM STORYVILLE TO 2000

Until it was abolished on October 2, 1917, Storyville was the most extraordinary spectacle of legalized vice in the United States. Patrons could pick up a copy of the "Blue Book" in a bar or hotel and find the names and addresses of 700 prostitutes listed with their prices and their color. Storyville also gave jazz a boost, because many early jazz artists began their musical lives in the brothels *(see pp20–21)*.

The Department of the Navy closed Storyville down in 1917, because it feared that it was too tempting to sailors shipping out from New Orleans to World War I battlefronts. Although the war briefly boosted business in the shipyards, the economy languished during the 1920s and early 1930s. The effects of the Depression were evident by 1933, when five New Orleans banks failed and 11 percent of the citizenry was on welfare. Under the New Deal, Mayor Robert Maestri used federal dollars to build roads, bridges, parks, and public buildings.

During World War II, business picked up again in the shipyards, and New Orleans produced thousands of the famous Higgins boats that were used in Allied amphibious landings on all war fronts.

In 1946 Mayor de Lesseps Story "Chep" Morrison was elected as a reformer and served until 1961. During his administration the city began to take on its current appearance. He constructed the Pontchartrain Expressway, a new airport, and, in 1958, the $65-million Mississippi Bridge (later renamed the Crescent City Connection Bridge), which opened the West Bank area to suburban development. In 1954, the Supreme Court ruling Brown vs. the Board of Education ordered the desegregation of public education. Schools were integrated by federal marshals in 1960.

During the 1960s there was some economic regeneration when NASA took over an old aviation plant to build the Saturn rocket booster, and a ship channel was opened, enabling very large ships to enter the port. In

The Crescent City Connection Bridge, reconstructed in the 1990s

TIMELINE

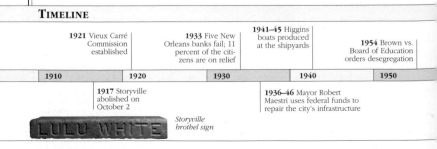

1921 Vieux Carré Commission established

1933 Five New Orleans banks fail; 11 percent of the citizens are on relief

1941–45 Higgins boats produced at the shipyards

1954 Brown vs. Board of Education orders desegregation

| 1910 | 1920 | 1930 | 1940 | 1950 |

1917 Storyville abolished on October 2

1936–46 Mayor Robert Maestri uses federal funds to repair the city's infrastructure

Storyville brothel sign

LULU WHITE

1969 the port was still the second in the nation. During the boom, new buildings like the World Trade Center, Rivergate, and One Shell Square were erected, and numerous hotels rose up along Canal Street. In 1967 the city was granted an NFL (National Football League) franchise and thereafter entered the major leagues.

The 1965 Voting Rights Act changed the political picture in the city. In 1969, Mayor Landrieu was elected primarily because he had the support of black voters, and he appointed the first black to a senior position in his administration, paving the way for the election of Ernest N. "Dutch" Morial, the first black mayor, in 1978.

At the beginning of his administration Morial benefited greatly from the oil boom, but by 1986 the bubble had burst, thanks to the drop in international oil prices; as a consequence, New Orleans' economy was devastated. Meanwhile, the white and middle class flight to the suburbs, which began in the 1950s, continued, leaving the inner city to the poor. Morial sought to salvage city fortunes by building the Convention Center, developing the waterfront, and encouraging tourism investment, but racial tensions increased, finally spilling over into Mardi Gras. In 1991 the City Council passed a stringent anti-discrimination law,

NASA Saturn rocket, built in the 1960s at the Michoud plant

refusing to grant parade permits to krewes that failed to open their ranks to all; the Comus, Proteus, and Momus krewes refused to comply, and canceled their parades. Subsequently, the ordinance was considerably toned down. Proteus resumed its parade in 2000. In 1994, Dutch's son, Marc Morial, age 34, was elected mayor. He continued to push his father's agenda, encouraging tourism and cleaning up corruption. Some economic diversification and the boom in the late 1990s helped restore prosperity, but the city still suffers from its dependence on the tourism and oil industries, and from the persistent problems of corruption.

Millennium celebrations on the Mississippi River

In spite of its troubles, however, the city continues to flourish, and still prides itself on what it does best; delivering the pleasures of food, drink, music, and art to the many visitors that flock here to enjoy its sensuality and individuality.

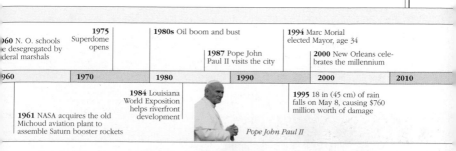

1960 N. O. schools are desegregated by federal marshals	1975 Superdome opens	1980s Oil boom and bust		1994 Marc Morial elected Mayor, age 34	
			1987 Pope John Paul II visits the city		2000 New Orleans celebrates the millennium
1960	1970	1980	1990	2000	2010
		1984 Louisiana World Exposition helps riverfront development		1995 18 in (45 cm) of rain falls on May 8, causing $760 million worth of damage	
1961 NASA acquires the old Michoud aviation plant to assemble Saturn booster rockets			Pope John Paul II		

History of Mardi Gras

CULMINATING ON MARDI GRAS – the day before Ash Wednesday – the Carnival celebrations in New Orleans attract visitors from across the United States and around the world. Since the 1700s the period between Twelfth Night (January 6) and Ash Wednesday, the start of Lent, has been celebrated with lavish balls, presented by groups of citizens known as "krewes." Although most balls are private, many krewes also put on parades, with ornate costumes and floats. These take place for ten days before Mardi Gras, with the biggest and most famous parades on Tuesday itself.

Mardi Gras costume

Bacchus Kings
The Krewe of Bacchus has invited Bob Hope, Kirk Douglas, and Charlton Heston to be their king.

Rex
This krewe was founded in 1872 to organize a spectacle for Grand Duke Alexis, a younger son of Czar Alexander II.

King Cake
The traditional food of Carnival, each king cake contains a small plastic figure of a baby, representing the baby Jesus.

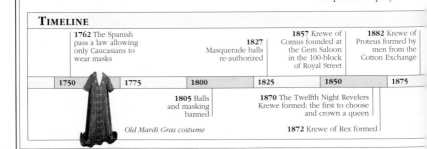

Parade Floats
Each Krewe has several colorful papier-mâché floats that are pulled through the city during the parades. Afterward many floats are put on public display.

TIMELINE

1750	1775	1800	1825	1850	1875

1762 The Spanish pass a law allowing only Caucasians to wear masks

1827 Masquerade balls re-authorized

1857 Krewe of Comus founded at the Gem Saloon in the 100-block of Royal Street

1882 Krewe of Proteus formed by men from the Cotton Exchange

1805 Balls and masking banned

Old Mardi Gras costume

1870 The Twelfth Night Revelers Krewe formed; the first to choose and crown a queen

1872 Krewe of Rex formed

Bourbon Street Celebrations
Crowds jam Bourbon Street to watch the Bourbon Street Awards, a competition for the best costumes.

WHERE TO SEE MARDI GRAS

The history of Mardi Gras is displayed at a permanent exhibition in the Presbytère *(see pp56–7)*. Many floats are constructed at Blaine Kern's Mardi Gras World *(see p88)* and can be seen there all year long.

The Presbytère presents a colorful display of Mardi Gras history.

Throws
Souvenir doubloons (coins), beads, and dolls are thrown from the floats to the crowds. This tradition began with Rex in 1881.

Blaine Kern's Mardi Gras World is the place where many of the floats are made.

MARDI GRAS COLORS
The purple, green, and gold masks, banners, and other decorations that adorn buildings everywhere during the Carnival season are derived from the original costume worn by Rex in the 1872 parade. He used a theatrical costume made for *Richard III*, consisting of a purple velvet cloak with green rhinestones and a golden scepter and crown. Today, these colors are still used: purple symbolizing justice, green for faith, and gold for power.

Rex's Scepter
The King of Mardi Gras, a prominent New Orleans citizen, is chosen by the Rex organization every year.

1968 Krewe of Bacchus breaks traditions. It opens its ranks to all and invites celebrities to become its king

1909 Zulu, the first black krewe, organized as a parody

1991 A city ordinance requires parading Krewes to open their membership to all. Comus, Momus, and Proteus cancel their parades

1900	1925	1950	1975	2000	2025

1889 The first marching krewe, Jefferson City Buzzards, founded

1935 The Elks organize the first truck krewe

2000 Mardi Gras parade celebrates the new millennium

Rex knight

New Orleans at a Glance

THERE ARE more than 100 places of interest described in this book. They range from the legendary Bourbon Street to the quiet and beautiful live oaks in City Park, and from Jackson Square, with its spontaneous jazz street-musicians, to the scientific exhibits in the Aquarium of the Americas. The following 16 pages are a time-saving guide to the best New Orleans has to offer. Architecture, wrought and cast iron, and cemeteries have their own sections. There is also a guide to the diverse cultures that have given this city its unique character and feeling. Below is a selection of sights that no visitor should miss.

New Orleans Top Ten Sights

Old US Mint
See pp74–75

Garden District
See pp98–113

Royal Street
See pp48–49

St. Charles Avenue Streetcar *See pp104–105*

Bourbon Street
See pp46–47

Aquarium of the Americas *See pp90–91*

Audubon Zoo
See pp112–13

Jackson Square
See p54

City Park
See pp116–17

Steamboat *Natchez*
See pp64–65

◁ **Chartres Street, near Jackson Square**

Multicultural New Orleans

BECAUSE NEW ORLEANS was one of the main ports of entry for the southern United States, as well as a very important commercial center, countless immigrants landed here. Many of them settled in or near the city, contributing their customs and ways of life to the unique blend of the Crescent City's distinctive Creole culture. Today, their influence can be seen throughout the city.

German Culture
The Oktoberfest is celebrated uproariously every year at the Deutsches Haus (see p42).

0 kilometers   1

0 miles   1

Irish Culture
A number of Irish bars dotted around the city provide lively evenings of traditional Celtic music and dancing.

Native Americans
American Indian tribes, such as the Natchez and the Chickasaw, lived in the delta of the Mississippi River before the arrival of Europeans.

Claiborne Avenue

Carrollton Avenue

St. Charles Ave.

GARDEN DISTRICT

Jewish Culture
Touro Synagogue (see p104) was built in 1828. It is the oldest Jewish place of worship in New Orleans.

American Culture
Newcomers from the Atlantic states settled on the upriver side of Canal Street, building beautiful homes in the Garden District (see pp100–101).

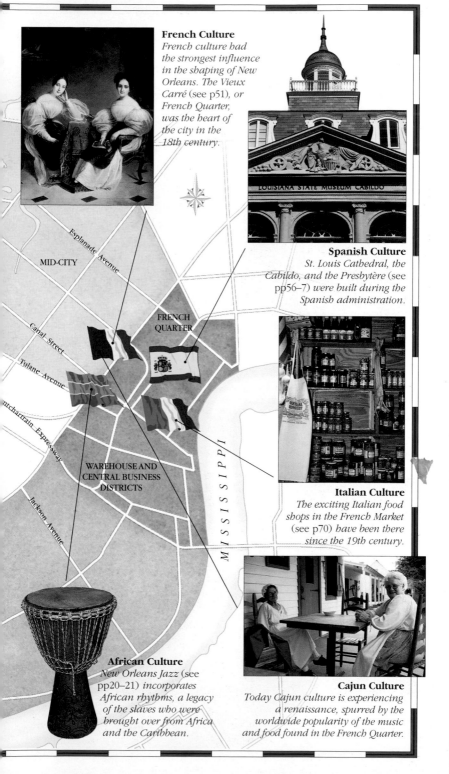

French Culture
French culture had the strongest influence in the shaping of New Orleans. The Vieux Carré (see p51), or French Quarter, was the heart of the city in the 18th century.

Spanish Culture
St. Louis Cathedral, the Cabildo, and the Presbytère (see pp56–7) were built during the Spanish administration.

Italian Culture
The exciting Italian food shops in the French Market (see p70) have been there since the 19th century.

African Culture
New Orleans Jazz (see pp20–21) incorporates African rhythms, a legacy of the slaves who were brought over from Africa and the Caribbean.

Cajun Culture
Today Cajun culture is experiencing a renaissance, spurred by the worldwide popularity of the music and food found in the French Quarter.

MID-CITY

FRENCH
QUARTER

Esplanade Avenue

Canal Street

Tulane Avenue

Pontchartrain Expressway

Jackson Avenue

WAREHOUSE AND
CENTRAL BUSINESS
DISTRICTS

M I S S I S S I P P I

LOUISIANA STATE MUSEUM CABILDO

Exploring New Orleans' Many Cultures

NEW ORLEANS' unique flavor derives from the incredible mix of peoples and cultures assembled on the banks of the Mississippi River; Native American, French, Spanish, African, Anglo-American, Jewish, Italian, German, Irish, and Cajun (Acadian). They have all contributed to the "gumbo" that is New Orleans.

African mask

French colonists signing a treaty with Native Americans

THE NATIVE AMERICANS

NUMEROUS Native American tribes lived in the Delta; Attakpas, Bayougoula, Oke-lousa, Choctaw, Houma, Tunica, and Chitimacha. They were either wiped out like the Natchez, who were de-stroyed in the war of 1730, or removed, like the Choctaw, to Oklahoma. Only scattered traces of these tribes remain, mostly outside the city.

THE FRENCH

THE FRENCH came down the Mississippi from Canada and explored and settled the region in the late 17th and

The French Market, where the city's diverse cultures mix

early 18th century. Refugees from the French colony of Saint Domingue added a dis-tinct West Indian flavor to the culture at the beginning of the 19th century. There was a continuous flow of immigration from France throughout the rest of the century. Their in-fluence is most clearly seen in the cuisine as well as in architecture and decorative arts, such as the furniture created by Prudence Mallard.

THE AFRICAN CULTURES

THE FIRST SLAVES arrived in 1720, and by 1724 there were enough slaves in the colony to justify establishing the *Code Noir* for their con-trol. New Orleans was known for the large number of free people of color who worked as artisans and operated busi-nesses of their own, many of whom had come from Haiti during the 1791–1808 Haitian Revolution. On the eve of the Civil War, the city had 13,000 blacks, slave and free. From Africa and the West Indies came voodoo practices and the chants and music that influenced the birth of jazz *(see pp20–21)* and blues.

THE SPANISH

THE SPANISH took over from the French as administra-tors of Louisiana from 1763 to 1800 *(see pp16–17)*, but few immigrants from Spain actually settled in New Or-leans. Spanish is still spoken by descendants of the "Isleños" – people who came at the request of the Spanish from the Canary Islands in the 1770s. In the 1950s, Latin American refugees from Cuba, Nicaragua, and Honduras flooded into the city. The most obvious Hispanic influence can be seen throughout the French Quarter in the design of the buildings, as well as in the cuisine.

THE GERMANS

THE FIRST GERMANS arrived in 1722, lured by John Law's promotion of the colony as an earthly paradise *(see p15)*. About 10,000 had left their homes in the Rhineland bet-ween 1719 and 1720 after the Thirty Years' War. Nearly 2,000 arrived in the region, settling as small farmers about 25 miles (40 km) upstream from New Orleans. A second wave followed between 1820 and 1850, bringing thousands more, who were fleeing political turmoil in Europe. Another wave followed just before the Civil War, and then another

African American in Indian-inspired Mardi Gras costume

from 1865 to the 1890s. Most German immigrants settled inland, but by 1870 there were more than 15,000 living in New Orleans itself. For a time they were the largest immigrant group in Louisiana.

THE CAJUNS

WHEN THE BRITISH gained control of French Canada, they insisted that the Acadians swear an oath to the British crown. When they refused, they were exiled. Many returned to France, but others traveled south to Catholic French Louisiana. The first 650 people arrived in the region in 1765 and settled as farmers along the bayous west of New Orleans. They continued to speak their 17th-century French until 1916, when the use of French was banned in all schools and government organizations. Today, Cajun culture is undergoing a renaissance, assisted by Cajun and zydeco artists and chefs such as the renowned Paul Prudhomme *(see p173)*.

Cajun craftsman sitting at a traditional workbench

THE ANGLO-AMERICANS

THE ROUGH-and-ready men who piloted the riverboats down the Mississippi were the first Americans to arrive in New Orleans and give it its reputation as a City of Sin. They came in search of "dixies," or ten-dollar bills, and their carousing became notorious. After the Louisiana Purchase in 1803 *(see p17)*, government workers and land speculators migrated from the east coast, all seeking fortunes in the new territory.

A jazz band marching in the French Quarter

Many of them were of Scots-Irish or English descent. They settled in what became the American Quarter on the up-river side of Canal Street, and brought another new architectural style to the city.

THE JEWS

THERE WAS a vibrant Jewish community in New Orleans as early as 1718, but it wasn't until 1828 that the first synagogue was organized. In the 19th century, many Jews emigrated from Germany and Eastern Europe. Samuel Zemurray, for one, started a fruit-importing company, which eventually became the United Fruit Company. He was a great philanthropist, and donated enormous sums of money to Tulane University *(see p110)*.

THE IRISH

THE IRISH arrived in the mid-19th century, fleeing the 1840 potato famine in Ireland. By 1860 there were 24,000 Irish in New Orleans, crowded into a narrow area dubbed the "Irish Channel" between the river and Magazine Street, east of Louisiana Avenue. The majority of them worked as laborers (building the New Basin Canal), and as stevedores. The later generations became very successful in politics.

THE ITALIANS

ALTHOUGH SOME Italians arrived before the Civil War, many more arrived later and replaced the blacks as agricultural laborers. By 1890 there were more than 25,000 living in New Orleans, and more arrived at the turn of the century. Most came from Sicily and settled in the poor French Quarter, where they started out as laborers, peddlers, and market vendors, bringing interesting new flavors to the French Market. Their influence can be seen mainly in the cuisine, including the popular *muffuletta* sandwich *(see p168)*.

A New Orleans canal, built by Irish laborers

The Architecture of New Orleans

French dormer

NEW ORLEANS is one of the few American cities that has managed to retain much of its historic architecture. The French Quarter has many buildings dating back 150 years or more, while the Garden District has splendid mansions designed in a variety of styles. Beautiful houses line Esplanade Avenue, historically the residential nucleus of the Creole elite, and the city also possesses a good stock of 19th-century public buildings built in Greek Revival style. It is not always easy to categorize buildings by style, for many of them are hybrids, like the Gallier House, which incorporated both Creole and American features.

Gothic-style Creole cottage on Esplanade Avenue

FRENCH COLONIAL

Only a few buildings, such as the Old Ursuline Convent (see p68) and Lafitte's Blacksmith Shop (see p78), remain from this period, which combines various French styles of the 18th century. Most were destroyed by a series of fires: one, in 1788, destroyed 856 wooden buildings; a second in 1794 destroyed 212 buildings.

Brick, stucco, and timber walls

The roof was made of wood tiles.

The brick chimney rose through the center of the house.

Lafitte's Blacksmith Shop *is a fine example of brick between posts, in which soft local bricks are supported by cypress timbers and protected by plaster.*

Water channels protected the wood from water damage.

Gas lamps were added in the 19th century.

SPANISH COLONIAL

After the 1788 and 1794 fires, the Spanish decreed that any building of more than one story must be constructed of brick. The houses that were subsequently built can still be seen in the French Quarter. They often combine residence and store, and feature arcaded walls, heavy doors and windows, and a flagstone alleyway leading to a loggia and fountain-graced courtyard.

The second floor was the family home.

The attic was used as a warehouse.

19th-century cast-iron balconies

Walls were built of brick instead of wood.

Napoleon House, *in the French Quarter, is a typical three-storied Spanish house. Only the crowning tower is unique.*

FEDERAL TOWNHOUSE

Americans from the Atlantic states brought their own architectural preferences with them, and the successful among them erected Federal-style homes that stand out from the French or Spanish cottages surrounding them in the Quarter.

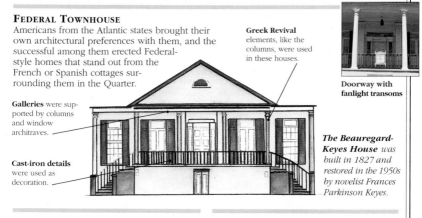

Greek Revival elements, like the columns, were used in these houses.

Doorway with fanlight transoms

Galleries were supported by columns and window architraves.

Cast-iron details were used as decoration.

The Beauregard-Keyes House was built in 1827 and restored in the 1950s by novelist Frances Parkinson Keyes.

THE CREOLE COTTAGE

Most of these raised houses were built flush to the streets, with extensive eaves and an alleyway leading to a rear courtyard. The interior usually contains two front and two back rooms with a loggia or gallery behind and a kitchen and servants' quarters in the courtyard.

Gabled roofs were popular and were often high enough for an attic.

Main bedrooms were usually at the front of the house.

A wide balcony faced the street.

Esplanade Avenue is lined with several kinds of Creole cottage.

The ground floor was used as a storage area.

SHOTGUN HOUSE

These cottages were so called because a bullet fired from a shotgun through the front door would go straight through the house and out the back as all the doors were aligned. They come in single and double versions, and usually have a set of box steps in front.

The main doorway leads directly into the first room.

Simple balconies overlook the porch.

The French Quarter has several examples of traditional shotgun houses.

Box steps

THE PLANTATION HOUSE

The refugees from Saint Domingue (Haiti) brought this Caribbean-style dwelling to New Orleans. This one-story residence is usually raised on brick pillars (to catch the breezes and to cope with flooding) and incorporates a wraparound veranda. The space below the house and the flagstone piazza below the veranda are used as service or storage areas.

French doors gave access to the veranda.

Wide verandas were built at the front entrance.

Brick pillars raised the house.

Plantation houses were the most popular style of residences built along the Bayou St. John.

Famous New Orleanians

BECAUSE OF its cultural roots, geographic importance, and easy-going ways, New Orleans has been a magnet for creative people since the 18th century. A great many writers and artists came here to live, and, like Tennessee Williams, called New Orleans their spiritual home. Others, like Louis Armstrong, were born here. Nurtured by its culture, they carried their musical, literary, and artistic creations to the rest of the world.

Marie Laveau
The most famous voodoo queen in New Orleans (see pp82–3). Laveau celebrated her rituals on the banks of Bayou St. John.

Truman Capote
This famous author was born in Touro Infirmary in the Garden District. He wrote his first work, Other Voices, Other Rooms, *in a rented room at 711 Royal St.*

GARDEN DISTRICT

Anne Rice
Born in New Orleans, author Anne Rice attended Redemptorist School and now lives at 1239 First Street in the Garden District. The city stars in her Vampire Chronicles *(see p107).*

Mahalia Jackson
This gospel singer (see p80) was born on Water Street and grew up at an aunt's house at 7467 Esther Street.

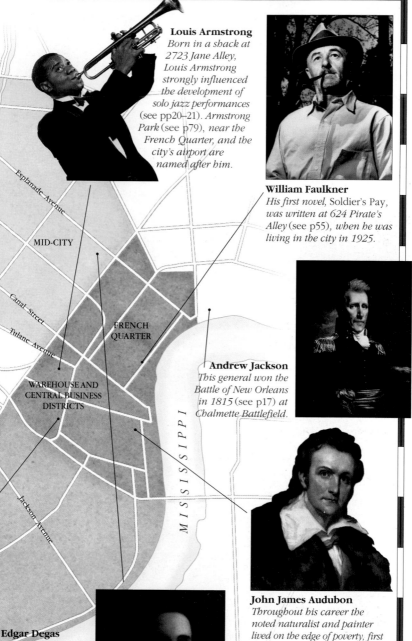

Louis Armstrong
Born in a shack at 2723 Jane Alley, Louis Armstrong strongly influenced the development of solo jazz performances (see pp20–21). Armstrong Park (see p79), near the French Quarter, and the city's airport are named after him.

William Faulkner
His first novel, Soldier's Pay, *was written at 624 Pirate's Alley (see p55), when he was living in the city in 1925.*

MID-CITY

FRENCH QUARTER

WAREHOUSE AND CENTRAL BUSINESS DISTRICTS

Andrew Jackson
This general won the Battle of New Orleans in 1815 (see p17) at Chalmette Battlefield.

MISSISSIPPI

Esplanade Avenue
Canal Street
Tulane Avenue
Jackson Avenue

Edgar Degas
The French painter visited the city in 1872–73 (see p126). During this period he painted many well-known pictures and portraits.

John James Audubon
Throughout his career the noted naturalist and painter lived on the edge of poverty, first at 706 Barracks Street, then at Oakley House plantation, where he stayed in 1821 (see p143).

0 kilometers 1

0 miles 1

New Orleans Ironwork

Cast iron detail

T HE SHADOWS CAST by New Orleans ironwork add a romantic touch to the city. Wrought iron, which came first, was fashioned by hand into beautiful shapes by German, Irish, and black artisans. Cast iron, on the other hand, was poured into wooden molds and allowed to set. As a result, the latter has a somewhat solid, fixed appearance, unlike wrought iron, which is handmade and has a more fluid aspect. Examples of both kinds of work can be seen throughout the city, particularly in the French Quarter and the Garden District.

Colonial-style house, Royal Street

Decorative Iron Balconies
Many galleries have elaborate iron rails with unique designs and patterns. They are admired as much today as they were in colonial times.

Royal Street's famous cornstalk fence

The Pontalba Buildings
These buildings, commissioned by Baroness Pontalba (see p55), started the craze for ironwork. Completed in 1850, they transformed the profile of Jackson Square (see p54). Some of the patterns were designed by the Baroness's son.

The Signature of New Orleans
Creole ironwork appears in many forms, including fences, gates, window grilles, balconies, hinges, doorknobs, and lanterns.

Cast Iron
This kind of ironwork was often used in homes in the Garden District. It was superior to wood because it withstood humidity.

Details
Many buildings were supplemented by ironwork in the 1850s. Lacy balconies depicting oak leaf and acorn were added to the LaBranch House at 700 Royal Street.

Wrought Iron
Wrought ironwork contains a purer iron. Handmade, and stronger than cast iron, it is very common in the French Quarter.

CORNSTALK FENCES
There are two "cornstalk" fences in New Orleans, so-called because of their decorative motifs. One is at 915 Royal Street (*see p77*), the other at Colonel Short's Villa in the Garden District (*see p107*). Both feature cornstalks entwined with morning glories and ears of corn; the former is painted in natural colors.

IRONWORK MOTIFS

Cast-iron railing detail

In the 1850s, Philadelphia iron-mongers Wood & Perot opened a branch office in New Orleans. Offering hundreds of patterns specially designed for the city, the company quickly grew, its motifs including abstracts, acorns, fruits, cherubs, bacchants, vines, and animals. These were soon seen in railings throughout the city.

Popular balcony motifs

New Orleans Cemeteries

IN NEW ORLEANS the dead are buried above, not below, ground, because the water table is so high. The early colony was dubbed "the Wet Grave," since coffins would often float to the surface after burial. The cemeteries are the only places where expensive imported stone was used for building. They take on the aspects of cities, complete with streets and mausoleums that reflect the social status of their deceased inhabitants.

St. Patrick's
Throughout this Irish cemetery, there are remarkable cast-iron sculptures representing the Way of the Cross.

Metairie
Located on the grounds of a former horse-racing track, Metairie (see p127) is laid out in concentric ovals. Established in 1872, it is one of the most attractive and interesting cemeteries in the city.

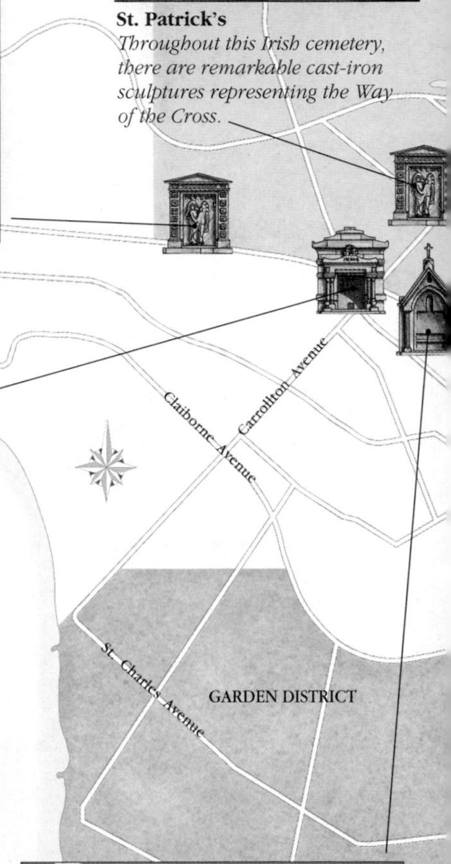

Claiborne Avenue

Carrollton Avenue

St. Charles Avenue

GARDEN DISTRICT

Cypress Grove
There are no cypress trees here, but other magnificent varieties of tree create a peaceful atmosphere (see p126).

Greenwood
Established in 1852 by the Firemen's Charitable and Benevolent Association, this cemetery is an extension of Cypress Grove (see p126).

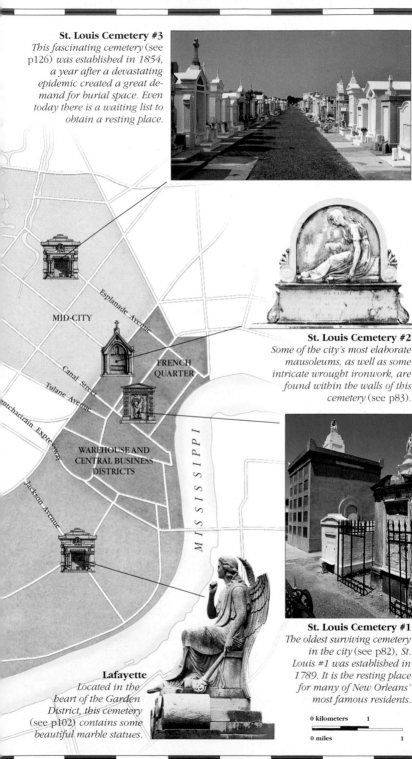

St. Louis Cemetery #3
This fascinating cemetery (see p126) *was established in 1854, a year after a devastating epidemic created a great demand for burial space. Even today there is a waiting list to obtain a resting place.*

MID-CITY

Esplanade Avenue

FRENCH QUARTER

Canal Street

Tulane Avenue

Pontchartrain Expressway

WAREHOUSE AND CENTRAL BUSINESS DISTRICTS

Jackson Avenue

MISSISSIPPI

St. Louis Cemetery #2
Some of the city's most elaborate mausoleums, as well as some intricate wrought ironwork, are found within the walls of this cemetery (see p83).

St. Louis Cemetery #1
The oldest surviving cemetery in the city (see p82)*, St. Louis #1 was established in 1789. It is the resting place for many of New Orleans' most famous residents.*

Lafayette
Located in the heart of the Garden District, this cemetery (see p102) *contains some beautiful marble statues.*

0 kilometers   1

0 miles   1

NEW ORLEANS
THROUGH THE YEAR

A WIDE VARIETY of activities and events takes place in New Orleans all through the year. The spring and fall, enjoying the most temperate weather, are the best times to visit. Although the pace slows with the heat of the summer, the city is still alive with indoor and outdoor events. Some festivities celebrate themes specific to New

Jazz Fest musician

Orleans, such as the French Quarter Festival in April. The city also throws parties for the major holidays, especially 4th of July and New Year's Eve. The high points of the year, however, are Mardi Gras with all the Carnival festivities, beginning in January and running through early March, and the New Orleans Jazz and Heritage Festival (Jazz Fest) in late April or early May.

SPRING

D URING THE SPRING the weather is at its best in New Orleans, neither too hot nor too humid. There are two main events in the city, both of which are internationally renowned: Mardi Gras, with its parades, street celebrations, and masked balls all over the city, and the Jazz Fest, which lasts for two weeks. It is very important to have confirmed reservations for transportation and lodging during this peak season.

MARCH

Mardi Gras *(early Feb to early Mar)*. The six-to-eight-week Carnival festivities *(see pp24–5)* begin with the four-day weekend before

A family dressed in colorful Mardi Gras costumes

Ash Wednesday and finish with the main parade on the Tuesday before Lent ("Fat Tuesday"). There are day and night parades, and some tickets are available for the masked balls. The whole city is on party time, so it's advisable to book hotels several months in advance. (www.mardigras.com)
St. Patrick's Day Parade *(week before and on Mar 17)*. The city commemorates Ireland's famous patron saint with parades through the French Quarter, Irish Channel, and Veteran's Boulevard, where potatoes, onions, and carrots are thrown to the public. An all-day street party around Parasol's Bar in the Irish Channel takes place on St. Patrick's Day itself.
St. Joseph's Day *(on and around Mar 19)*. The city's Italian population honors the patron saint of Sicily with elaborate altars of food. Angelo Broccato's ice cream parlor (214 North Carrollton Ave) is one of the best places to see an altar.
Crescent City Classic *(last Saturday)*. Since 1979 world-class runners have gathered in New Orleans for this 10,000-meter race from the French Quarter to City Park. Thousands of amateur runners also join in.
Tennessee Williams New Orleans Literary Festival and Writers' Conference *(late Mar)*. This five-day

cultural festival takes place in various locations to honor the celebrated writer, with theatrical productions, lectures, readings, literary walking tours, and panel discussions on New Orleans-based authors and books. Don't miss the "Stella and Stanley" screamfest in Jackson Square.

A huge jazz brunch at the French Quarter Festival

APRIL

French Quarter Festival *(second weekend)*. To celebrate the food and music of New Orleans, this festival is held in the French Quarter, with free musical entertainment, "the world's largest jazz brunch," fireworks over the Mississippi River, and children's activities. (www. frenchquarterfestivals.org)
Spring Fiesta *(begins Fri night after Easter, lasting five days)*. With the French Quarter's historic homes as the main attraction, this celebration also has a parade

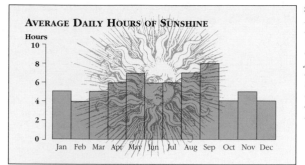

AVERAGE DAILY HOURS OF SUNSHINE

Hours

Jan Feb Mar Apr May Jun Jul Aug Sep Oct Nov Dec

Sunshine Chart
From May through September the weather is hot and humid, and the sun shines for six to eight hours a day. From October through March the temperature is colder, and there are often heavy fogs.

Crowds enjoying the music at the Jazz Fest

that ends with the coronation of a local queen. **New Orleans Jazz and Heritage Festival (Jazz Fest)** *(last weekend in Apr to first weekend in May)*. In this ten-day festival, held at the Fair Grounds, more than 4,000 jazz musicians entertain, with a large selection of traditional food, crafts, and evening concerts. (www. nojazzfest.com)

MAY

Zoo-to-Do *(first Fri in May)*. The largest one-night fundraising event in the country takes place at Audubon Zoo *(see pp112–13)*, with unforgettable dances among the animals, under the stars. **Greek Festival** *(weekend before Memorial Day weekend)*. The Hellenic Cultural Center, near Lake Pontchartrain, hosts two days of Greek dances, cuisine, music, and various arts and crafts. **New Orleans Wine & Food Experience** *(fourth week)*. US and European wineries come to town for parties, discussions, and wine tastings.

SUMMER

H OT AND EXTREMELY humid weather along with daily thunderstorms make summertime in New Orleans the off-season period. Since this is also the time when hurricanes and tropical storms are frequent, it is wise to be prepared for weather alerts. The biggest celebration in the city is 4th of July (Independence Day).

JUNE

Great French Market Tomato Festival *(first weekend)*. Held in and around the French Market, this unique festival offers cooking demonstrations and local cuisine. **Reggae Riddums Festival** *(second weekend)*. Caribbean culture is the main theme of this annual event at Marconi Meadows in City Park *(see pp116–17)*, which features some of the very best reggae, calypso, and soca music.

JULY

Go 4th on the River *(Jul 4)*. The riverfront hosts the Independence Day celebrations. There is music, food, and entertainment suitable for the whole family. The festivities conclude with a spectacular fireworks display over the river.

AUGUST

White Linen Night *(first Sat)*. An open-air event in which a number of art galleries take their exhibits outdoors to the Warehouse Art District. **Southern Decadence** *(last week of Aug to Labor Day)*. There is Mardi Gras, and then there is Southern Decadence, a gay street party that has over-the-top costumes, spontaneous parades, rowdy behavior, and a great time for adults. Centered in the French Quarter, it culminates on Labor Day, the first Monday of September. (www. southerndecadence.com)

Go 4th on the River celebration at Woldenberg Park

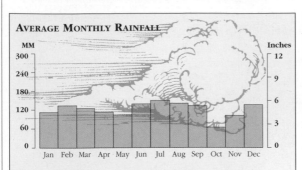

MM
Inches

300
240
180
120
60
0

Jan Feb Mar Apr May Jun Jul Aug Sep Oct Nov Dec

12
9
6
3
0

Rainfall Chart
New Orleans is one of the rainiest cities in the United States, and July and August are its rainiest months, with daily showers. Tropical storms can cause widespread power failures. The hurricane season lasts from June to November.

Alligator close-up at the Louisiana Swamp Festival

FALL

ALTHOUGH THERE MAY still be rainy days in September, the driest months of the year are October and November, when both humidity and heat decrease. Thanksgiving is the most important celebration of this season, and it launches the biggest selling period of the year. The New Orleans' Saints football team starts the NFL season which lasts through December.

SEPTEMBER

Madisonville Wooden Boat Festival *(last weekend Sep).* The largest gathering of wooden water craft in the the New Orleans area, at picturesque Madisonville on the Tchefuncte River. A Kids Dingy Workshop, Quick and Dirty Boat Building Contest, and live entertainment.
Saints Football *(Sep–Dec, Louisiana Superdome).* The NFL football season starts in September with games at the Louisiana Superdome *(see p95)* through December or January *(see pp190–91).*

Louisiana Swamp Festival *(late Sep, early Oct).* For two weekends, both at the Audubon Zoo *(see pp112–3)* and the Woldenberg Riverfront Park *(see p88)*, live Louisiana swamp animals are the center of attention. Those brave enough to touch them are allowed to do so, under close supervision. There is also Cajun food, music, and crafts.

OCTOBER

Oktoberfest *(every weekend).* The German community celebrates its cultural roots at the Deutsches Haus (200 Galvez St (504) 522-8014) with music, food, and beer.
New Orleans Film and Video Festival *(early to mid-Oct).* This week-long event at the Canal Place Landmark Theater presents the works of filmmakers from all over the world. Visiting celebrities, authors, and film stars always attend the event.
Jazz Awareness Month *(all month).* Celebrating jazz at its

birthplace, daily concerts are held throughout the city.
Lesbian and Gay Pride Festival *(weekend nearest Oct 11).* This festival takes place at Washington Square Park in Marigny, and includes music, food, shopping opportunities, and plenty of live entertainment.
Halloween in New Orleans *(31 Oct).* Moonlight Witches Run, Boo-at-the-Zoo for kids, and costume parties are the most important events in this spooky celebration that has a unique atmosphere.

NOVEMBER

Thanksgiving Day Race *(fourth Thu in Nov).* This 5-mile (8-km) run celebrates Thanksgiving.
New Orleans Fair Grounds Horse Racing Season *(last week).* The thoroughbred racing season lasts through March, at the country's third oldest racetrack *(see p126).*
Celebration in the Oaks *(late Nov through early Jan).* City Park *(see pp116–17)* is transformed by countless sparkling Christmas lights illuminating carriage tours.

The Fair Grounds, home to thoroughbred racing in the Deep South

AVERAGE MONTHLY TEMPERATURE

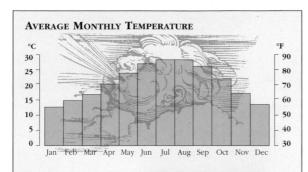

°C / °F
30 / 90
25 / 80
20 / 70
15 / 60
10 / 50
5 / 40
0 / 30

Jan Feb Mar Apr May Jun Jul Aug Sep Oct Nov Dec

Temperature Chart
New Orleans is a semi-tropical city, and during the summer the temperature may rise above 90°F (33°C). Winters are relatively mild, as are spring and fall, which are the the most comfortable times of year to visit.

WINTER

THE WINTER MONTHS are enlivened by the holiday spirit of Christmas and New Year. As soon as Christmas festivities end on Twelfth Night (Jan 6), the excitement of Mardi Gras begins to build with events and preparations for the main celebrations before Lent.

DECEMBER

Christmas *(all month).* Candlelight caroling in Jackson Square *(see p52–3),* madrigal dinners, and historic homes decorated for Christmas in the French Quarter and Garden District.
Festival of Bonfires *(early to mid-Dec and on Christmas Eve).* Both riverboats *(see pp64–5)* and paddlewheelers ply the Mississippi River in this blazing festival in which local people build bonfires to guide Santa Claus to their hometown for Christmas.
Countdown *(Dec 31).* On New Year's Eve, people gather at Jackson Square *(see pp52–3)* to await and celebrate the arrival of the New Year with live music, food, and fireworks.

JANUARY

Sugar Bowl *(first week).* Hundreds of college football fans gather in the Louisiana Superdome *(see p95)* for this important postseason game. An accompanying sports festival also has sailing, tennis, basketball, and track events.

Mardi Gras Parade at the Central Business District

Battle of New Orleans Anniversary *(weekend closest to Jan 8).* A live reenactment of this 1815 battle *(see p17)* is performed at Chalmette Battlefield in St. Bernard Parish, featuring colorful period costumes and artillery demonstrations.

FEBRUARY

New Orleans Boat & Sportfishing Show *(second week).* A display at the Louisiana Superdome *(see p95),* with the latest fishing accessories.
Mardi Gras *(early Feb to early Mar).* Carnival begins on Jan 6 with masked balls and other celebrations; the majority of the parades do not take place until the second weekend before Mardi Gras itself (the Tuesday before Lent).

PUBLIC HOLIDAYS

New Year's Day (Jan 1)
Martin Luther King Day (3rd Mon, Jan)
President's Day (3rd Mon, Feb)
Memorial Day (last Mon, May)
Independence Day (Jul 4)
Labor Day (1st Mon, Sep)
Columbus Day (2nd Mon, Oct)
Veterans Day (Nov 11)
Thanksgiving (4th Thu, Nov)
Christmas Day (Dec 25)

Fireworks at the traditional Countdown on New Year's Eve

NEW ORLEANS
AREA BY AREA

A View of Bourbon Street

**Tile street sign on
Bourbon Street**

Today BOURBON STREET, rather than Basin Street, is synonymous with sin. The name has nothing to do with bourbon, despite the string of bars that line this legendary street; it is named after the French royal family of Bourbon. One bar after another proffers vats of such lethal concoctions as Nuclear Kamikaze, Brain Freeze, and Sex on the Bayou, most often to the accompaniment of blasting rock or blues. Other emporiums offer everything from peep shows and topless and go-go dancers, to drag shows and gay action. During Mardi Gras, the lacy balconies above the sidewalks literally sag from the weight of drinking revelers.

John Wehner's Famous Door
This nightclub lives with the beat of live 1970s and 1980s rock music.

Storyville District
Currently closed, this hip and funky restaurant-bar gave a real boost to jazz on Bourbon St.

Arnaud's
Count Arnaud Cazenave opened the original Arnaud's in 1833. It has been at this location since 1918. There are 17 dining rooms with mosaic tiles, mirrored walls, and paddle fans (see p172).

Old Absinthe House
This building is notable for its entresol, the half-story between the first and second floors.

The World Jeweler
Lafcadio Hearn, the famous American journalist, rented a room here in 1827.

Preservation Hall
An aptly named music venue, Preservation Hall has helped preserve traditional New Orleans jazz. It opened in 1961, and still provides top-quality jazz.

Razoo
This bar is well known for its "shooters" – different cocktails served in uniquely designed glasses.

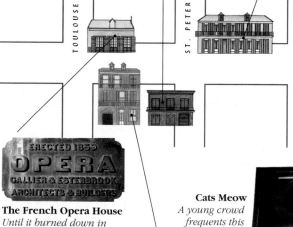

TOULOUSE ST

ST. PETER ST

ORLEANS ST

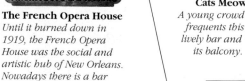

The French Opera House
Until it burned down in 1919, the French Opera House was the social and artistic hub of New Orleans. Nowadays there is a bar on the spot.

Cats Meow
A young crowd frequents this lively bar and its balcony.

Pat O'Brien's
The birthplace of the internationally renowned "Hurricane" cocktail, O'Brien's has a spectacular fire fountain in the main courtyard.

Fritzel's
This is the only traditional European jazz club in New Orleans.

A View of Royal Street

**Tile street sign
on Royal**

THIS IS THE MOST fetching street in the French Quarter. It is lined with antique shops that are filled with beautiful, often French, treasures associated with an opulent Southern lifestyle; crystal chandeliers, massive inlaid armoires, ormolu furnishings, and more. In the early colony this was the city's financial center and its main and most fashionable street. Today, many stores occupy handsome landmarks.

**Street musicians provide open-air
entertainment on Royal Street**

↕ CONTI ST •

**Louisiana State
Bank (# 403)**
*Built in 1821, this
building, now a fine
antique shop, was
designed by Benjamin
Latrobe, who also designed
the southern wing of the
US Capitol.*

Brennan's (# 417)
*Built around 1802 for a
Spanish merchant, this building later became a bank
and the property of Judge
Alonzo Morphy. Brennan's
restaurant moved here in
1954 (see p172). Its balcony
seal is made of cast iron.*

| 0 meters | 10 |
| 0 yards | 10 |

↕ ST. LOUIS ST • TOULOUSE ST ↕

Rumors
*This gift shop sells Mardi
Gras paraphernalia all year
long. Masks, beads, krewe
costumes, and posters are
all for sale (see p186).*

The Historic New Orleans Collection (# 533)
*Occupying a complex of houses built in 1792 for Jean-
François Merieult and his wife, this museum boasts a
magnificent collection of art and artifacts (see pp60–61).*

A Street of Living Tradition

Royal Street is the pride of the French Quarter. Its beautiful buildings have been carefully maintained and are today occupied by fine stores and restaurants.

LOCATOR MAP

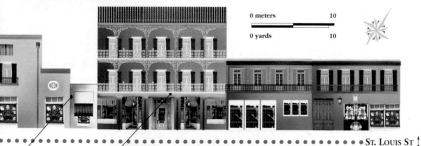

0 meters   10
0 yards   10

● ●St. Louis St ↕

Moss Antiques
offers a fine range of French antiques.

0 meters   10
0 yards   10

Antoine Peychaud's Pharmacy (# 437)

The cocktail was born here when pharmacist Antoine Peychaud mixed brandy with his bitters and served the potion in a coquetier *(see p170). Today it is an antique shop.*

↕ St. Peter St ● Orleans St ↕

St. Anthony's Garden

This beautiful garden (see p55) stands at the back of St. Louis Cathedral. Its serenity hides the fact that it was a staging ground for duels in the 18th century.

The LaBranche Buildings (# 700)
Embellished with fine oak-leaf ironwork, these buildings were constructed in 1835 for sugar planter Jean Baptiste LaBranche.

Upper French Quarter

The French Quarter is synonymous with New Orleans. The original 20 blocks were laid out around the Place d' Armes (present-day Jackson Square) by engineer Adrien de Pauger in 1721. The Upper French Quarter runs from Iberville Street to St. Ann and incorporates the busiest blocks of Decatur, Chartres, Royal, and Bourbon streets. The last of these is particularly lively, offering several popular bars that promise rollicking good times. Architecturally, the Vieux Carré (meaning Old Square) is quintessential New Orleans. The Creole-style cottages painted in reds, greens, mauves, and blues, featuring jalousie-shuttered windows, stand flush along the sidewalks. There are also several Spanish-style buildings decorated with typically elaborate lacy iron galleries.

Cupid statue in Le Petit Théâtre

Sights at a Glance

Historic Buildings
Louisiana Supreme Court Building 11
Napoleon House 12
Père Antoine Alley and St. Anthony's Garden 7
Pirate's Alley 6
Pontalba Buildings 4
St. Louis Cathedral, Cabildo, and Presbytère pp56–7 2

Museums and Galleries
The 1850 House 3
Hermann-Grima Historic House 9
Historic New Orleans Collection pp60–61 10
Jean Lafitte National Historical Park Visitor Center 14
Musée Conti Wax Museum 8
New Orleans Pharmacy Museum 13

Theaters
Le Petit Théâtre du Vieux Carré 5

Parks and Gardens
Jackson Square 1

Boat Trips
Steamboat *Natchez* 15

Key
Street-by-Street map *See pp52–3*
Streetcar stop
[P] Parking

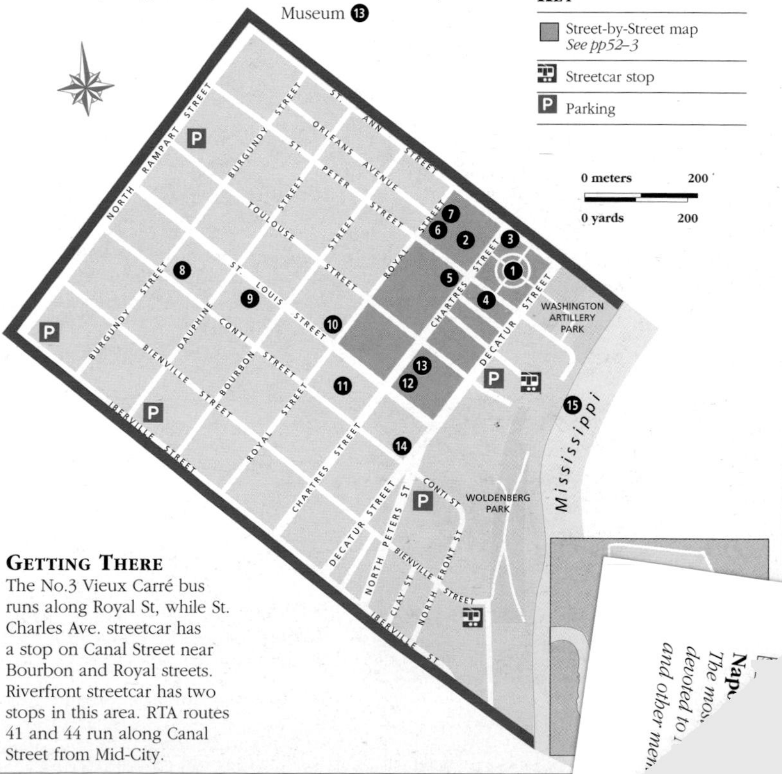
0 meters 200
0 yards 200
NORTH RAMPART STREET
BURGUNDY STREET
ST. ANN STREET
ORLEANS AVENUE
ST. PETER STREET
TOULOUSE STREET
ROYAL STREET
CHARTRES STREET
DECATUR STREET
ST. LOUIS STREET
CONTI STREET
DAUPHINE STREET
BOURBON STREET
BIENVILLE STREET
IBERVILLE STREET
WASHINGTON ARTILLERY PARK
WOLDENBERG PARK
NORTH PETERS ST
CLAY ST
NORTH FRONT ST
CONTI ST
BIENVILLE STREET
IBERVILLE ST
Mississippi

Getting There

The No.3 Vieux Carré bus runs along Royal St, while St. Charles Ave. streetcar has a stop on Canal Street near Bourbon and Royal streets. Riverfront streetcar has two stops in this area. RTA routes 41 and 44 run along Canal Street from Mid-City.

◁ **St. Louis Cathedral in Jackson Square**

Street-by-Street: Upper French Quarter

**Leech jar,
Pharmacy
Museum**

Tʜɪs ɪs ᴛʜᴇ ʜᴇᴀʀᴛ of the French Quarter, containing a striking and harmonious collection of buildings. The lively Jackson Square initially served as a military parade ground, or *place d'armes*, where troops were trained and drilled, executions carried out, and public meetings held. The Cathedral, Cabildo, and Presbytère face the square. It was redesigned in 1848, when Baroness Pontalba built the two elegant apartment buildings on the upriver and downriver sides of the square. A statue was also unveiled in the center; it is said that General Jackson is doffing his hat to his one-time mistress, the Baroness herself, who lived in an apartment opposite.

Père Antoine Alley and St. Anthony's Garden
This garden was a favorite local dueling place in the 19th century ❼

Tennesee Williams
wrote *A Streetcar Named Desire* in an apartment at 632 St. Peter Street.

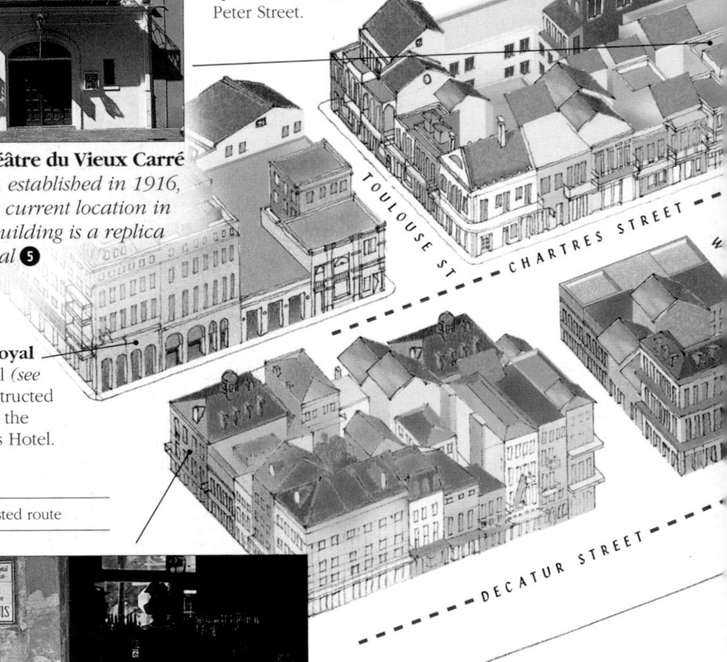

Le Petit Théâtre du Vieux Carré
This theater, established in 1916, moved to its current location in 1919. The building is a replica of the original ❺

The Omni Royal Orleans hotel *(see p155)* is constructed on the site of the 1836 St. Louis Hotel.

Kᴇʏ

– – – Suggested route

TOULOUSE ST.

CHARTRES STREET

DECATUR STREET

...leon House
...beloved bar in the French Quarter is ...apoleon's memory. His portraits ...orabilia adorn the walls ⓬

Sᴛᴀʀ Sɪɢʜᴛs

★ St. Louis Cathedral, Cabildo, and Presbytère

★ The 1850 House

★ Jackson Square

★ **St. Louis Cathedral, Cabildo, and Presbytère**
These were the most important religious and administrative buildings in the French and Spanish periods ②

Street musicians
play in front of the cathedral.

LOCATOR MAP
See Street Finder maps 4 and 5

ST. ANN STREET

ST. PETER ST.

★ **The 1850 House**
This small museum displays opulent furniture and decorations that convey the middle-class lifestyles of the antebellum era ③

★ **Jackson Square**
A magnificent statue of General Jackson takes center stage in the square, where artists hang their works "on the fence" ①

Pontalba Buildings
The handsome Pontalba apartments were built in 1848 for $302,000. The Baroness herself supervised their construction ④

0 meters	30
0 yards	30

Jackson Square ❶

Map 5 D2. 🚋 *Riverfront.* 🚌 3, 55.

Jazz band playing in Jackson Square

TODAY AN ATTRACTIVE and lively meeting place, this square was named the *Place d'Armes* in the early French colony, when it was little more than a muddy field. Here the troops were drilled, criminals were placed in the stocks, and executions were carried out. When Andrew Jackson defeated the British at the Battle of New Orleans in 1815 *(see p17)*, the square was renamed in his honor. It was not until 1848 that the Baroness Pontalba paid for its beautification and laid out the gardens and pathways of the square as they exist to-day. Under her auspices, the Pelanne brothers designed the hand-some wrought-iron fence that encloses the square. At the center stands a statue of General Jackson astride a rearing horse, which was sculpted by Clark Mills for $30,000. Baroness Pontalba insisted that the sculptor depict General Jackson doffing his hat toward the Pontalba apartments on the uptown side of the square. It is said that she was taking her revenge on the General, with whom she had had a love affair, for his failure on one occasion to raise his hat, an omission that had infuriated her. Today he pays his respects eternally. The inscription, "The Union must and shall be preserved," on the plinth was added by Union General Benjamin "Beast" Butler, when he occupied the city during the American Civil War *(see p18)*.

Water vessel in The 1850 House

Today, diverse artists rent space and hang their works on the enclosing fence, while on the flagstones around the square, tarot-card readers, jazz musicians, and clowns entertain visitors throughout the week.

St. Louis Cathedral, Cabildo, and Presbytère ❷

See pp56–7.

The 1850 House ❸

523 St. Ann St. **Map** 5 D2. 🖀 568-6968. 🚌 3, 55, 82. ◯ 9am–5pm Tue–Sun. ● Public hols. 🏚 ⚃

IN THE LOWER Pontalba building, this museum recreates an antebellum apartment. The three-story residence above the ground-floor space is accessed by a dramatic circular staircase. The bedrooms contain all the innovations of their day, including walk-in closets

The Pontalba Buildings, the upriver side of Jackson Square

and private bathrooms. Also displayed are decorative arts and everyday artifacts of the period. A gift shop occupies the ground floor.

Pontalba Buildings ❹

St. Peter and St. Ann Sts. **Map** 5 D2. 🚈 *Riverfront.* 🚌 *3, 55, 82.* ▣ 🗋

I N 1848, Baroness Micaela Pontalba supervised the building of these block-long apartments flanking the up-town and downtown sides of Jackson Square. They were erected for over $300,000, and at the time they were considered the best and the largest apartments of their kind.

At the age of 15, Micaela had married the foppish aristocrat Celestin Pontalba, a distant cousin, and moved to Paris. There, her father-in-law tried to force her to sign over her entire estate. When she refused, he attempted to kill her, but succeeded only in shooting off two of her fingers.

She courageously separated from her husband in 1848 and returned to New Orleans. The baroness, like her father the philanthropist Don Andrés Almonester y Rojas, was a developer. With plans brought back from Paris, she proceeded to build apartments like the ones she had seen in Paris. The architect of the apartment buildings is unknown. The design of the initials A and P (for Almonester and Pontalba) in the cast-iron railings of the galleries and balconies is attributed to one of the baroness's sons, an artist.

Le Petit Théâtre du Vieux Carré ❺

616 St. Peter St. **Map** 5 D2. 🕿 522-2081. 🚌 45, 87. 🕙 10:30am–5:30pm Tue–Sat, noon–4pm Sun. 🔵 Public hols. 🖼

T HIS SMALL theater was the brainchild of a group of actors called the Drawing Room Players, who came together in 1916 under the management of Mrs. Oscar

Interior of Le Petit Théâtre du Vieux Carré

Nixon. Their first theater was located in the Lower Pontalba Building, but in 1922 the current site was bought and was used for the first American productions of Eugene O'Neill's *Beyond the Horizon* and Oscar Wilde's *Lady Windermere's Fan*. It is a pretty building with a beguiling courtyard and fountain.

The structure is actually a 1962 reconstruction of a house that was built here in 1796. Some of the original grillwork, by the brilliant iron-worker Marcellino Hernandez, was reused, but little else, in an effort to create a modern theater space.

Today, the theater presents an annual season of performances between September and June, and functions as a headquarters during the Tennessee Williams New Orleans Literary Festival and Writers' Conference.

Pirate's Alley ❻

Map 5 D2. 🚌 3, 55, 82.

A LTHOUGH it is named after the famous pirate brothers, Jean and Pierre Lafitte *(see p17)*, there is no evidence here that this was once a pirates' haunt or a slave market. Today, the alley's classic bohemian atmosphere and open-air cafés are what make it worth seeking out.

The Faulkner House, a bookstore where the shelves are lined with William Faulkner first editions as well as works by other major

Southern authors, is located in the building where Faulkner wrote his first novel, *Soldier's Pay*, in 1925.

Père Antoine Alley and St. Anthony's Garden ❼

Map 5 D2. 🚈 *Riverfront.* 🚌 3, 55, 82.

T HIS ALLEY is named after one of the city's most beloved clergymen, Father Antonio de Sedella (Père Antoine), who served as pastor of St. Louis Cathedral for 40 years. He was loved for his compassionate ministry to the poor, whom he assiduously fed and clothed. The fenced garden, once a popular dueling ground, features a great sculpture of the Sacred Heart. In the early morning and evening the scent of sweet olive lingers in the air.

Faulkner House, a bookstore in Pirate's Alley

St. Louis Cathedral, Cabildo, and Presbytère ❷

THIS COMPLEX OF BUILDINGS was the most important ensemble in the early colony. The Cabildo, designed by Guilberto Guillemard, was built and financed in 1795 by Don Andrés Almonester y Rojas. It served as a capitol for the legislative assembly of the Spanish colonial government, and subsequently as the City Hall. From 1853 to 1911 it housed the state Supreme Court. The Casa Curial, or Presbytère, was built between 1794 and 1813, and served as a courthouse until 1911. Two earlier churches on the site of the St. Louis Cathedral were destroyed, the first by a hurricane in 1722, the second by a fire in 1788. The current building was begun in 1789 and dedicated as a cathedral in 1794. It has been substantially modified since then.

★ Main Altar
The carved-wood Baroque altars were constructed in Ghent, Belgium, and brought to the cathedral in pieces.

Cathedral Dome
A great mural of St. Louis announcing the Seventh Crusade was painted above the altar.

Old Press
Printing presses were widely used from colonial times. This one is displayed on the third floor of the Cabildo.

Cabildo

★ Sala Capitular
The Louisiana Purchase (see p17) *was signed in this room; this is the pen used in the official act.*

Ceiling Murals
Painted by Alsatian artist Erasme Humbrecht in 1872, the murals portray different biblical stories.

VISITORS' CHECKLIST

Jackson Square. **Map** 5 D2.
525-9585 (St. Louis Cathedral); 568-6968 (Cabildo and Presbytère). St. Charles Ave. 3, 55, 81, 82. 9am–5pm daily (St. Louis Cathedral); 9am–5pm Tue–Sun. (Cabildo and Presbytère). Cabildo and Presbytère. St. Louis Cathedral, regular services throughout the day.
W www.saintlouiscathedral.org

Stained-glass windows with figures of Catholic saints adorn the cathedral's interior.

Mardi Gras Exhibit
Various Mardi Gras objects and memorabilia are displayed here.

Presbytère

Presbytère Façade
The American emblems were added to the pediment in 1821, replacing the royal arms of Spain.

St. Louis Cathedral

The clock bell, given the name "Victoire" by Père Antoine, was cast in Paris. It has tolled hourly since 1819.

The steeples, the portico, and the pilasters were added in 1851.

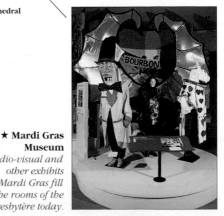

STAR FEATURES

★ **Main Altar**

★ **Mardi Gras Museum**

★ **Sala Capitular**

★ **Mardi Gras Museum**
Audio-visual and other exhibits about Mardi Gras fill the rooms of the Presbytère today.

Master bedroom, the Hermann-Grima Historic House

Musée Conti Wax Museum **8**

917 Conti St. **Map** 4 C2. [525-2605. [3.] 10am–5:30pm Mon–Sat; noon–5:30pm Sun. Thanksgiving, Dec 25, Mardi Gras.

THE MAJOR PART OF this museum's space is taken up with a series of 25 vivid tableaus featuring lifelike historical figures. The museum presents the tempestuous story of New Orleans' development, from its founding in the 18th century to the lynching of 11 Italians accused of gunning down the police chief in 1891. One of the most imaginatively conceived scenes depicts Napoleon in his bathtub gesticulating madly as he informs onlookers of his decision to sell Louisiana

Recreation of America's purchase of Louisiana, Musée Conti

to America *(see p17)*. The museum also features wax representations of political figures such as the legendary governor of Louisiana, Huey Long (1893–1935). Also present is four-time Governor Edwin Edwards, who was found guilty of racketeering.

The tour ends with a series of tableaus featuring stock horror figures such as Dracula and Frankenstein in dungeon-like surroundings. Statues of Andrew Jackson, the pirate Jean Lafitte, and Marie Laveau also compete for your attention.

Hermann-Grima Historic House **9**

820 St. Louis St. **Map** 4 C2. [525-5661. [3.] 10am–3:30pm Mon–Fri. Public hols.

THIS GABLED BRICK HOUSE stands out from those around it because it is one of the few examples of American Creole-style architecture in the French Quarter. William Brand built it in 1831 for Samuel Hermann, a German-Jewish merchant. Unfortunately, he lost his fortune in 1837 and had to give the house to Judge Felix Grima. The house features a central doorway with a fanlight and marble steps; another window with a fanlight graces the second floor.

Inside, the floors and doors are made of cypress, and the rooms feature elegant marble fireplaces. The three-story service quarters, located in a separate building off the parterre behind the house, are also striking. They feature slave quarters and a kitchen containing a rare four-burner wood-fired stove with a beehive oven.

Historic New Orleans Collection **10**

See pp60–61.

Louisiana Supreme Court Building **11**

400 Royal St. **Map** 4 C2. [3. Riverfront.

WHEN THIS massive granite and marble structure was built in 1908–1910, the French Quarter was little more than a slum, and no one protested the destruction of an entire block of buildings to make way for it. Until the 1950s it housed the city's municipal court, then the Louisiana Wild Life and Fisheries Museum moved in and occupied the building until it closed. Over the years it was allowed to decay, windows fell out, and it became a sorry-looking hulk.

Façade of the Louisiana Supreme Court Building

Napoleon House, surmounted by its landmark cupola

The building has recently been renovated, and from 2003 it will serve as the home of the Louisiana Supreme Court, the Louisiana Law Library, and other state legal offices. A small Supreme Court Museum will explain Louisiana legal history and the role of the court, and will also exhibit important state documents. Supreme Court sessions, which have always been open to the public, will also be available to view via closed-circuit television screens, for visitors who would like just a brief glimpse.

Marble detail from the Supreme Court Building

Napoleon House ⑫

500 Chartres St. **Map** 5 D1.
📞 524-9752. 🚌 3, 55, 81, 82.
🕐 11am–midnight Mon–Thu, 11am–1am Fri–Sat, 11am–7pm Sun.
♿ 🍽 🖥 🍸

ONE OF THE city's most atmospheric bars, Napoleon House is famous for its Pimm's Cup and for a warm version of the *muffuletta*, a traditional New Orleans deli sandwich (*see p168*). It occupies two buildings, one of which is a two-story structure, built in 1798, facing St. Louis Street; the second, built in 1814, is a three–story building with a mezzanine. Together, they were the home of Mayor Nicholas Girod, who planned to free Napoleon from impris-

onment on St. Helena Island. With the help of Dominique You and a pirate band (*see p17*), Girod intended to bring Napoleon to this refuge, but Napoleon died before the mission could be undertaken. Today, the walls of the house are adorned with all kinds of Napoleonic decor and memorabilia. Both buildings are attributed to Hyacinthe Laclotte, and the balcony railings were crafted by William Malus. The cupola on the roof is a local landmark.

New Orleans Pharmacy Museum ⑬

514 Chartres St. **Map** 5 D2.
📞 565-8027. 🚌 3, 55, 81, 82.
🕐 10am–5pm Tue–Sun. ● Public hols. 🎟 📷 ♿

THIS MUSEUM is located on the site of the first licensed pharmacy in the United States, operated by Louis Joseph Dufilho from 1823 to 1855. The original display cases and mahogany cabinets contain some gruesome-looking early surgical tools – saws, axes, knives, and bloodletting instruments – as well as early herbal remedies, many of which were forerunners of today's drugs. These include a bottle of salicin, an early

form of aspirin produced by Bayer & Co. from black willow bark. The museum also features a splendid 1855 marble soda fountain at which appealing sodas were first concocted to help the medicine go down. The second floor features a 19th-century sick room, a fine collection of eye glasses, plus homeopathic remedies and an impressive collection of 19th-century dental instruments. The walled courtyard garden is filled with medicinal herbs.

Jean Lafitte National Historical Park Visitor Center ⑭

419 Decatur St. **Map** 4 C3.
📞 589-2636. 🚌 3, 55, 81, 82.
🕐 9am–5pm daily. ● Dec 25, Mardi Gras. 🎟 📷 ♿ 🎵

THIS VISITOR CENTER has some excellent displays on the geography, history, and culture of the Mississippi River Delta region. It also offers slide shows and ranger-led walking tours of the French Quarter at 10:30 every morning. The Williams Research Center, the reading room of the Historic New Orleans Collection (*see pp60–61*), is located nearby.

The Jean Lafitte National Historical Park comprises six sites in all, including three in Cajun Country (*see pp144, 146*) and the Chalmette Battlefield (*see p88*).

A 19th-century soda fountain at the Pharmacy Museum

Historic New Orleans Collection ❿

THIS MASSIVE COLLECTION, born of one couple's interest in the Battle of New Orleans, is housed in several 18th and 19th century structures. The Merieult House (1792) features 10 galleries displaying historical artifacts, ranging from maps and paintings to furnishings and decorative objects. Free temporary exhibitions are

Spanish coat of arms

held in a gallery on the first-floor. The Williams residence, at the rear of the courtyard, was the home of the collectors, General and Mrs. L. Kemper Williams, who lived here from the 1940s to the 1960s. The Williams Research Center at 410 Chartres Street offers changing exhibitions in its small public areas.

Williams Research Center
This facility houses the largest collection of historical documents in the city.

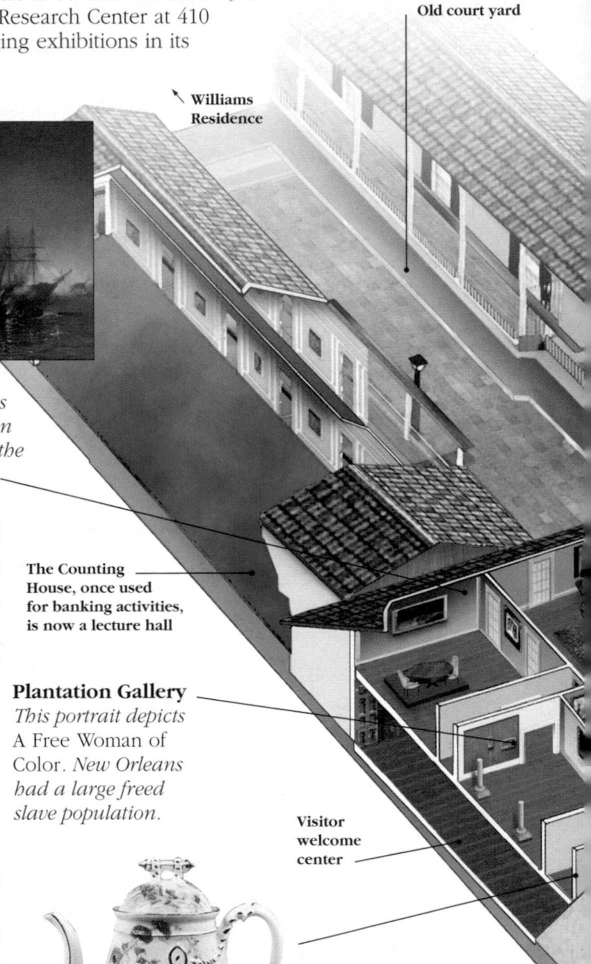

Old court yard

Williams Residence

River Gallery
On display here are paintings showing commercial activity in the port of New Orleans and the vessels that made it wealthy.

The Counting House, once used for banking activities, is now a lecture hall

Plantation Gallery
This portrait depicts A Free Woman of Color. *New Orleans had a large freed slave population.*

Visitor welcome center

STAR EXHIBITS

★ **Empire Gallery**

★ **Spanish Colonial Gallery**

★ **Victorian Gallery**

★ **Victorian Gallery**
This gallery features elaborate furniture, plus smaller objects, such as this teapot.

Slave Funeral
One of a series of paintings by John Antrobus evokes life on a Louisiana plantation in the Plantation Gallery.

VISITORS' CHECKLIST

533 Royal St. **Map** 4 C2.
523-4662. St. Charles
Ave. 3, 55, 81, 82.
10am–4:30pm Tue–Sat.

French Colonial Gallery
French period items such as this refectory table, used in the Old Ursuline Convent, are displayed here.

A dining room in 1792, this area is now closed to the public

★ **Spanish Colonial Gallery**
Portraits of residents during the Spanish colonial era are shown here.

Louisiana Purchase Gallery
This detailed carved-wood sculpture commemorates Napoleon (see p17).

★ **Empire Gallery**
Superb Empire furnishings, including tables, chests, and sofas, are displayed alongside portraits of such native New Orleanian figures as Madame Auguste de Gas, mother of artist Edgar Degas.

Main entrance

The French Quarter, open for business at dusk ▷

Steamboat *Natchez*

Upper deck light

Fok a reminder of the old days of river travel, visitors can take a two-hour cruise on the Steamboat *Natchez*. In the 19th century, steamboats traveled the length of the Mississippi, taking between three and five days to get from Louisville, Kentucky, to New Orleans. The boatmen were notorious brawlers who went looking for women and liquor at the end of a trip and established New Orleans' reputation as the "City of Sin." In their heyday, from 1830 to 1860, some 30 steamboats lined up at the levee. Their steamboat era ended by the close of the 19th century as railroads and highways replaced them.

Steam Whistle
The genuine copper-and-steel steam whistle is a treasured antique.

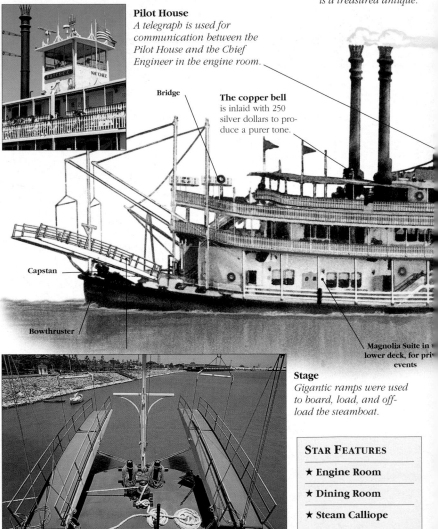

Pilot House
A telegraph is used for communication between the Pilot House and the Chief Engineer in the engine room.

Bridge

The copper bell is inlaid with 250 silver dollars to produce a purer tone.

Capstan

Bowthruster

Magnolia Suite in lower deck, for priv events

Stage
Gigantic ramps were used to board, load, and off-load the steamboat.

STAR FEATURES
★ **Engine Room**
★ **Dining Room**
★ **Steam Calliope**

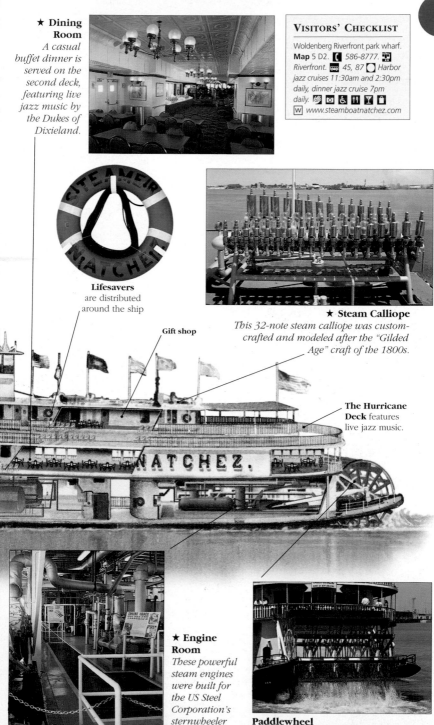

★ **Dining Room**
A casual buffet dinner is served on the second deck, featuring live jazz music by the Dukes of Dixieland.

VISITORS' CHECKLIST

Woldenberg Riverfront park wharf.
Map 5 D2. ☎ 586-8777. ☐
Riverfront. ☐ 45, 87 ○ Harbor
jazz cruises 11:30am and 2:30pm
daily, dinner jazz cruise 7pm
daily. ☐ ☐ ☐ ☐ ☐ ☐
Ⓦ www.steamboatnatchez.com

Lifesavers
are distributed around the ship

★ **Steam Calliope**
This 32-note steam calliope was custom-crafted and modeled after the "Gilded Age" craft of the 1800s.

Gift shop

The Hurricane Deck features live jazz music.

NATCHEZ.

★ **Engine Room**
These powerful steam engines were built for the US Steel Corporation's sternwheeler Clairton in 1925.

Paddlewheel
Twenty-five tons of white oak propel the steamboat along the river.

LOWER FRENCH QUARTER AND MARIGNY

EXTENDING from St. Ann Street to Esplanade Avenue, this is the quieter, more residential part of the French Quarter. Within this area the busiest sidewalks are those around the French Market, where people gather at the Café du Monde for coffee and *beignets*. A popular pastime among local people is wandering among the stalls of the arcade, with its hot sauces, strings of garlic and peppers, and other Creole and Cajun specialties.

Louis Armstrong statue

The surrounding streets are lined with Creole-style cottages and other handsome residences. Esplanade Avenue acts as the dividing line between the French Quarter and the Faubourg Marigny. Soon after the Louisiana Purchase *(see p17)*, the Marigny Plantation was subdivided, and the area known as the Faubourg Marigny was settled (*faubourg* is French for suburb). Today the Marigny is the most arty section of the city.

SIGHTS AT A GLANCE

Museums and Galleries
Beauregard-Keyes House **6**
Gallier House Museum **8**
Madame John's Legacy **15**
New Orleans Historic Voodoo Museum **17**
New Orleans Jazz Historical Park **4**
Old US Mint pp74–5 **1**

Parks and Gardens
American Aquatic Gardens **20**
Armstrong Park **21**
Congo Square **22**
Washington Square **19**

Cemeteries
St. Louis Cemetery #1 **25**
St. Louis Cemetery #2 **26**

Historic Buildings
Cornstalk Fence **16**
Gauche Villa **11**

Lafitte's Blacksmith Shop **18**
Lalaurie House **9**
Latrobe House **10**
Old Ursuline Convent **5**
Soniat House **7**

Landmarks
Café du Monde **14**
Central Grocery **13**
Esplanade Avenue **12**

Flea Market **2**
French Market **3**

Churches
Our Lady of Guadalupe **24**

Theaters
Mahalia Jackson Theater of the Performing Arts **23**

GETTING THERE
The 48 bus runs from Mid-City to the Esplanade; the 3 circles the Quarter on Dauphine and Chartres. The Riverfront Streetcar has two stops here.

KEY

▨	Street-by-Street map *See pp68–9*
🚋	Streetcar stop
P	Parking

0 meters 300
0 yards 300

◁ **Lacy, New Orleans ironwork, Royal Street**

Street-by-Street: Lower French Quarter

THE AREA SURROUNDING the French Market is loaded with atmosphere. It has long been a place for meeting and mixing. In the city's early days, Native Americans came to this area to sell wild herbs, and today the district still offers a range of exotic goods. French Market Place, formerly Gallatin Street, was once the most notorious street in the Quarter, populated by prostitutes, rowdies, criminals (like the Black Hand Gang), and visiting sailors, who ventured there at their peril. It was lined with so many brothels and bars that it was dubbed "Louisiana's Barbary Coast." Today, it still has plenty of bars, and some of the oldest and most important buildings in the French Quarter.

Gallier House Museum
Set in a former residence, this is an informative showcase of 19th-century life ❽

Soniat House
This residence has been restored to its original splendor, and serves as a lovely small hotel (see p158) ❼

Beauregard-Keyes House, former home of Frances Parkinson Keyes, is now a museum ❻

★ **Old Ursuline Convent**
Designed in 1745, and built in 1752, this is the oldest building in the Mississippi Valley ❺

CHARTRES STREET

GOV. NICHOLLS ST

Sbisa's Café is one of the oldest bars in the French Quarter.

★ **French Market**
Brimming with appetizing fruit and vegetables, the French Market has been a New Orleans institution since 1791 ❸

KEY

- - - Suggested route

Gauche Villa
Built in 1856, this house is notable for its beautiful cast-iron balcony. Architect James Freret designed the house ⑪

LOCATOR MAP
See Street Finder maps 4 and 5

Esplanade Avenue
This beautiful avenue was the aristocratic residential street of the Creole community in the 19th century. It marks the division between the French Quarter and the Faubourg Marigny ⑫

| 0 meters | 30 |
| 0 yards | 30 |

DECATUR STREET

ESPLANADE AVENUE

BARRACKS ST

★ Old US Mint
Coins were minted here until 1909. Today the building is home to the Jazz Museum ❶

Flea Market
Handcrafts, souvenirs, and curiosities can be found at this ever-popular flea market ❷

STAR FEATURES

★ French Market

★ Old US Mint

★ Old Ursuline Convent

Old US Mint ❶

See pp74–5.

Flea Market ❷

French Market Pl. and Barracks St.
Map 5 D1. 🚋 *Riverfront.* 🚌 *3, 55.*
🕐 *9am–7pm daily.* 🔧 🏠 🍽

A<small>T STALLS AND TABLES</small> inside and outside the French Market buildings, all kinds of items can be bought, from jewelry and pottery to African arts and crafts. The flea market stands on the site of the notorious neighborhood around Gallatin, once called the "port of missing men," because so many men who visited the neighborhood's bars and brothels were either shanghaied or killed.

Dramatic African sculptures, the Flea Market

French Market ❸

French Market Pl. and Ursulines St.
Map 5 D1. 🚋 *Riverfront.* 🚌 *3, 55.*
🕐 *9am–7pm daily.* 🏠 🍽 🛒 🍴 🍷

E<small>VEN THOUGH</small> it is called the French Market, this New Orleans institution has been a gathering place for the many different ethnic inhabitants of New Orleans, be they Native American, French, Italian, German, or African American. Originally it was a market where Native Americans came to sell their baskets, beads, pottery, and filé (ground sassafras leaves used in gumbo). Later, they were joined by African American women selling various wares including calas (hot rice cakes), German

Typical French Market stand displaying fresh garlic and vegetables

farmers from upriver selling agricultural produce, and still later by Italians who operated most of the market stalls in the late 19th century.

Today, the French Market is a favorite place to purchase hot sauce, filé, coffee, crawfish, and many other New Orleans specialties.

New Orleans Jazz Historical Park ❹

916 N Peters St. **Map** 5 D1.
🚋 *Riverfront.* 🚌 *3, 82.* 🕐 *9am–5pm daily.* 🔧

A<small> NEW, LARGE</small> complex in Armstrong Park, devoted to the history and development of jazz, is planned for construction in 2003. Until its completion, this temporary visitors' center offers live programs of seminars, lectures, and free afternoon jazz concerts. There is also a permanent collection of photographs charting the history of jazz, as well as guided walks to nearby sites of interest.

Old Ursuline Convent ❺

1100 Chartres St. **Map** 5 D1. 📞 *529-3040.* 🚋 *Riverfront.* 🚌 *3, 55.*
🕐 *10am–3pm Tue–Fri, 11am–2pm Sat, Sun. (Guided tours only.)* 🌐 🔧

D<small>ATING FROM</small> 1752, this is the oldest building in the Mississippi Valley. With its steep-pitched roof punctuated by a row of dormers and tall chimneys, it is typically French Colonial.

In the 1820s, when the nuns departed to new quarters, the convent became the first official residence for the bishops and archbishops of New Orleans, and the home of the archdiocesan archives. Later, the convent became part of a parish complex and the old nuns' kitchen and laundry became (as it remains today) the rectory for Our Lady of Victory Church.

The current chapel, consecrated in 1845, was originally known as St. Mary's, but today it is called Our Lady of

Main façade, Old Ursuline Convent

Beautiful ironwork adorning the Soniat House

his name is still associated with the building.

Novelist Frances Parkinson Keyes, who wintered and wrote many of her 51 novels here, including *Dinner at Antoine's*, restored the property. Today, many of her personal possessions are on display, including all of her novels, plus a collection of dolls from all over the world. The rooms are arranged around an attractive courtyard, which contains a fountain that Mrs. Keyes brought from Vermont, her home state.

Soniat House ❼

1133 Chartres St. **Map** 5 D1.
522-0570. *Riverfront.* 3,
55. *See Where to Stay, p158.*

THIS HISTORIC RESIDENCE was built in 1829 as a townhouse for wealthy sugar planter Joseph Soniat Dufossat and his family. Joseph was the second son of Chevalier Guy Saunhac du Fossat, who had been sent to Louisiana by Louis XV of France in 1751 to help the fight against the Native Americans.

The house combines Creole style – the flagstone carriageway, a garden courtyard, an external spiral staircase, and lacy iron galleries – with Greek Revival detail in the mantels and moldings. In the 1940s, the Nathaniel Felton family restored it completely. Today it is a small hotel, exquisitely furnished with authentic antiques and decoration.

Victory. Inside, visitors can admire the splendid pine and cypress ceiling, two fine Bavarian stained-glass windows, and a window depicting the Battle of New Orleans *(see p17)* beneath an image of Our Lady of Prompt Succor.

A formal French garden containing a handsome iron gazebo lies in front of the building. It is accessed via the porter's lodge.

Beauregard-Keyes House ❻

1113 Chartres St. **Map** 5 D1.
523-7257. *Riverfront.* 3, 55.
10am–3pm Mon-Sat.

TWIN STAIRCASES lead up to this Federal-style townhouse, designed by François Correjolles in 1826. It is associated with several famous New Orleanians,

including master chess player Paul Morphy who was born here in 1837, when it was the residence of his grandfather, Joseph Le Carpentier. General P. G. T. Beauregard lived here briefly for six weeks in 1866–7, and because he was such a famous Civil War hero

Grand entrance to the Beauregard-Keyes House

Gallier House Museum ❽

1132 Royal St. **Map** 5 D1.
📞 525-5661. 🚌 3, 55, 81, 82.
🕐 10am–3:30pm Mon–Fri.
⬤ Public hols. ♿ 📷 📷

Iᴺ 1857, JAMES GALLIER, JR. designed this attractive residence, which combines architectural elements of the Creole, with great height and verticality, and the American townhouse, with Federal-style windows and doorways *(see pp32–3)*. The interior incorporated many innovations of its time, including an ingenious hot-water and ventilation system. The kitchen was also inside the house, which was unusual for the period because of the danger of fire. On the exterior, the rosebud design of the railings is striking.

Inside, visitors can view the "isolation room," a sparsely furnished room designed for the sick. Every household had such a room, which was not surprising in a city that experienced 23 yellow fever epidemics between 1718 and 1860.

James Gallier, Jr. was the son of the city's renowned architect James Gallier, Sr., who built Gallier Hall *(see p95)*. Gallier Hall served as the City Hall during the 1950s. James Gallier, Jr. also designed the portico of the Louisiana State Bank building *(see p48)*.

Lalaurie House, associated with ghostly visions

Lalaurie House ❾

1140 Royal St. **Map** 5 D1.
🚌 45, 87. ⬤ Closed to the public.

Rᴇꜱɪᴅᴇɴᴛꜱ of the French Quarter still hurry past this otherwise lovely building because of its grim associations and reputation for ghosts. It was built in 1832 for a distinguished couple, Dr. Leonard Louis Nicolas Lalaurie and his wife, Delphine, who were well known for their fashionable and lavish parties.

At these social events, though, guests could not help but notice the condition of the servants, who were painfully thin and seemed to be terrified of their mistress. The gossip about how she treated her slaves was confirmed on April 10, 1834, when a fire broke out at the residence. When neighbors rushed in to extinguish the fire and save the contents, they found seven half-starved and manacled slaves, plus a number of grim-looking torture instruments. A story in the local press further fueled

Front door at Lalaurie House

the outrage, and a mob arrived intent on destroying the place. During the melee, Madame Lalaurie and her husband escaped unharmed. After she died in 1842, it is believed that her body was secretly returned from Paris and was buried in St. Louis Cemetery #1 *(see p82)* or #2 *(see p83)*. During the Civil War *(see pp18–19)* the house served as a Union headquarters; later it was used variously as a school, conservatory of music, and gaming house.

A private residence now, some locals still swear that the house is haunted, that a slave girl can be seen leaping to her death, and that the clanking of chains can be heard.

Latrobe House ❿

721 Governor Nicholls St. **Map** 5 D1.
🚌 45, 87. ⬤ Closed to the public.

Wʜᴇɴ Benjamin Henry Latrobe designed this building in 1814, with its sturdy Doric columns, he helped launch the mania in New Orleans for Greek

Gallier House, an innovative 19th-century residence

Revival-style architecture. Known as the first professional architect in the US, Benjamin Henry Latrobe (1764–1820) was born in England, and after working as a professional architect for several years in Europe he came to the United States in 1796. Latrobe was highly influential, and built a variety of private residences and public buildings, the latter ranging from waterworks to cathedrals. He is largely responsible for the interior of the US Capitol Building, and for the East Portico of the White House. He died in New Orleans of yellow fever while supervising the building of a new waterworks.

Gauche Villa, with its superb original ironwork

Gauche Villa ⓫

704 Esplanade Ave at Royal. **Map 5** D1. 🚌 *45, 87.*

THE BEAUTIFUL ironwork of this residence is uniquely integral to the villa's overall design, which accounts for the building's harmonious appearance. Little of the cast iron-work in New Orleans was constructed at the same time as the building – mostly it was added as an afterthought. Numerous patterns are used on the fence, the gate, the balconies, and the parapet, casting lovely shadows on the stucco exterior on sun-filled days. A bacchant surrounded by grapevines adorns the balcony, cast in Saarbrucken, Germany, and shipped to New Orleans. Rows of anthema and other Greek floral motifs decorate the edge of the roof and the fence posts. Architect James Freret designed the house for crockery merchant John Gauche in 1856.

Esplanade Avenue ⓬

Map 2 B2–3 E4. 🚌 *45, 87.*

TODAY, Esplanade Avenue acts as the dividing line between the French Quarter and Faubourg Marigny, and extends from the Mississippi to Bayou St. John.

As early as the 1830s, this broad, tree-lined 3-mile (2-km)-long street cut through what was the most aristocratic Creole neighborhood of impressive villas and townhouses. The fashionable elite paraded in their carriages past the many elegant residences, some of which have survived to this day.

Many of these homes were designed by the city's foremost architects, including Henry Howard, James Gallier, Sr., and William and James Freret. Their styles range from Greek Revival to Italianate and Queen Anne.

Most are still private residences, but some have been converted into handsome bed-and-breakfasts. A stroll along this street will reveal over 190 homes that were built before 1900. Every block contains numerous architectural gems.

Elegant residences lining Esplanade Avenue

Old US Mint ●

THIS GREEK REVIVAL building, built in 1835 by William Strickland, functioned as a mint until 1909, turning out a variety of coinage, including Confederate and Mexican currency. In 1931, it was converted into a federal prison by the addition of cell blocks. Later, it was used by the Coast Guard until the late 1970s, when it was taken over by the state as a museum to house the New Orleans Jazz Collection. This exhibit tells the story of jazz through paintings, instruments, recordings, photographs, and scrapbooks. Fort St. Charles formerly stood on the site; it was here that Andrew Jackson reviewed his troops before the Battle of New Orleans *(see p17).*

Trombone slide detail

★ History of the Old US Mint Exhibition
A selection of the gold and silver coins formely minted here are displayed in this glittering exhibit.

Early Jazz
Vintage photographs depict the early bands with their jug and tin drums, washboards, kazoos, and other homemade instruments.

Ironwork
The balconies and railings display some of the city's beautiful wrought iron.

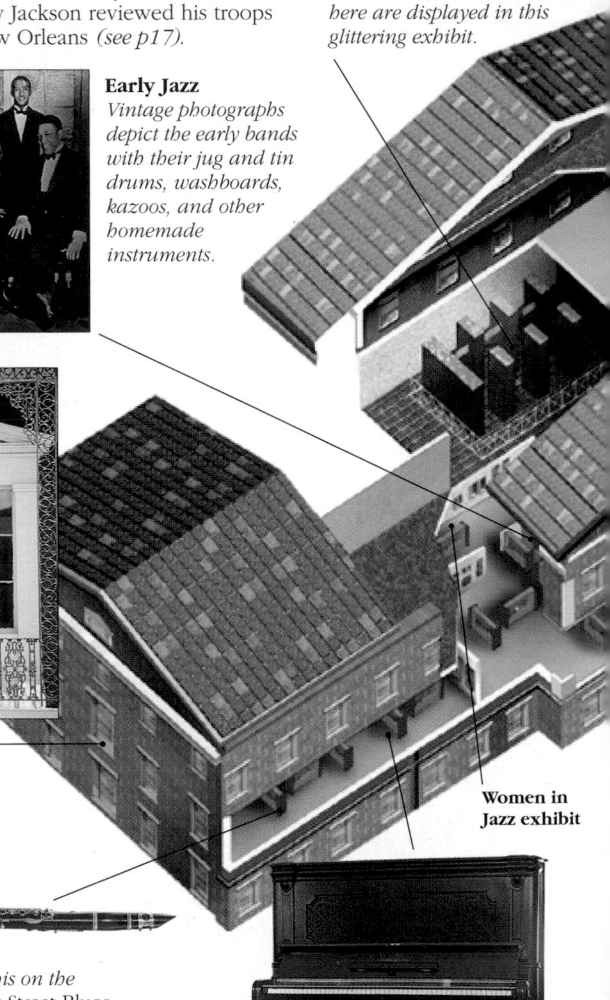

Women in Jazz exhibit

Ebony Clarinet
George Lewis played this on the recording of Burgundy Street Blues.

★ New Orleans Jazz Collection
Original musical instruments, vintage photographs, and historic documents show the evolution from Dixieland to modern jazz music.

Cornet
Louis Armstrong learned to play jazz on this horn.

VISITORS' CHECKLIST

400 Esplanade Ave. **Map** 5 E1.
(*(504) 568-6968.* 🚊 *River-front.* 🚌 *3, 55.* ◯ *9am–5pm, Tue–Sun.* ● *Public hols.* 🎫 ⬆️
📷 🚻 W *http://lsm.crt.state.la.us/mintex.htm*

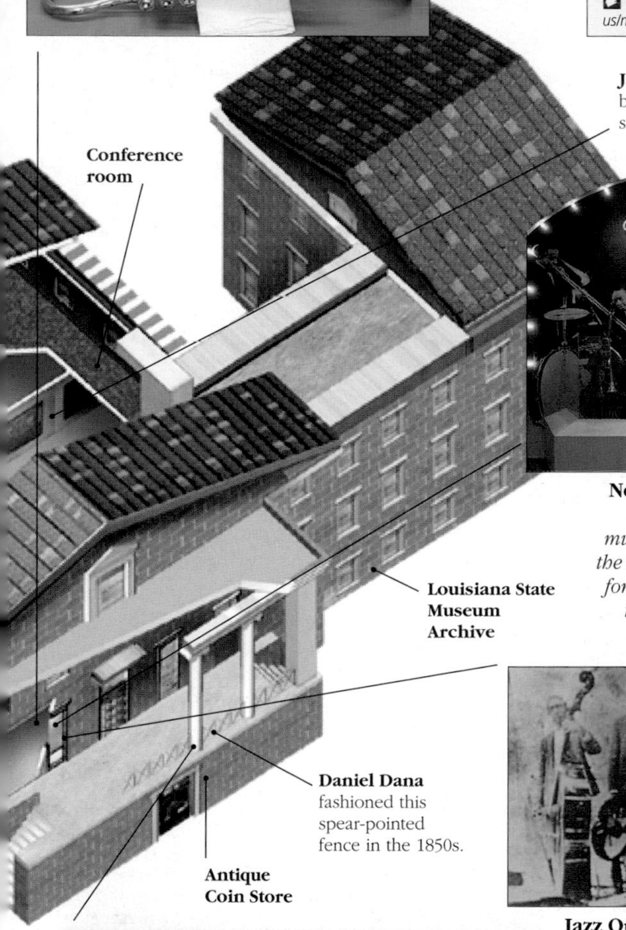

Conference room

Jazz murals painted by Tony Green show scenes of Storyville.

New Orleans-style Band
This mural with real musical instruments shows the traditional jazz line-up, formed by cornet, clarinet, trombone, drums, string bass, and banjo.

Louisiana State Museum Archive

Daniel Dana fashioned this spear-pointed fence in the 1850s.

Antique Coin Store

Jazz Origins
A selection of photographs of early jazz bands and musicians, as well as a steamboat scale model, are displayed at the Jazz Collection entrance.

STAR EXHIBITS

★ **History of the Old US Mint Exhibition**

★ **New Orleans Jazz Collection**

Main Façade
Visitors enter the Old US Mint through a grand Neo-Classical portico, which has been carefully restored along with the rest of the building.

Central Grocery ⑬

923 Decatur. **Map** 5 D2. 523-1620.
3, 55, 81, 82. 8am–5:30pm
Mon–Sat, 9am–5:30pm Sun.

THIS HISTORIC STORE, one of
the few Italian delis left
in the city, sells all kinds of
Italian food, from pasta, pro-
volone, and mozzarella, to
sausages, parmesan, and olive
oil. In the 1890s many Italians
began to move to the French
Quarter, and became major
stallholders at the nearby
French Market *(see p68)*.
Today, customers gather at
the counters at the back
of the store to order another
specialty, the *muffuletta (see
p168)*, which is a sizable
sandwich filled with deli
meats and cheeses. The most
vital ingredient, however, is
the olive salad – a blend of
pickled olives, celery, carrots,
cauliflower, and capers. This
delicious salad can also be
purchased at the store.

**Olive salad and other deli
specialties at the Central Grocery**

Café du Monde ⑭

800 Decatur. **Map** 5 D2. 587-
0833. 3, 55, 81, 82. 24 hours
daily.

EVERYONE WHO visits New
Orleans stops here for a
plate of sugar-dusted *beignets*
(square French donuts) accompanied by either plain *café
au lait* or the famous chicory-
flavored version. These are
the only items offered at this
100-year old coffeehouse,
where you can relax at a
table under the arcade and
listen to the street musicians
entertain, or just people-watch.

Taking a break at Café du Monde, with *beignets* and coffee

During the mid-19th century
there were as many as 500
similar coffee houses in the
French Quarter. Coffee was
one of New Orleans' most
important commodities, and
the coffee trade helped the
economy recover after the
Civil War, when New Orleans
vied with New York City to
control coffee imports.
Chicory-flavored coffee was
invented during the Civil War,
when the root was used to
stretch the coffee supply.

Madame John's Legacy ⑮

632 Dumaine St. **Map** 5 D2. 568-
6968. 3, 55, 81, 82. 9am–
5pm Tue–Sun. Public hols.

DATING FROM 1788, this is
the oldest surviving residence in the Mississippi
Valley. It is a typical Creole
plantation-style house, supported on brick piers which
rise some 9 ft (3m) off
the ground. A
veranda,
accessible via French windows
from all the rooms, extends
around the first floor.
The name Madame John's
Legacy refers to George
Washington Cable's famous
story *Tite Poulette* (1873), in
which the hero leaves a residence as a legacy to his quadroon mistress, who sells the
building, deposits the cash in
a bank, and loses it all when
the bank fails. Cable used this
residence as a model of the
home in his story. In the late
19th century, the house was
converted into rental apartments, which were occupied
by a broad mixture of
immigrant families.
Today, exhibits in the
first-floor galleries relate the
history of the house and its
many owner-residents.
Among them were Jean Pascal,
a Provençal sea captain who
built the original house on
this site before being killed
by Natchez Indians in 1729;
pirate-admiral René Beluche,
who was born here and
later served in the
Venezuelan

Madame John's Legacy, the oldest residence in the Mississippi Valley

Revolutionary Navy; and the Segher family, whose household inventory featured four slaves, including a mulatto, valued at $2,500, and his daughter, who was valued at only $1,200, because she had been promised her freedom at age 30. The second-floor galleries are currently used for changing contemporary art exhibitions.

Cornstalk Fence ⑯

915 Royal St. **Map** 5 D2. ▦ 45, 87.

Voodoo altar with voodoo dolls, rum bottles, and Catholic saints

THIS HANDSOME cast-iron landmark fence is one of two remaining in the city (see p106). It was erected around 1850, when cast iron began replacing wrought iron (see pp36–7). The cornstalks are entwined with morning glories, and each element is painted in its natural color – yellow for the ears of corn, green for the stalks, and blue for the morning glories. A butterfly decorates the central portion of the gate, and a spray of holly adorns the bottom. It was cast by the prestigious Philadelphia company, Wood & Perot.

New Orleans Historic Voodoo Museum ⑰

724 Dumaine St. **Map** 5 D2. [522-5223. ▦ 45, 87. ○ 10am–8pm daily. ⬚ ✔ ⬚

THIS SMALL museum traces the origin and development of voodoo, a cult-religion brought to the city by slaves from Martinique and Saint Domingue in the late 1700s. An amalgam of West Indian fetish worship and Roman Catholic saint-worship, voodoo had its most famous practitioner in the mulatto hairdresser, Marie Laveau (see p83), who performed her ritual celebrations in public along the Bayou St. John (see p119). Citizens consulted her for charms, amulets, and magical gris-gris powders (dried frog, dried lizard, and many more), which were believed to help accomplish any purpose, from evicting a neighbor to inspiring love. The museum displays some of her alleged possessions. The cramped rooms are filled with altars,

Voodoo candle

including one dedicated to the "alligator man," which is considered a very powerful image. There are also ritual objects, spirit portraits, charms for curing and preventing illness, and a coiled live python in a box (the serpent is believed to be the earthly form of the voodoo god and the source of the religion's power).

In a room off the back courtyard, visitors can watch a detailed documentary video, which explains what voodoo is, and what role it has played in the New Orleans community. The museum's store sells love oil, "boss fix" powder, gris-gris for safe travel, voodoo dolls, African drums, and other magical accoutrements.

Cast-iron Cornstalk Fence and hotel (see p154)

Tree-shaded passage in Washington Square

Lafitte's Blacksmith Shop ⑱

941 Bourbon St. **Map** 5 D1.
☎ 523-0066. 🚌 3, 55, 81, 82.
🕐 11:30am–4am daily. ♿ 🚻 🖥
🍸 🍴 🎵

THIS IS ONE of the finest bars in the French Quarter. It is an example of the brick between posts *(see p32)* French-style building, and was constructed sometime before 1772, although the precise date is unknown. Inside, several small fireplaces warm the place on cool evenings, and there is also a small patio containing a sculpture of Adam and Eve embracing on a bed of ivy. The sculpture was created by an artist as payment for his bar bill.

Despite its name, there is no proof that the pirate brothers, Jean and Pierre Lafitte, operated a smithy here as a front for their smuggling activities. Very little documentation of their lives exists, so that many myths have been woven around these two legendary figures. They operated as smugglers and were prominent slave traffickers, selling "black ivory" to all of the important slave-holding families in Louisiana, particularly after 1808 when the importation of slaves into the United States was forbidden. The auctions were conducted in the rotunda of the St. Louis Hotel (1836),

which stood on the site of today's Omni Royal Orleans *(see p155)* at Royal and St. Louis street. They earned local gratitude by warning the Americans of the planned British attack on New Orleans, and with their band they fought bravely in the ensuing battle *(see p17)*.

Just up Bourbon Street from Lafitte's stands another bar, called Lafitte's in Exile. It is so called because, until the early 1950s, gays frequented the old Lafitte's; when the bar changed hands, its new owner refused to renew the lease, and in 1953 its gay patrons were driven into exile. They established their new quarters just up the street at Lafitte's in Exile. It has remained a popular alternative ever since.

Washington Square ⑲

Frenchman between Royal and Dauphine. **Map** 5 E1. 🕐 9am–6pm daily. 🚌 45, 87. ♿

WASHINGTON SQUARE, one of the earliest parks to be laid out in New Orleans, was created in 1808. It lies at the center of the Faubourg Marigny, today the most "bohemian" section of the city and home to most of the city's gay community.

The park is a good place to throw a frisbee and for ball games, or just to relax on the vast green areas it offers. There are also open-air concerts here in summer, and a wine festival in September.

Water lily at the American Aquatic Gardens

American Aquatic Gardens ⑳

621 Elysian Fields. **Map** 5 E1.
☎ 944-0410. 🚌 45, 87.
🕐 9am–5pm daily. 🖥

A DELIGHTFUL, relaxing place, this "store," which occupies half a city block, is the largest – and widely considered the best – aquatic plant nursery and garden

The historic Lafitte's Blacksmith Shop

Main entrance to Armstrong Park

supply store in the United States. It is certainly worth visiting for its glorious display of aquatic and exotic plants in the outdoor gardens, which include an Asian garden complete with decorative Buddhas and Oriental lanterns. The water gardens contain exquisite water lilies in a whole spectrum of colors, and there are also spectacular sculpted fountains, handsome statuary, attractive pond designs, plus a variety of garden benches and ornamental wall planters.

Armstrong Park ㉑

Rampart St between St. Peter St and St. Ann St. **Map** 4 C1.
🚌 45, 87. 🎵

Named after the legendary trumpeter, Louis "Satchmo" Armstrong *(see pp20–21)*, this spacious park stands on hallowed jazz ground. It occupies what used to be a section of Storyville *(see p81)*, the legal red-light district that nurtured so many of the early jazz artists.

Armstrong's statue stands in the park, and his name is emblazoned on the arch at St. Ann Street. He was born in New Orleans on August 4, 1901, and as a boy he spent his time singing on the streets

in a quartet until he was sent to the Colored Waifs' Home after firing a pistol in public. It was there that he learned to play the trumpet, and soon he was talented enough to challenge such leading players as Joe "King" Oliver and Freddie Keppard. He left New Orleans in 1922 to join King Oliver in Chicago, and went on to build an international career, entertaining

audiences until his death in 1971. The park features an artificial lake, City Auditorium, the Mahalia Jackson Theater of the Performing Arts *(see p80)*, and Congo Square *(p80)*, and has a bust of Sidney Bechet, the great clarinetist and soprano saxophone player. Bechet was born in New Orleans in 1897, but spent most of his life performing in London, Paris, and New York.

WOMEN IN JAZZ

Jazz was not solely a male preserve; many noted female singers and musicians also made their names in New Orleans. Blanche Thomas declined the life of endless one-night stands and stayed in the city singing the blues with such artists as Al Hirt and Pete Fountain. She could be heard in the bars along Bourbon Street in the early 1970s, where her command of traditional jazz and big blues voice made her a particular favorite. Singer Louise

Blanche Thomas

"Blue Lu" Barker is said to have influenced both Billie Holiday and Eartha Kitt. Lizzie Miles dazzled the crowds in the 1920s, and Esther Bigeou was dubbed the "Creole songbird" in the 1930s. There were also some prominent female instrumentalists in the early jazz bands – pianists like Sweet Emma Barrett and Lil Hardin. The most famous female jazz musicians to emerge from New Orleans were the Boswell Sisters *(see p21)*, a trio of middle-class white girls who learned jazz from their black maids. Their close harmonies and up-tempo tunes propelled them out of New Orleans and on to a national weekly radio program in the 1930s, and then into movies.

Congo Square ㉒

N Rampart St, between St. Peter St and St. Philip St. **Map** 4 C1. ⌨ 48, 57. ♿

U NDER THE *Code Noir* (an edict concerning the treatment of slaves), slaveholders were forbidden to work slaves on Sunday in order to encourage them to attend church and become good Roman Catholics. Such minimal amounts of freedom allowed the blacks of New Orleans to retain more of their African heritage than those in other parts of the South. On Sunday afternoons, during the 18th and early 19th century, slaves and free people of color would gather in Congo Square

Armstrong's statue

(also known as *Place des Nègres*), part of Armstrong Park *(see p79)*, to speak in their native African tongues. They would sing and dance, and perform the *calinda*, an African line dance, and the *bamboula*. These dances were one of the chief origins of jazz, and Congo Square is thus remembered as one of the birthplaces of jazz music. The famous Marie Laveau *(see p83)* is said to have performed voodoo rituals here.

Congo Square, home of the *calinda* and *bamboula* dances

Mahalia Jackson Theater of the Performing Arts ㉓

Armstrong Park, Rampart St between St. Peter St and St. Ann St. **Map** 4 C1. 🎟 565-7470. ⌨ 48, 46, 52, 57. 📷 ♿

N AMED AFTER the globally celebrated gospel singer Mahalia Jackson (1911–72), who was born in New Orleans, this theater is used by local and visiting dance, music, and theater companies.

Jackson began her career singing in the local church, where her father was a pastor.

At the age of 16 she moved to Chicago and opened first a successful beauty shop, then a flower store. Despite her strict upbringing, she fell in love with the syncopated rhythms of blues, but she never sang the more bawdy songs in its repertoire. Her talent was discovered in the 1930s, and she made her first recording in 1934, launching a career that took her to Carnegie Hall, the Newport Jazz Festival, and other major music venues. She was also very active in the civil rights movement and was a passionate supporter of activist Martin Luther King, Jr.

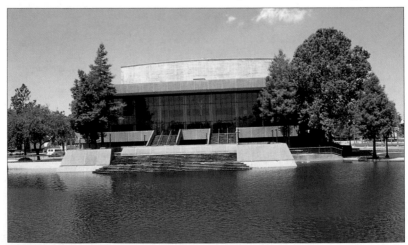

The Mahalia Jackson Theater of the Performing Arts

Stained-glass window, Our Lady of Guadelupe

Our Lady of Guadelupe ㉔

411 N. Rampart. **Map** 4 B2.
📞 525-1551. 🚌 48, 46, 52, 57.
🕐 7am–6pm daily. ♿

Renamed Our Lady of Guade-lupe in 1875, when it served an Italian congregation,

St. Anthony's Chapel was built on the outskirts of the French Quarter in 1826, when fune-rals were no longer being held in St. Louis Cathedral, for fear of spreading yellow fever (see p18). It was originally known as "Mortuary Chapel" because all the bodies were taken directly from the chapel to St. Louis Cemetery #1 (see p82), via the back entrance. It displays several brilliantly colored stained-glass win-dows, representing different saints honored by devoted New Orleanians.

The most visited altar is de-dicated to St. Jude, the "patron saint of hopeless causes," but a more interesting one stands to the left of the exit; this is dedicated to New Orleans' very own St. Expedite, whose name is not in any official dictionary of saints. According to legend, a crate marked with the word "Spedito!" (meaning "rush") arrived in the chapel one day. The statue inside it was removed and mounted on the wall, and its name was confused with the word on the box. To this day, New

Orleanians visit the altar to pray for help when they need something in a hurry. St. Expedite is also associated with voodoo (see p83), which is why the church is called the "voodoo church." Guadelupe is the official place of worship for the police and fire departments, whose altar stands to the right of the main altar.

Our Lady of Guadelupe

STORYVILLE

From 1897 to 1917 the 38 blocks roughly bounded by Iberville, Basin, Robertson, and St. Louis streets were set aside as a legal red-light district (see p22). Saloons and high-class brothels lined Basin Street, cheap bawdy houses clustered along Dauphine, Burgundy, St. Louis, Conti, and Bienville streets, while the poorest huts, furnished with bed, table, and chair, were found along Rampart and Iberville streets. Names and addresses of 700 prostitutes were listed in the Blue Book, which was available at bars like the Annex, which was operated by state legislator and

political boss Tom Anderson, the informal "Mayor" of Storyville. Many of the brothels were quite luxurious, furnished with velvet drapes, gilt-framed paintings, leopard-skin fabrics, and plenty of ormolu. At No. 317 Basin Street, Countess Willie Piazza held court. She regularly employed pianist Jelly Roll Morton, who played behind a screen, as did most musicians at these establish-ments, so they were not able to observe the patrons who frequented the brothels. The district was officially closed in 1917 by the Department of the Navy (see p22).

Mahogany Hall in Basin Street, one of Storyville's notorious bordellos

Poignant statue atop an above-ground tomb at St. Louis Cemetery #1

St. Louis Cemetery #1 ㉕

Basin St. between St. Louis and Conti.
Map 4 B1. ☎ *596-3050.* 🚌 *48, 46, 52, 57.* ◐ *9am–3pm daily.* ♿ ✔

THIS CEMETERY opened in 1789 and is the oldest in the city. Because of its age, it is one of the most fascinating to visit. However, this cemetery and its neighbor, St. Louis Cemetery #2, should not be visited alone; both are ideal places for muggers and pickpockets to operate.

By 1829 St. Louis #1 was already filled, mostly with victims of yellow fever. Today the narrow alleyways are jammed with mausoleums, many in advanced stages of decay. It is divided into a larger Catholic section and a smaller Protestant section. There are numerous legendary local figures buried here: Homer Adolph Plessy (1862–1925), who challenged the segregation laws in the 1890s *(see p19)*; Bernard de Marigny (1788-1871), who inherited $7 million at age 15 and squandered it playing craps (dice), the game he introduced to the United States *(see p102)*. Daniel Clark (1766-1813), the wealthy Irish merchant who challenged Governor Claiborne *(see p17)* to a duel and wounded him in the leg, lies here, along with his daughter Myra Clark Gaines (1803–1885). She fought for 65 years to secure her father's estate, in a case that generated 8,000 pages of court documents. Jean Etienne Boré (1741–1820), the plantation owner who was the colony's first mayor,

A beseeching angel

is buried in a low brick vault. Boré contributed much to the city's prosperity as he was the first to granulate sugar on a commercial scale in 1796. Boré's grandson, the historian Charles Gayarré, is also buried here, as is Paul Morphy (1837–1884), the genius chess player who was a world champion at age 13 but who later went mad. The most famous of all is probably Marie Laveau (c.1794–1881), known as the voodoo queen. Crowds visit her tomb, marking it with X's (symbolically requesting that she grant a particular wish) or leaving unusual voodoo "gifts." A more contemporary figure who rests here is Ernest "Dutch" Morial (1929–1989), the first black mayor and the father of mayor Marc Morial. The largest tomb is that belonging to the Société Française de Bienfaisance, which contains 70 vaults. The tallest monument, sculpted by Pietro Gualdi in 1857 for $40,000, belongs to the Italian Society. It served as the background in the psychedelic scenes in the film *Easy Rider*. A plaque memorializes Benjamin Henry Latrobe *(see p72)*, the architect who came to New Orleans to build a waterworks and died in 1820 of yellow fever *(see p18)*. No one knows where his remains are. Many bodies were moved from the St. Louis Cemetery #1 in 1823 to Lafayette Cemetery *(see p102)*, and from there to Metairie Cemetery *(see p127)* in the 1950s. Somehow, Latrobe's body got lost in the shuffle.

Recommended tours *(see p190)* are given by the Save our Cemeteries organization, and by New Orleans Tours, Inc. Both provide plenty of excellent local information.

Ornate family mausoleums in St. Louis Cemetery #1

VOODOO WORSHIP

Voodoo arrived in New Orleans from Africa, via the Caribbean, where it originated as a form of ancestor worship among the West African tribes who were brought to North America as slaves. During the slave uprising in Saint Domingue in 1793, many of the planters from Haiti fled to New Orleans, bringing their slaves (and voodoo) with them. Voodoo enabled those slaves to preserve their African culture and roots beneath the mask of the Roman Catholic religion, for it mixed both traditions. The most famous of all 19th-century voodoo leaders was Marie Laveau, a mulatto and a great marketer. She used such Catholic elements as prayer, incense, and saints in her rituals, which she opened to the public for an admission fee. The high point of the voodoo calendar was the celebration she held along the Bayou St. John on St. John's Eve. She is believed to be buried at St. Louis Cemetery #1.

Portrait of Marie Laveau

The Barelli tomb

St. Louis Cemetery #2 ㉖

Iberville to St. Louis St, between N. Claiborne Ave and N. Robertson St. **Map** 4 B1. 596-3050. 48, 46, 52, 57. 9am–9pm Mon–Sat.

B Y THE END of the colonial period, and mostly because of a devastating series of epidemics, this cemetery was established as the natural extension of St. Louis Cemetery #1 around 1823. The final resting place for much of New Orleans' 19th-century Creole aristocracy, it contains remarkably ornate mausoleums. Many of them were designed by Jacques Nicholas Bussière De Pouilly, who arrived in New Orleans from France in the 1830s. His plans were inspired

Tree-shaped statue

by the tombs in Paris's Père Lachaise Cemetery. Grand in design and scale, and modeled on Greek, Egyptian, and other classical styles, the patterns for these ambitious mausoleums became very popular in New Orleans. The tombs are like impressive residences, often enclosed within beautiful wrought-iron gates, featuring such motifs as lyres, winged hourglasses, hearts, inverted torches, and urns with arrows. The fences around the tombs are some of the finest wrought-iron work in the city. The intricate immortelles made of wire, beads, and glass are also unique and represent everlasting tributes to the dead.

Among the notables buried here are General Jean Baptiste Plauché, who fought with Andrew Jackson at the Battle of New Orleans (see p17). J. N. B. DePouilly himself is humbly buried in a modest wall vault with his brother, who was also an architect. Other famous New Orleans figures buried here include jazz musician Danny Barker, and the pirate Dominique You (see p17), who rests in the main aisle in a tomb marked with a Masonic emblem and the inscription: "This New Bayard could have witnessed the end of the world without fear or trembling."

Near the cemetery office, the Barelli tomb recalls the tragedy that occurred on November 15, 1849, when the steamer *Louisiana* exploded, killing 86 people, including the young son of Joseph Barelli, who erected the memorial in 1856. Five sculpted angels hover around the tomb and a bas-relief depicts the explosion.

A common legend says that Napoleon Bonaparte's followers were waiting for his arrival in New Orleans from his exile in St. Helena, but since he died beforehand on December 20, 1821, a funeral service for him was held here.

Like St. Louis #1, the cemetery is in a secluded area where lone visitors have been robbed. Guided visits, which are available from several organizations (see p190), are advisable.

Creole family mausoleum, fallen into disrepair

WAREHOUSE AND CENTRAL BUSINESS DISTRICTS

WHEN THE AMERICANS arrived after the Louisiana Purchase *(see p17)* they developed a community of their own on the upriver side of Canal Street. It was called the Faubourg St. Mary and extended from Canal Street to Louisiana Avenue. Between 1820 and 1860 the waterfront was developed, and behind it grew a

Contemporary statues in the CBD

commercial and residential district that matched the Creole district downriver. Today the CBD incorporates narrow streets lined with Victorian warehouses, banks, and office buildings, as well as such broad thoroughfares as Poydras, which is lined with skyscrapers belonging to oil companies, hotels, and financial institutions.

SIGHTS AT A GLANCE

Museums and Galleries
Confederate Memorial Hall **16**
Custom House **9**
Gallier Hall **11**
Louisiana Children's
  Museum **18**
The National D-Day Museum **19**
New Orleans Contemporary
  Arts Center **17**
Ogden Museum of
  Southern Art **15**

Shopping Areas
Canal Place **8**
Riverwalk
  Marketplace **4**

Entertainment
*Aquarium of the
  Americas pp90–91* **7**
Harrah's Casino **6**
Louisiana Superdome **12**
Orpheum Theater **13**

Landmarks
World Trade Center **5**

Churches
St. Patrick's Church **10**

Parks and Squares
Lee Circle **14**
Spanish Plaza **3**
Woldenberg Riverfront Park **1**

Boat Trips
Ferry to Algiers and Mardi
  Gras World **2**

0 meters 500
0 yards 500

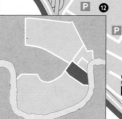

KEY

▪ Street-by-Street map
  See pp86–7

🚉 Railroad station

🚌 Bus station

🚋 Streetcar stop

⛴ Ferry boarding point

P Parking

GETTING THERE
RTA routes 44, 41, and 34 run from the Lakefront, Mid-City, and Uptown to this area. The St. Charles Avenue and Riverfront streetcars also have several stops in the area.

◁ **Canal Street at dusk**

Street-by-Street: CBD

Spanish coat-of-arms

WHEN THE AMERICANS ARRIVED from the North in the early 1800s they developed the uptown side of Canal Street. It is still the city's commercial area, where the head-quarters of oil, sugar, and cotton corporations and many public institutions are located. The median running through the middle of Canal Street was the neutral ground separating the English-speaking Americans from the French-speaking Creole community. Today, Canal Street is lined with hotels, restaurants, and stores. A casino and the ferry to Algiers are located at the riverfront end. During the last three decades the riverfront has been totally redeveloped with parks, walks, and such major attractions as the Aquarium and Riverwalk Marketplace.

Harrah's Casino
This enormous casino, with its garish over-the-top decor, offers jazz in the central court café **6**

World Trade Center
Built in the shape of a Greek cross, this 1960s skyscraper towers over the river, port, and Warehouse District **5**

TCHOPITOULAS

Riverwalk Marketplace
Containing more than 120 stores, including a huge food court, this is one of the largest malls in the city **4**

Spanish Plaza
Spanish music is played at this plaza, which has a beautiful fountain at its center **3**

MISSISSIPPI RIVER

Ferry to Algiers and Mardi Gras World
A free ferry takes visitors across the Mississippi to Algiers and the fasci-nating warehouse of Blaine Kern's Mardi Gras World **2**

STAR SIGHTS

★ **Aquarium of the Americas**

★ **River Cruises**

Canal Place

The city's most upscale shopping mall features big names such as Saks, Gucci, Jaeger, and Williams-Sonoma. There is also a theater on the third floor **8**

LOCATOR MAP
See Street Finder, maps 4, 5, and 8.

The Custom House

Four identical classical façades define this massive granite building, which took 33 years (from 1848 to 1881) to complete **9**

★ Aquarium of the Americas

Opened in 1990, it has striking marine life sculptures by Ida Kohlmeyer at the entrance **7**

★ River Cruises

The Cajun Queen *and* John James Audubon *offer daily cruises from the Aquarium of the Americas (see p209).*

Woldenberg Riverfront Park

Named for local businessman Malcolm Woldenberg, the park contains a charming statue of Woldenberg, but the most notable sculpture is the 16-ft (5-m) tall kinetic steel Ocean Song, *by John Scott* **1**

| 0 meters | | 100 |
| 0 yards | | 100 |

KEY

- - - Suggested route

Woldenberg Riverfront Park ❶

2 Canal St. **Map** 5 D3. 🚋 *Riverfront.*
🚌 *3, 55, 57, 65.* ♿

THE 16-ACRE Woldenberg
Park extends all the way
along the riverfront from St.
Peter Street to the Riverwalk
Marketplace, providing a
pleasant garden setting
studded with contemporary
sculpture. From Jackson
Square, visitors can access
Woldenberg Riverfront Park
via Washington Artillery Park
and the Moonwalk. The
former is an amphitheater-
shaped space, where many of
the city's street mimes and
other artists can be found; the
latter is named after Moon
Landrieu, who is widely regarded as paving the way for the
first black mayor, "Dutch"
Morial, to be elected in 1978
(*see p23*). The park is open
from dawn till dusk daily.

River view from the Woldenberg Riverfront Park

Ferry to Algiers and Mardi Gras World ❷

Take the ferry at the end of Canal St.
In Algiers take the Shuttle.
Map 5 D4. 🚋 *Riverfront.* 🚌 *55,
57, 65.* ⏰ *9am–5pm daily.*
🎨 🚻 ♿

FROM THE FOOT of Canal
Street, a free ferry crosses
the river to Algiers on the west
bank, where a minibus takes
visitors from the ferry landing
to Blaine Kern's Mardi Gras
World. Blaine Kern is often
called "Mr. Mardi Gras,"
because so many of the massive floats that roll through
the streets of New Orleans
during Carnival (*see pp24–5*)
are constructed here in the
20 warehouse-dens of his
company. The tour begins
with coffee and King Cake
and a short film showing the
floats in the Mardi Gras
parades and the stages of
their production, from the
original drawings and molds
to the manufacture of the
final pieces. Visitors are then
free to don some of the
costumes that krewe mem-
bers have worn in past
parades. Many of these are
extremely heavy and ornate.
Visitors can also wander
through the warehouses and
view gigantic decorative
figures, which are made of
either fiberglass or Styrofoam
overlaid with papier-mâché.
It is also possible to climb on
to the floats to get an idea
of what it is like to ride

aboard. The cost of making
the floats is borne by the
krewes themselves, which
collect contributions from
their members. These dues
can range anywhere between
$300 and $3,000, depending
on the krewe.

Spanish Plaza ❸

2 Canal St. **Map** 5 D4. 🚋 *Riverfront.*
🚌 *3, 55, 57, 65.* ⏰ *24 hrs daily.*
🍽 🚻 🏛 📷

THIS SMALL plaza at the
entrance to the Riverwalk
Marketplace is a good place
to take a rest and enjoy an
uninterrupted view of the
river. A fountain stands at its
center, surrounded by a
circular mosaic bench on
which the coats of arms of all
the New Orleans Spanish
immigrants are depicted.
The *Creole Queen* paddlewheeler departs from the
Plaza and takes passengers
downriver to the Chalmette
Battlefield Park, the site of
Andrew Jackson's victory at
the Battle of New Orleans
(*see p17*). Rangers provide a
40-minute tour of the site.
Adjacent to the battlefield is
Chalmette National Cemetery,
where thousands of Union
soldiers are buried. An antebellum house, the Malus-
Beauregard home stands on
park property. This residence
was built in 1833 and purchased in 1880 by the son of
General P. G. T. Beauregard
(*see p71*).

Fountain at the center of the Spanish Plaza

Riverwalk Marketplace ❹

1 Poydras St. **Map** 5 D4. 522-1555. Riverfront. 3, 55, 57, 65.

THIS MASSIVE riverside shopping mall, designed by the same company that developed Boston's Faneuil Hall, contains more than 140 stores, most of which are brand-name favorites like Eddie Bauer, Brookstone, Banana Republic, and the Museum Company. The entire top floor is devoted to the food court, while a highlight of the ground floor is the Creole Delicacies Gourmet Shop *(see p185)*, which offers a two-hour course in cooking.

In addition to plentiful shopping opportunities, the mall has an outdoor walkway that runs along the Mississippi River, giving visitors one of the best views of the river and river traffic in the city. International and other cruise ships dock alongside the marketplace, the most notable being those operated by the Delta Queen Steamboat Company, which was established in 1890. A number of information plaques attached to railings along the walkway describe everything from the types of boats plying their trade on the river to the seagulls that drift up from the Gulf of Mexico.

Entrance to the Riverwalk Marketplace

World Trade Center ❺

2 Canal St. **Map** 5 D4. 581-4888. Riverfront. 57, 65.

THE WORLD TRADE CENTER building was designed by Edward Durrell Stone in the 1960s. Originally called the International Trade Mart Building, it housed the headquarters of various mercantile companies and consulates. Architecturally it has little to recommend it; however, being built in the shape of a Greek cross, it serves as a useful landmark. The *Skybar* revolving cocktail lounge on the 33rd floor, which once gave spectacular views over New Orleans, has now closed. A plan to develop the building as part of a new hotel consortium is pending.

Riverside view of the WTC Building

Harrah's Casino ❻

601 Poydras St. **Map** 5 D4. 533-6000. Riverfront. 3, 57, 65. 24 hrs daily.

THIS CASINO, which opened in October 1999, is conveniently situated close to the riverfront. Covering 100,000 sq ft (9,290 sq m) of floor space, Harrah's offers a vast ballroom in addition to a wide selection of games, including 2,900 slot machines and 117 table games featuring baccarat, blackjack, craps, and roulette. All these are arranged around five highly decorated courts, each of which has a New Orleans theme. There is no accommodation at the casino, but there are several dining areas, including a 250-seat buffet restaurant.

Aquarium of the Americas ❼

See pp90–91.

The modern and lively Harrah's, a popular New Orleans casino

Aquarium of the Americas ❼

CONCENTRATING on the waters around New Orleans, from the Mississippi and the swamps to the Gulf of Mexico and the Caribbean, the Aquarium of the Americas complex features some 560 species of marine life. Highlights include a tank containing a Caribbean reef, and a replica of an oil rig. Other tanks contain species that illustrate everything there is to know about life beneath the sea, including how fish communicate and how they camouflage themselves.

Sea Horses
These are among the many creatures that can be seen being fed by divers in the Caribbean Reef tank.

The Amazon Rainforest
Piranhas lurk in the waters that flow under the forest canopy, which is inhabited by tropical birds and wild orchids.

Shark cove

Food Court
with several different kinds of restaurants.

Main entrance and information center

Gift shop

★ The Caribbean Reef
An acrylic tunnel underneath a 132,000-gallon tank provides a startling perspective from which to view the rays, parrot fish, and other denizens that float above.

Jellyfish
These transparent, fluid creatures sway and dance in an exhibit that is one of the largest of its kind anywhere in the United States.

★ The Gulf of Mexico
A 400,000-gallon tank holds a replica of an offshore oil rig, around which swim the species that share the waters – sharks, tarpon, sting rays, and sea turtles.

VISITORS' CHECKLIST

Canal Street at Mississippi River.
Map 5 D3. 581-4629.
Riverfront. 45, 87.
9:30am–5pm daily (7pm in summer). Dec 25 and Mardi Gras.

Doc's Lab has touch tanks where children may pet a small shark, or examine starfish, hermit crabs, and sea snails.

Sea Otter Gallery
A lovable pair of sea otters frolic in this exhibit where a waterfall creates waves for their amusement.

Changing-exhibits gallery

The Entergy IMAX Theater
This cinema adds a high-tech dimension to the complex. The screen is 5 ½ stories high.

★ The Mississippi River and Delta Habitat
Check out the blue-eyed, white alligator that hangs suspended in the water along with some other Mississippi regulars – catfish, gar, and turtles.

STAR FEATURES

★ The Caribbean Reef

★ The Gulf of Mexico

★ The Mississippi River and Delta Habitat

Mardi Gras float, passing through the Central Business District ▷

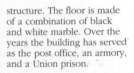

Main entrance to Canal Place and its many luxury stores

Canal Place ⑧

Canal and N Peters St. **Map** 4 C3.
🚌 3, 41. ⏱ 10am–7pm Mon–Sat,
noon–6pm Sun. ⛱ ⬛ ⬛ ⬛

DOWNTOWN'S most upscale
shopping mall is anchored
by Saks Fifth Avenue, and
contains such fashionable
stores as Ann Taylor, Jaeger,
Brooks Brothers, Bally,
Williams-Sonoma, Kenneth
Cole, Banana Republic, Gucci,
and Laura Ashley. The third
floor features the enormous
food court, plus the only
cinemas in the city that show
a mixture of first-run
movies, arthouse
films, and indepen-
dent productions.
    The third floor also
houses the Southern
Repertory Theater,
which stages excellent
productions in its
small auditorium. The
theater offers support
to contemporary local
playwrights, often by
providing a showcase
for their work.

Custom House ⑨

423 Canal St. **Map** 4 C3.
🚌 3, 41. ⬤ Closed to
the public.

THIS QUINCY granite
building, extending
340 ft (103 m) along
Canal Street, is
perhaps the most
important Federal-style

building in the South. Alexander Thompson Wood was the
original architect, and the
building reflects his genius,
even though he was
succeeded by James Dakin,
Confederate General Beauregard (see p71), and Thomas K.
Wharton. Construction began
in 1847, and was completed in
1881.
    Inside, the Marble Hall is
a dramatic space under a
ground-glass ceiling with a
decorative stained-glass
border and a skylight above.
Juno and Mercury embellish
the capitals of the 14 marble
columns, each 41-ft (12.5-m)
high, which support the

structure. The floor is made
of a combination of black
and white marble. Over the
years the building has served
as the post office, an armory,
and a Union prison.

St. Patrick's Church ⑩

724 Camp St. **Map** 4 C4. 📞 525-
4413. 🚌 3, 41. ⏱ 11am–1pm
Mon–Sat, 9am–1pm Sun. (Guided
tours only.) ⛱ ⬛

ESTABLISHED IN 1833 to
minister to the Irish
Catholic population, the
original St. Patrick's Church
was replaced in 1841 at the
urging of Father James
Ignatius Mullon. The brothers
Charles and James Dakin
were the original architects,
but James Gallier, Sr. replaced
them. It is an impressive
church with a 185-ft (60-m)
high tower, a Gothic-inspired
interior, and splendid stained-
glass vaulting in the sanctuary.
    Behind the altar are three
paintings by French-born
artist Leon Pomarede. At the
center is a copy of *Raphael's
Transfiguration of Christ*,
flanked by *St. Patrick Baptiz-
ing the Irish Princesses* and
Christ Walking on Water. Each
of these works dates to
1841. Although the
Irish community has
largely moved away
from the neighbor-
hood, the congregation
still draws loyal
followers from other
districts. Father Mullon
is still remembered as
an ardent Confederate.
He prayed publicly for
a Confederate victory,
and when General
Benjamin "Beast"
Butler (see pp18–19)
accused him of
refusing to bury a
Union soldier, he
volunteered that he
would be "very happy
to bury them all." At
noon on St. Patrick's
Day, a mass is
attended by most
Catholics as an
important part of the
festivities held all
over the city.

The impressive tower of St. Patrick's Church

Greek Revival-style façade of Gallier Hall

Gallier Hall ⓫

543 St. Charles Ave. **Map** 5 D1.
🚌 3, 41. 🔘 Mon–Fri.

JAMES GALLIER, SR.'s sole surviving masterpiece was built between 1845 and 1850, at a cost of $342,000. Constructed of bricks that were plastered and scored to look like stone, the building is 215 ft (65.5 m) deep, extending behind a façade only 90 ft (27 m) wide. Six fluted Ionic columns support the tympanum on the façade, which is decorated with bas-reliefs of Justice and Commerce created by Robert A. Launitz.

Gallier Hall was built to serve as the headquarters of the Second Municipality when the city was briefly served by three separate governments. In 1852 it became City Hall, when the three "cities" (or districts) were reunited. Many great historical figures have lain in state here, including Jefferson Davis, president of the Confederacy, and General Beauregard.

The building faces Lafayette Square, which was laid out in 1788 as Place Gravier, and renamed in 1824. The square contains statues of statesman Benjamin Franklin by Hiram Powers, and famed Southern States Rights Senator Henry Clay by Joel T. Hart. John McDonogh, a native of Baltimore and a great benefactor of the New Orleans public schools, is remembered with a

statue by Atallio Piccirilli. Today, the building is a popular vantage point during the famous Mardi Gras parades *(see pp24–5)*.

Louisiana Superdome ⓬

Poydras St. **Map** 4 A3. 🎟 587-3808.
🚌 45, 87. 🔘 10:30am–noon and noon–1:30pm Sun. (Guided tours only.) ♿ 🎟 📷

THIS FLYING saucer-shaped New Orleans landmark is home to local football teams the Saints and Tulane's Green Wave, as well as being the venue for the Sugar Bowl and other sports and entertainment events. Being the world's largest steel-constructed stadium unobstructed by posts, it has been the site of the Super Bowl more times than any other facility: Super Bowl XXXVI in 2002 was the sixth one to be held here.

A guided tour allows visitors to see the stadium's main arena, the working press area (which accommodates 334 journalists), the 137 private box suites, and the locker rooms. However, the route of the tour is subject to changes at any time, depending on what is going on at the Dome, so phone ahead if there is a particular area you would like to see. In total, the stadium caters to an audience of 100,000, ranging from 24,500

at arena concerts, 72,675 at football games, and up to 87,500 at festival concerts. It occupies 52 acres, has a roof area of 8 acres, and stands 27 stories high. Among some of its more impressive statistics, there are 400 miles (645 km) of electrical wiring, and 15,200 lighting fixtures. Its construction took four years from 1971 to 1975.

The New Orleans NFL football team, the Saints, started playing here in November 1966. The Sugar Bowl was launched in New Orleans and was first played in 1935 at Tulane Stadium. Today the Sugar Bowl is a national New Year's Day event.

Orpheum Theater ⓭

129 University Place. **Map** 4 B3.
🎟 524-3285. 🚌 3, 41. 🔘 For performances only. ♿ 🎵

NOW HOME TO the Louisiana Philharmonic Orchestra, which plays a season from fall to spring, this Beaux-Arts terra-cotta building opened in 1918 as a vaudeville theater. The building was designed by G. Albert Lansburgh and Samuel Stone, who lavished impressive detailing on the façade. It was restored in 1981, and today it plays host to a variety of music festivals and plays, plus all kinds of public and private events.

Orpheum Theater detail

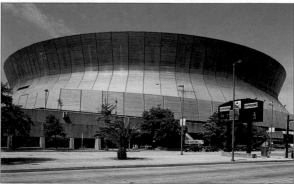

Louisiana Superdome, one of the world's largest indoor stadiums

Memorial to Robert E. Lee at Lee Circle

Lee Circle ⑭

St. Charles Ave. & Howard Ave.
Map 4 B5. 🚋 3, 41. ♿

THE TOWERING 60-ft (18-m) column at the center of Lee Circle, topped by a 16-ft (5-m) statue of Confederate general Robert E. Lee, is one of the city's key landmarks. For many years the Lee Circle area was merely a grubby intersection favored by homeless people. More recently, however, it has become the anchor of an attractive new museum district. The brand new Ogden Museum of Southern Art opens on to the circle and the D-Day Museum is just a block away. Meanwhile, these additions have boosted the regeneration of existing museums nearby, such as the New Orleans Contemporary Arts Center and the Confederate Memorial Hall.

The Lee Monument, which was sculpted by New Yorker Alexander Doyle and inaugurated in 1884, has been the subject of controversy over the years. Critics highlight the incongruity of a monument to the leader of a white, pro-slavery army having such a prominent place in a black majority city. But the prevailing view is that Lee deserves his highly visible spot, for accepting defeat gracefully at the end of the Civil War and urging his soldiers to renew their allegiance to the United States and its laws.

Ogden Museum of Southern Art ⑮

Camp St. at Howard Ave. **Map** 4 B5.
📞 539-9600. 🚋 11. **Temporary gallery** 603 Julia St. ⏰ phone to check. 🅿 🄲 ♿
🌐 www.ogdenmuseum.org

THIS MUSEUM is named after Roger H. Ogden, the philanthropist art collector who donated the core collection of some 1,200 works by more than 400 Southern artists. Due to open in late 2002, the collection will be displayed in a unique two-building complex connected by a corridor gallery. The Romanesque-style Howard Memorial Library was designed by native-born Henry Hobson Richardson in 1888. This architectural masterpiece, with its splendid wood-paneled rotunda, will be incorporated into the newly designed, post-modern Goldring Hall. These two structures are designed to wrap around the Confederate Memorial Hall, so that the finished complex will front both Camp Street and Lee Circle.

The museum will contain works from the 18th to the 21st century, and will portray the diversity of urban and rural life in the South from the Depression and War years right up to the modern day. The collection includes works by William Henry Buck, Clarence Millet, Richard Claque, John McCrady, George Dureau, Robert Gordy, Clementine Hunter, and Ida Kohlmeyer.

Confederate Memorial Hall ⑯

929 Camp St. at Howard Ave.
Map 4 B5. 📞 523-4522. 🚋 3, 41.
⏰ 10am–4pm Mon–Sat.
⬛ Thanksgiving, Dec 24, 25, Mardi Gras and Jan 1. 🅿 🄲

ONE OF THE OLDEST MUSEUMS in the city, Confederate Memorial Hall offers a moving experience. The memorabilia in the display cases tell the often tragic, personal stories of the many young men who fought in the Civil War. Some were teenagers, like Landon Creek, who had fought in seven battles and been wounded

The Howard Memorial Library, now part of the Ogden Museum

three times by the age of 15. Several display cases contain objects relating to the occupation of the city by General "Beast" Butler *(see p18)*, including the document ordering that all women who insulted Union officers, wore Confederate colors, or sang Southern songs, were to be locked up as if they were common prostitutes.

The museum also possesses a large collection associated with the Confederate president Jefferson Davis, from his cradle to his military boots. Several interesting exhibits are devoted to the black regiments, which served on both sides during the Civil War. The cypress hall of the museum was originally constructed in 1891 as a meeting place for Confederate veterans to reflect on their Civil War experiences and to house and protect their relics.

Modern art bench, at the Contemporary Arts Center

New Orleans Contemporary Arts Center ⑰

900 Camp St. **Map** 4 C5. [528-3805. 3, 41. 11am–5pm Tue–Sun. Public hols.

THIS WAREHOUSE-STYLE center is the city's premier space for all of the contemporary arts, from dance, painting, film, and video, to performance art, theater, and music. The museum combines the original structure with modern designs to its full advantage, presenting a unique, modern space mostly illuminated with natural light that houses four galleries and two theaters. The rotating shows in the galleries usually remain for four to eight weeks. The café at the entrance provides free Internet access.

Replica of one of the Higgins boats in The National D-Day Museum

Louisiana Children's Museum ⑱

420 Julia St. **Map** 4 C5. [523-1357. 3, 41. 9:30am–4pm Mon–Sat, noon–4:30pm Sun. Public hols.

THIS ACTIVITY-ORIENTED museum allows children to entertain themselves with a variety of role-playing games, plus other interactive exhibits with a didactic focus. Kids can anchor their own news show in the TV studio, go shopping in the supermarket, or pilot their own tugboat, and there is an area designed for one- to three-year-olds. The museum is housed in a huge 45,000-sq-ft (4,180-sq-m) warehouse with Tuscan-style arched doors and enormous windows.

The Louisiana Children's Museum, playground for children of all ages

The National D-Day Museum ⑲

945 Magazine St. and Howard Ave. **Map** 4 C5. [527-6012. 3, 41. 9am–5pm daily. Thanksgiving, Dec 25, Mardi Gras.

A NEW ORLEANS shipbuilder, Andrew Higgins, played a major role in the D-Day invasion of Normandy in June 1944 *(see p22)*, and both he and his company are celebrated at this museum. More than 20,000 of Higgins's crafts were deployed in US landings on all fronts during the war, from North Africa to Sicily and the Pacific Islands. Among the most inspiring exhibits on display are nine oral history stations which feature real-life stories narrated by the participants. They are accompanied by all kinds of wartime memorabilia donated by veterans, including letters, uniforms, and weapons. Various electronic maps, mini-theaters, and photomurals illustrate the role played by the United States in World War II.

In 2001 the museum added a new wing devoted to the war in the Pacific. There are oral histories from both army veterans and civilians, as well as a moving depiction of the bombing of Hiroshima.

Loyola University

SIGHTS AT A GLANCE

Historic Buildings

Museums and Galleries

Cemeteries

Universities

Entertainment

Landmarks

GARDEN DISTRICT
AND UPTOWN

Iᴺ 1832 ᴀ ʀᴇѕɪᴅᴇɴᴛɪᴀʟ quarter was established uptown on the Livaudais Plantation. Celeste de Marigny, wife of Jacques François de Livaudais, sold it to developers for half a million dollars. The land was subdivided and developed to create the city of Lafayette, which was eventually incorporated into New Orleans in 1852. Here, between Jackson and Louisiana avenues, and St. Charles Avenue and Magazine Street, the wealthy merchants, planters, bankers, and real estate moguls built mansions in a variety of styles, ranging from Greek Revival to Italianate and Queen Anne. The minimum building plot was a quarter block to ensure that only grand residences owned by substantial citizens would be built in this neighborhood. It became known as the Garden District because of the lush tropical gardens that were laid out around the mansions.

Stone sculpture at Tulane University

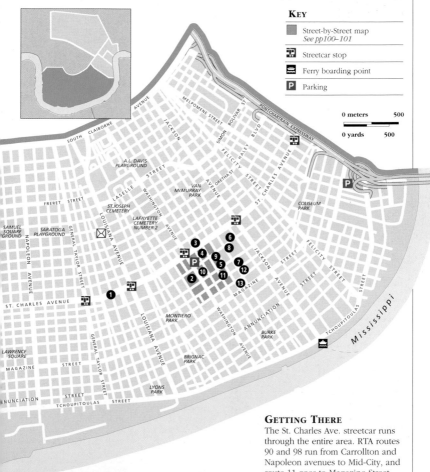

KEY

Street-by-Street map
See pp100–101

Streetcar stop

Ferry boarding point

P Parking

0 meters 500

0 yards 500

GETTING THERE
The St. Charles Ave. streetcar runs through the entire area. RTA routes 90 and 98 run from Carrollton and Napoleon avenues to Mid-City, and route 11 goes to Magazine Street.

Street-by-Street: Garden District

WHEN THE AMERICANS arrived in New Orleans they settled upriver from the French Quarter. The plantations that lined St. Charles Avenue in the 1820s were subdivided and the city of Lafayette established. It was incorporated into the city of New Orleans in 1852. Today, this area is referred to as the Garden District, a residential neighborhood filled with grand Victorian mansions built by wealthy city merchants and planters. The gardens, planted with magnolia, camellia, sweet olive, jasmine, and azalea, are as stunning as the residences themselves.

Claiborne Cottage
This cottage was built in 1857 for the daughter of the first governor of Louisiana. It has served as a school and a convent ❸

★ **Lafayette Cemetery**
Confederate General Harry T. Hays and Samuel Jarvis Peters, a wealthy 19th-century developer of the Garden District, are buried in this cemetery, which often appears in Anne Rice's books ❷

KEY

– – – Suggested route

Commander's Palace
Excellent Creole food is the specialty of this landmark restaurant, one of the best in the city (see p177).

Briggs-Staub House
This handsome Gothic Revival mansion was designed by James Gallier, Sr. in 1849 ❹

0 meters   40

0 yards   40

LOCATOR MAP
See Street Finder maps 6 and 7

★ **Colonel Short's Villa**
Built in 1859 for Colonel Robert Short of Kentucky and designed by Henry Howard, the house has an exquisite morning glory and cornstalk fence (see p37) **10**

Women's Guild Opera House
This Greek Revival mansion was designed in 1858 by William Freret **9**

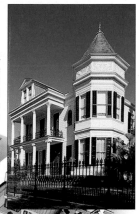

STREET

3RD STREET

★ **Robinson House**
One of the grandest residences in the Garden District, Robinson House was built between 1859 and 1865 for Virginia tobacco merchant Walter Robinson **5**

Musson-Bell House
This was the home of Michel Musson, uncle of artist Edgar Degas; an iron merchant added the lacy galleries later **11**

STAR SIGHTS

★ **Colonel Short's Villa**

★ **Lafayette Cemetery**

★ **Robinson House**

St. Charles Avenue Streetcar ❶

See pp104–105.

Lafayette Cemetery ❷

1600 block of Washington Ave.
Map 7 F3. 🕾 529 3040.
🚋 St. Charles. 🚌 11, 14, 87.
🕙 9am–2:30pm. 📷

THIS WALLED CEMETERY was laid out in 1833 by Benjamin Buisson to accommodate the residents of the adjacent Garden District. The second Protestant cemetery to open in New Orleans, it is the resting place of many German and Irish Protestants, as well as numerous Americans who had migrated here from the east coast. By 1840 it was full, mostly with yellow fever victims, and a new cemetery was needed.

Among the notables buried here are Confederate general Harry T. Hays and Samuel Jarvis Peters (1801–1885), an influential city politician and land developer. A Canadian, Peters arrived in New Orleans and ascended to a powerful

Angel statue at Lafayette

position by the time he was 30. He was one of the movers and shakers who developed the area north of Canal Street, fashioning it into a Second Municipality comparable to the downtown Creole community south of Canal Street. It had its own fashionable hotel, the St. Charles, which was equal to the St. Louis and mirrored its Creole counterpart in other ways.

One of the most striking memorials in this cemetery is the one built in 1852 to commemorate the Jefferson Fire Company #22. It is embellished with a typical pumper.

In her book *Interview with the Vampire* Anne Rice often gives Lestat and Claudia free rein to wander around this cemetery. The author herself staged a mock burial here on July 14, 1995, to promote her book, *Memnoch the Devil*.

The wall vaults were added to the cemetery in 1858.

Greek columns, Claiborne Cottage

Claiborne Cottage ❸

2524 St. Charles Ave. **Map** 7 F3. 🚋
St. Charles. 🚌 11, 14, 87. ● Closed
to the public.

THE HISTORY of this Greek Revival-style cottage is disputed, but the plaque in front states that it was built in 1857 for Louise Claiborne, the daughter of the first governor of Louisiana. She was married to Mandeville Marigny, the youngest son of Bernard de Marigny *(see p82)*, who introduced dice to the United States. His gambling friends thought he resembled a frog, and so he was nicknamed "Le Crapaud," after which the game "craps" takes its name.

Some experts date the house to 1860 and claim that it was built for a Virginian, James Dameron.

Briggs-Staub House ❹

2605 Prytania St. **Map** 7 F3. 🚋 St.
Charles. 🚌 11, 14, 87. ● Closed to
the public.

A RARITY in New Orleans, this Gothic Revival home was built for gambler Cuthbert Bullitt in 1849. The Gothic style is uncommon in this part of the city, because

![Above-ground vaults at Lafayette Cemetery]
Above-ground vaults at Lafayette Cemetery

Gothic arched windows, Briggs-Staub House

many Protestant Americans claimed it reminded them of Roman Catholic France. After James Gallier, Sr. had designed it, Bullitt refused to pay for the building, perhaps because of a gambling loss, and the house became the property of Englishman Charles Briggs, an insurance executive.

The second-floor galleries at Robinson House

Robinson House ❺

1415 3rd St. **Map** 8 A3. 🚋 *St. Charles.* 🚌 *11, 14, 87.* ◑

ONE OF THE grandest and largest residences in the Garden District, this house was built for the Virginia tobacco merchant, Walter Robinson. Designed by Henry Howard, it was built between 1859 and 1865. The galleries of this Italian-style villa are supported with Doric columns on the first floor and Corinthian on the second. Domenico Canova, a famous European craftsman, was hired to decorate the interior, which boasts elaborate

painted ceilings. It also featured the first indoor plumbing in the city. An unusual feature of this mansion is the curved portico.

Louis S. McGehee School ❻

2343 Prytania St. **Map** 8 A3. 🚋 *St. Charles.* 🚌 *11, 14, 87.* ◻ *9am–5pm daily.*

JAMES FRERET designed this elaborate French Second Empire home in 1872 for sugar planter Bradish Johnson, for $100,000. Freret had recently returned from Paris and was enamored of the École des Beaux-Arts, which shows in this mansion's Renaissance Revival style. When it was built, the house incorporated all of the fashionable interior design elements and conveniences –

a conservatory, a marble pantry, a passenger elevator, and a magnificent circular staircase. It is one of the few houses in the city to have a basement.

Since 1929 it has served as a private school for girls. The cafeteria was once a stable, and the gym is a refurbished carriage house. Note the steep mansard roof with its wrought-iron parapet and the unique bull's-eye window on the façade. The gardens contain some magnificent magnolias and ginger trees.

Carroll-Crawford House ❼

1315 First St. **Map** 8 A3. 🚋 *St. Charles.* 🚌 *11, 14, 87.* ● *Closed to the public.*

THIS BROADLY proportioned house was designed by Samuel Jamison in 1869 for Joseph Carroll, a cotton merchant from Virginia. The surrounding gardens include venerable live oaks and other lush plantings. A two-story home with octagonal wings, the house is Italianate in design with fine cast-iron galleries, made in New Orleans by Jacob Baumiller.

The original carriage house can still be seen around the corner on Chestnut Street. Jamison also constructed an identical building at 1331 First Street for cordage dealer Joseph C. Morris.

The ornate façade of the Carroll-Crawford House

St. Charles Avenue Streetcar ●

Statue of John McDonogh, Lafayette Square

FOR A SLOW-MOVING ROMANCE take a ride on the St. Charles Avenue streetcar, which passes many of New Orleans' most famous landmarks. It is the last streetcar operating of the sort that inspired Tennessee Williams's drama *A Streetcar Named Desire*. It travels 6.5 miles (10 km) from Canal Street through the Central Business District, along tree-shaded St. Charles Avenue to Carrollton Avenue. It began operating in 1835, under steam power until 1867 when mule power took over. In 1893 it was electrified. This famous streetcar was one of a network that carried 15 million people annually in the 1870s. By 1900 there were four companies operating 173 miles (278 km) of track, but from the 1930s on, they were replaced by motor buses. By 1964 they had all ceased operating, except for this beloved survivor.

Claiborne Cottage
This classic raised cottage was built in 1857 for the daughter of the first Louisiana governor (see p102).

Touro Synagogue
This building is named after Judah Touro, who came to New Orleans from Newport, Rhode Island, and donated the money for its construction.

A metal pole conducts power from an overhead cable.

Lee Circle
This 60-ft (18-m)- tall Doric column supports a statue of General Robert E. Lee, looking north (see p96).

Christ Church
This building is one of the few examples of Gothic Revival style in the city.

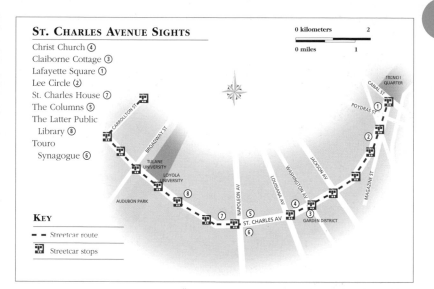

St. Charles Avenue Sights

Christ Church ④
Claiborne Cottage ③
Lafayette Square ①
Lee Circle ②
St. Charles House ⑦
The Columns ⑤
The Latter Public Library ⑧
Touro Synagogue ⑥

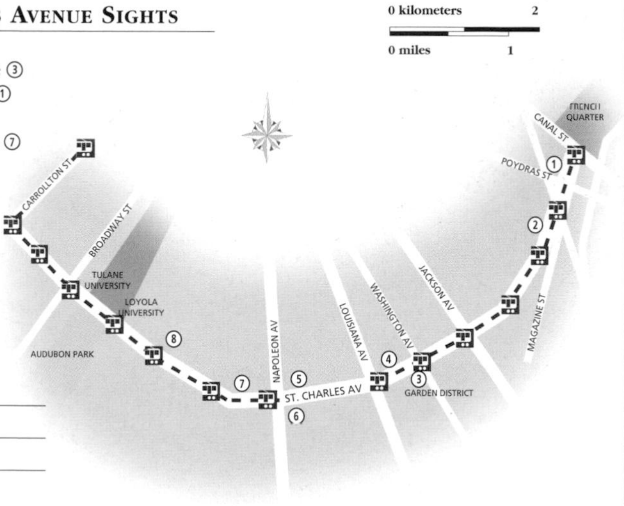
0 kilometers 2
0 miles 1
FRENCH QUARTER
CANAL ST
POYDRAS ST
CARROLLTON ST
BROADWAY ST
TULANE UNIVERSITY
LOYOLA UNIVERSITY
AUDUBON PARK
NAPOLEON AV
ST. CHARLES AV
LOUISIANA AV
WASHINGTON AV
JACKSON AV
MAGAZINE ST
GARDEN DISTRICT

Key

Streetcar route

Streetcar stops

The seats are made of slatted polished wood with brass handles and can be reversed for the return trip.
Blinds protect against the sun.
Windows open wide for a fresh breeze.

St. Charles House
Dating from the 1850s, this house may be the oldest on the street.

The Columns
Built for a wealthy cigar manufacturer, this imposing building was used by director Louis Malle as one of the sets for his movie Pretty Baby *(1970).*

MILTON H. LATTER MEMORIAL LIBRARY

The Latter Public Library
One of the most elegant libraries anywhere, the Latter started life in 1907 as a private mansion and was donated to the city by film star Marguerite Clark in the 1940s.

Toby's Corner, a 19th-century Greek Revival-style residence

Toby's Corner ❽

2340 Prytania St. **Map** 8 A3. 🚋 *St. Charles.* 🚌 *11, 14, 27.* ⬤ *Closed to the public.*

BUILT AROUND 1838, this house was constructed for Thomas Toby and is believed to be the oldest residence in the Garden District. Toby was a native Philadelphian, who moved to New Orleans and became a very successful wheelwright. He amassed a huge fortune but lost it financing Sam Houston and the cause for Texas independence from Mexico. It was, in fact, his wife who paid for the construction of the house. Subsequently, Toby worked as a plantation manager until he died.

After the Civil War *(see pp18–19)* the house was foreclosed and sold at auction for $5,000. The grounds contain an interesting fountain, which was fashioned from a large sugar kettle.

Nowadays, it is privately owned and closed to the public. However, its façade is an impressive example of the Greek Revival style, and it remains one of the most beautiful houses in the Garden District.

Women's Guild Opera House ❾

2504 Prytania St. **Map** 8 A3. ❰ *899-1945.* 🚋 *St. Charles.* 🚌 *11, 14, 27.* ⬤ *1pm–4pm Mon, groups of 20 or more.* 🏷️ ✔️

WILLIAM FRERET designed the original Greek Revival section of this house in 1858 for a wealthy merchant. The octagonal tower was added later. In 1996 the house was bequeathed to the Women's Guild of the New Orleans Opera Association, and it is now used for meetings and receptions. It also features some exhibits relating to the history of opera in New Orleans.

The city built the first opera house in the United States and in the 19th century it was a major opera center.

As early as the 1820s, French singers and musicians were being brought over to perform at the *Théâtre d'Orleans.* The French Opera House, at Bourbon and Toulouse, opened on December 1, 1859, with a performance of Rossini's *William Tell.* All of the great singers performed here, including Léonce Escalais, Julia Calvé, Etta Roehl, and Adelina Patti, who saved the season in 1860. The house seated more than 2,000 patrons in four tiers, with a splendid red-and-white mirrored interior. The fourth tier was reserved for blacks. A fire destroyed the Opera House in 1919, and it has never been replaced. The Women's Guild Opera House is open to the public for guided tours for 20 or more people with advance reservations.

Colonel Short's Villa ❿

1448 Fourth St. **Map** 7 F3. 🚋 *St. Charles.* 🚌 *11, 14, 27.* ⬤ *Closed to the public.*

Cornstalk fence detail

HENRY HOWARD designed this large Italian-style residence in 1859 for native Kentuckian Colonel Robert Short. The veranda, with fine iron railings, extends around three sides of the house. An

The Women's Guild Opera House, combining an octagonal tower and a Greek Revival main house

Colonel Short's Villa, with its remarkable cornstalk fence

exquisite ironwork fence, incorporating a morning glory and cornstalk motif, encloses the gardens *(see pp36–7)*. The story goes that the Colonel had it installed to please his wife. Unlike a similar fence on Royal Street in the French Quarter *(see p77)*, famous for its detailed ironwork, this one has not been painted and shows its original colors. In September 1863, the Union troops seized the residence. It was returned to the family after the Civil War *(see pp18–19)*. Although closed to the public, the famous cornstalk fence is much visited.

Musson-Bell House ⓫

1331 Third St. **Map** 8 A4. 🚊 *St. Charles.* 🚌 *11, 14, 27.* ⬤ *Closed to the public.*

WHEN THIS handsome Italianate villa was built in 1853 for Michel Musson (1812–1885), he was a successful cotton merchant and prominent Creole, and was also the New Orleans postmaster *(see p126)*. Musson had close ties with his extended family, including his sister Celestine Musson Degas, who lived in France. Celestine's son, Edgar Degas, was to become one of the world's great artists.

After the Civil War Degas came to visit Louisiana but it is unlikely he ever saw this house. The war had dealt Musson's fortunes a severe

blow and he sold the house in 1869, moving his family to a rented house on Esplanade Avenue *(see p126)*.

Brevard-Wisdom-Rice House ⓬

1239 First St . **Map** 8 A3. 🚊 *St. Charles.* 🚌 *11, 14, 27.*

FANS OF THE GOTHIC author, Anne Rice, stop to gawk at the Brevard-Wisdom-Rice House, her current home, which she purchased in 1989. The house was designed by James Calrow for merchant Albert Hamilton Brevard in 1857 and cost $13,000, at the time a formidable sum. It is adorned with ornate iron-work, including a fence incorporating a charming rose motif, for which reason the house is referred to as "Rosegate." Ionic and Corinthian columns support the galleries. The second owners of the pro-perty, the Clapp family, added the hexagonal wing in 1869. The gardens are splendid and feature some stunning camellias.

Anne Rice, who was born in New Orleans and

grew up in the Irish Channel, has portrayed the city in many of her best selling *Vampire Chronicles,* which began with the *Interview with the Vampire,* published in 1976. She and her husband, poet-scholar Stan Rice, returned to New Orleans from San Francisco in 1988. Rice used this house as the setting for her book *The Witching Hour* (1990). Rice spent her teenage years at 2524 St. Charles Avenue, which inspired much of her novel *Violin.* The author also owns several historic buildings, including the former St. Elizabeth's Orphanage at 1314 Napoleon Avenue.

Payne-Strachan House ⓭

1134 First St. **Map** 8 A4. 🚊 *St. Charles.* 🚌 *11, 14, 27.*

THIS GRAND HOME was built in the 1850s by Judge Jacob U. Payne, who brought slaves from his plantation in Kentucky to help construct it. The two-story Greek Revival residence features Ionic columns on the first gallery and Corinthian on the second. The house passed to Payne's son-in-law, Charles Erasmus Fenner, a close friend of Jefferson Davis, United States senator and president of the Confederacy *(see pp96–7)*. Davis died here on December 6, 1889, in the first-floor guest room. Because of its historic tradition, the house is popular with visitors.

Brevard-Wisdom-Rice House, Anne Rice's home

A stately Greek Revival home, the Garden District ▷

A side window of Loyola University's chapel

Loyola University ⑭

6363 St. Charles Ave. ☎ 865-3737. **Map** 6 B2. ☷ St. Charles. ☷ 22, 15. ◯ 9am–7pm daily.

THE JESUIT ORDER established the College of the Immaculate Conception downtown in 1840. It merged with Loyola College in 1912, and together they became Loyola University. The Tudor-Gothic buildings house the largest Catholic university in the South. The three buildings facing St. Charles Avenue are Marquette Hall, the adjacent Thomas Hall, and the Most Holy Name of Jesus Roman Catholic Church, the design of which was inspired by Canterbury Cathedral in the UK.

The statue of Jesus with uplifted arms in front of Marquette is referred to locally as "Touchdown Jesus," for obvious reasons.

Tulane University ⑮

6823 St. Charles Ave. **Map** 6 B2. ☎ 865-5000. ☷ St. Charles. ☷ 22, 15. ◯ 9am–5pm daily.

FOUNDED IN 1834 as a medical college, the precursor of Tulane University was given its present name in 1882 after it received a substantial gift from Paul Tulane, a native of Princeton, New Jersey. He made a fortune from a merchandising business, which he launched in New Orleans in 1822. Tulane's School of Business is the oldest college of commerce in the country.

The University moved to its current location in 1894. The 110-acre campus has 79 buildings, designed in a variety of styles. The Howard Tilton Memorial Library houses the Hogan Jazz Archive, plus other special collections. About 12,000 students attend the university.

Amistad Collection ⑯

Tulane University. **Map** 6 B3. ☎ 865-55 35. ☷ St. Charles. ☷ 45, 87. ◯ 9am–4:30pm Mon–Sat. ☉

THIS RESEARCH CENTER is named after the now famous slave mutiny aboard the Cuban slave ship *Amistad* in 1839. After a trial in Hartford, Connecticut, the slaves were acquitted and allowed to return home. The American Missionary Association, an organization formed to defend the slaves, established the center's archive, which moved from Fisk University to New Orleans in 1969. It consists of documents, photographs, pamphlets, and oral history records. A small gallery shows the works of artists including such names as Henry O. Tanner and Elizabeth Catlett.

Newcomb Art Gallery ⑰

Tulane University. **Map** 6 B2. ☎ 865-5000. ☷ St. Charles. ☷ 22, 15. ◯ 9am–5pm daily. ☉

IN 1886 Josephine Le Monnier Newcomb founded a women's college that was allied with Tulane University. Initially she donated $100,000

Stately Tulane University's Gibson Hall, built in Richardson-Romanesque style

Taking a rest on a hot day in Audubon Park

his first studio in 1821 at 706 Barracks Street. He stayed only four months before taking off for another brief sojourn as tutor to a young girl at Oakley House in West Feliciana Parish *(see p143)*. Here, in this rich ornithological environment, he began many of his bird portraits, but he stayed only a short time because of a dispute with his employer. He returned to New Orleans and took up residence at a studio at 505 Dauphine Street.

Audubon Zoo ⑲

See pp112–13.

Riverbend ⑳

Riverfront of St. Charles St. **Map** 6 A1. 📷 *St. Charles.* 🚌 *34.*

in memory of her daughter Harriot Sophie Newcomb, who died at the age of 15 in 1870. When Josephine herself died, she left an additional estate of more than $2.5 million to the college.

The Woldenberg Art Center houses the Newcomb Art Gallery and a smaller space to display student and faculty works. The Newcomb Gallery focuses on presenting traveling shows and also curates its own exhibitions.

The name of Newcomb is more familiarly associated with the arts-and-crafts style of pottery that was made at the Newcomb College of Art from 1895 to 1940. The gallery has some typical pieces on display.

Bronze statue in Audubon Park

morale. The main building alone covered almost four times the surface of the Superdome *(see p95)*. The first streetcar was introduced at the Expo, and so entranced Thomas Lipton of tea company fame that he became a motorman. The Mardi Gras Krewe of Rex *(see pp24–5)* arrived at the Expo aboard a yacht, establishing a tradition that survives to this day. Inside the park there is a golf course, several lakes, recreation areas, sport facilities, and the Audubon Zoo, which occupies 58 acres of the grounds. The park was named after naturalist John James Audubon, whose statue stands in its grounds. Audubon, the artist of *Birds of America*, was born in the West Indies. He came to New Orleans and rented

W ITH MORE THAN 300 billion gallons of water flowing by the city each day, New Orleans lives under the constant threat of flood. A system of spillways, pumps, and levees, like this one along the St. Charles Street Riverfront, forms a line of defense against the Mississippi. Still, certain sections of the city are prone to flooding, particularly after heavy rains. The pumping system was installed soon after 1927 when the city was so threatened that the authorities cut the levee below the city in St. Bernard Parish to forestall urban flooding. This part of the levee has been adapted as a recreation area, where visitors can enjoy a beautiful view of the river.

Audubon Park ⑱

6500 Magazine St. **Map** 6 B3. 📷 *St. Charles.* 🚌 *22, 11.* 📷 ♿

A UDUBON PARK was carved out of the plantations owned by the Foucher and Boré families in 1871. In 1884 the World's Industrial and Cotton Exposition, celebrating the first shipment of cotton, was held here. New Orleans was still recovering from the double devastations of the Civil War and Reconstruction *(see pp18–19)*, and the exposition helped boost the city's

Riverbend, a popular place for outdoor recreation

Audubon Zoo ⑲

Elephant giving a show

THIS APPEALING 58-ACRE ZOO, landscaped with fountains and water gardens, can be toured easily in a few hours. It opened in 1938 but was completely redesigned in the 1980s; today most of the animals are living in open paddocks that replicate their natural habitats. Only a few of the 1930s buildings remain. The swamp exhibit is one of the most engaging, showcasing Louisiana white alligators, as well as Acadian culture and music. The world-class zoo is part of Audubon Park *(see p111)*, one of the loveliest urban parks in the country. Originally, the 340-acre park was the sugar plantation of Jean Etienne Boré, who developed the commercially successful sugar granulation process. It was also the location of the 1884 World Exposition.

★ **Louisiana Swamp**
White alligators bask along the banks or float in the muddy lagoon.

Primates, such as orangutans and gorillas, play here.

The African Savannah
Rhinos, hippos, marabou storks, zebra, kudu, and white pelicans all live together with a host of opportunistic visitors such as ibis, heron, and egrets.

Tropical Bird House

Sea Lions
The sea lion pool is one of the oldest features of the zoo. Feeding time draws the crowds.

Reptile Encounter
King cobra, python, boa constrictors, and the impressive Komodo dragon hold court here.

★ **Jaguar Jungle**
Sloths, scarlet ibis, jabiru storks, and anteaters cohabit with jaguars in this exhibit, which is built around a replica of Mayan ruins set in a super-lush jungle.

VISITORS' CHECKLIST

6500 Magazine St. **Map** 6 B3.
861-2537. St. Charles Ave. 9:30am–5pm daily.
Dec 24–25, Thanksgiving, first Friday in May, and Mardi Gras.

The River Cruise landing
is a stop for the *John James Audubon* riverboat *(see p209).*

Flamingos
Near the river cruise landing, a peaceful lake is home to dozens of beautiful flamingos.

Elephant Plaza
An elephant show is presented in front of the plaza, while children are able to enjoy the unique experience of riding one.

Main entrance

St. Charles Streetcar free shuttle stop

Australian Outback
This area recreates the Australian outback with its kangaroos and kookaburras.

STAR FEATURES

★ **Louisiana Swamp**

★ **Jaguar Jungle**

Evocative statue at the New Orleans Botanical Gardens

Sights at a Glance

Museums & Galleries
Degas House [10]
Longue Vue House and Gardens [13]
New Orleans Museum of Art pp120–23 [1]
Pitot House [7]
Storyland and Carousel Gardens [3]

Parks and Gardens
Bayou St. John [6]
Dueling Oaks [2]
The New Orleans Botanical Garden [4]

Cemeteries
Cypress Grove Cemetery [11]
Metairie Cemetery [12]
St. Louis Cemetery #3 [8]

Entertainment
Fair Grounds [9]
Sports Facilities in City Park (Golf Course) [5]

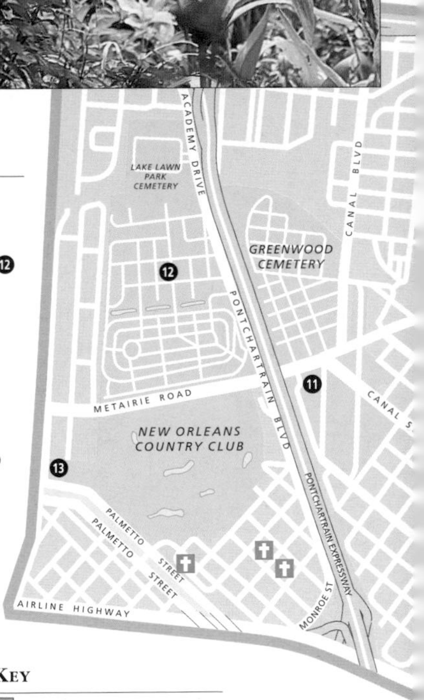

Rose garden entrance, Botanical Gardens

Key

Street-by-Street map *pp116–17*

[+] Hospital

✝ Church

Getting There

Routes 22, 33, 48 and 54 and a Cemetery Bus route run along Canal Street and Esplanade Street from the French Quarter.

MID-CITY

EXTENDING FROM the French Quarter to the shore of Lake Pontchartrain, Mid-City encompasses a variety of different neighborhoods. It is the greenest part of New Orleans, and the largest swath of land is taken up by City Park, which is carved out of the old Allard Plantation. The plantation had been obtained at auction by John McDonogh, a one-time Director of the Louisiana State Bank, who donated the area to the city on his death in 1850, provided that the funds from its sale be used for the city's public

Angel statue in Greenwood cemetery

schools. However, the city bent the rules a little after he died, and decided instead to create a park, which was landscaped in 1898. The other pockets of greenery in Mid-City are given over to various cemeteries such as Greenwood, Metairie, St. Louis Cemetery #3, and Cypress Grove. The two major streets that cut through the area are Esplanade Avenue and Canal Street. Esplanade is lined with beautiful Creole mansions, while Canal cuts through a series of ethnic neighborhoods, each boasting its own favorite eateries.

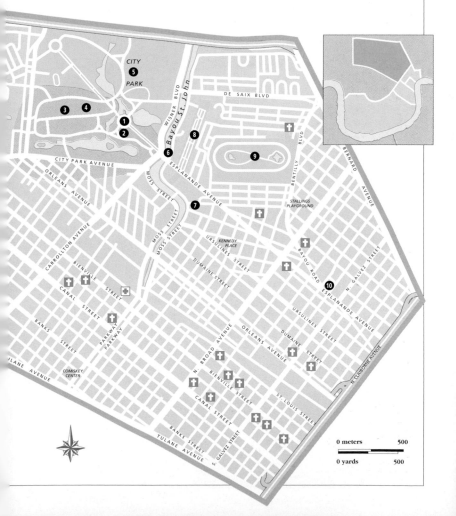

Street-by-Street: City Park

THIS 1,500-ACRE PARK is the fifth largest urban park in the US. The 10-acre Botanical Gardens and the world-class New Orleans Museum of Art share this space with moss-draped live oaks, 8 miles (13 km) of lagoons for boating and fishing,

Sculpture at NOMA

and the championship Bayou Oaks Golf Course. Children love the antique carousel and Storyland, a mini-theme park with Mardi Gras exhibits and a kid-sized carnival with rides. City Park is a real New Orleans institution, where visitors can relax and enjoy the semi-tropical Louisiana weather.

Storyland and Carousel
The wooden carousel is one of the main attractions in this children's park ❸

Sports Facilities
The Bayou Oaks Golf Course is on the park's periphery, while tennis courts are here in the center ❺   VICTORIA AVENUE

Popp's Bandstand
Named after lumber magnate John Popp, this bandstand is often used by jazz bands and mime artists.

DREYFOUS AVENUE

0 meters	100	**KEY**
0 yards	100	- - - Suggested route

The Peristyle
An entrance to a building that was never erected, the Peristyle formerly functioned as a dancehall. Today it is a picnic area.

★ **New Orleans Botanical Gardens**
Botanical exhibits and themed gardens – including the famous rose gardens – cover 10 acres of this ever-popular park. Statues by Mexican artist Enrique Alferez stand among the trees ❹

LOCATOR MAP
See Street Finder map 1

★ **New Orleans Museum of Art**
A Beaux-Arts building houses a collection of American and international art ❶

Dueling Oaks
As many as ten duels a day were once fought here. The last one was a challenge with sabers and took place in 1939 ❷

STAR SIGHTS

★ **New Orleans Botanical Gardens**

★ **New Orleans Museum of Art**

The Casino (1912)
Originally a casino, this Mission Revival build-ing houses a visitors' center, offering tourist information, a gift shop, and food concessions.

The Flute Player, by Enrique Alferez, at the Botanical Gardens

New Orleans Museum of Art ❶

See pp120–23.

Dueling Oaks ❷

City Park. **Map** 2 A1. 🚌 *46, 90.* ♿

B EHIND the famous statue of Confederate General P. G. T. Beauregard *(see p71)*, which guards the entrance to City Park, Lelong Avenue passes a cluster of massive live oaks, commonly called the Dueling Oaks.

Many duels were fought in New Orleans, and most of these took place in the bosky acres of what has since become City Park. Under the massive branches of live oaks, as many as ten duels a day were fought. Reports indicate that one particular dueler called for the use of whaling harpoons, after which the offended party decided he wasn't so offended after all. The last duel was fought in 1939 between two students from

a local fencing academy, who chose sabers as their weapons. The owner of the original plantation from which City Park was carved, Louis Allard, is said to be buried at the foot of one of the oaks.

Storyland and Carousel Gardens ❸

City Park. **Map** 2 A1. 📞 *483-9381.* 🚌 *46, 48, 90.* ◷ *10am–12:30pm Mon–Fri, 10am–4:30pm Sat–Sun.* ● *Dec 25, weekdays in Jan and Feb.* ♿ &

S TORYLAND, a beguiling theme park for children, is filled with all kinds of entertainments derived from traditional folk tales and well-known nursery rhymes. Kids can enjoy Jack and Jill's slide, climb around Miss Muffet's spider web, or challenge Captain Hook to a duel. Along the way, they may also encounter fairytale characters

such as Jack (of the Beanstalk), Puss in Boots, Rapunzel, and many others. Story reading, puppet shows in the Puppet Castle, and face painting are also on the agenda.

The carousel, situated in the southwest corner of the gardens, was built in 1906 and is one of the few wooden carousels to have survived in the United States. Nearby, visitors can climb aboard a miniature train, which has threaded its way around the park since 1896.

New Orleans Botanical Gardens ❹

Victory Ave, City Park. **Map** 2 A1. 📞 *483-9386.* 🚌 *46, 48, 90.* ◷ *10am–4:30pm Tue–Sun.* ● *Dec 25, Jan 1, Mardi Gras.* ♿ & ⬚

T HIS 10-ACRE public garden was created in the 1930s by the WPA, a public works agency. Back then, it was primarily a rose garden, but today there are also spring and perennial gardens, featuring azaleas, camellias, and magnolias, as well as tropical plants and trees, including palms and ginger. Several statues by Mexican artist Enrique Alferez, including his *Women in Huipil* and *The Flute Player*, stand among live oaks and other flora.

The Garden Study Center and the Pavilion of the Two Sisters are reminiscent of European garden architecture. The Conservatory houses orchids and two major exhibits: Living Fossils, showcasing plants that grew on the earth before flowering plants, and the impressive Tropical Rainforest exhibit.

The carousel in City Park, one of the oldest enclosed carousels in the United States

Sports Facilities in City Park ❺

Map 1 B1. *Riverfront.* ☎ 482-4888. 🚌 4C, 4B, 90.

THE MAJESTIC City Park contains many excellent sports facilities. The Wisner Tennis Center has 34 lighted courts, which can be reserved by phone 30 days ahead of time. Balls and rackets may also be rented here. The Bayou Oaks Golf Club has four 18-hole golf courses, plus a 100-tee lighted double-deck driving range.

The park's 8 miles (13 kilometers) of lagoons provide ample opportunities for boating, and for fishing for bass and trout. Egrets, heron, and the occasional alligator also inhabit the lagoons. Fishing permits can be obtained at the Administrative Center. There is also a stable, offering riding lessons and trail rides.

The Wisner Tennis Center, City Park

Bayou St. John ❻

Map 2 B1. 🚌 46, 48, 90.

THE FRENCH recognized this bayou as a key strategic asset, providing access to the Gulf of Mexico via Lake Pontchartrain. As New Orleans grew, plantations grew along the bayou and

a canal was dug, linking it to the downtown, ending in Basin Street at Congo Square. Today, the canal is filled in, but the name Basin Street has survived.

In the 18th and 19th centuries the bayou was the scene of voodoo ceremonies. Marie Laveau *(see p83)* was the most infamous practitioner.

Pitot House ❼

1440 Moss St. **Map** 2 B2. ☎ 482-0312. 🚌 46, 48, 90. ⏰ 10am–3pm Wed–Sat. ● *Major holidays.* 🖼

THIS CLASSIC West Indian-style raised house was built in 1799, on the banks of Bayou St. John. Once a

working plantation, it was carefully moved in the 1960s to this location, the site of the first French settlement in New Orleans. In 1810, the house was purchased by James Pitot, who had been the second mayor of the city five years earlier. Pitot had arrived from Haiti in 1796 after the slave uprising led by Toussaint L'Ouverture. He directed a bank and ran the New Orleans Navigation Company before being appointed to a judgeship.

In 1904, the house was bought by Mother Cabrini, later to become America's first saint, and converted into a convent. It is now a museum with original antiques and furnishings from the house.

Bayou St. John, where plantations developed a unique way of life

New Orleans Museum of Art ❶

Aztec maize goddesss

CONSIDERING ITS SIZE, this museum has an astonishingly varied collection. Originally the Delgado Museum of Art, it was founded in 1910 when Isaac Delgado, a millionaire bachelor, donated the original $150,000 to construct an art museum in City Park. It is housed in an impressive Beaux-Arts building designed by Samuel A. Marx of Chicago. Since its opening, the museum has tripled in size, and in 1971 it was renamed the New Orleans Museum of Art in deference to some of its later benefactors.

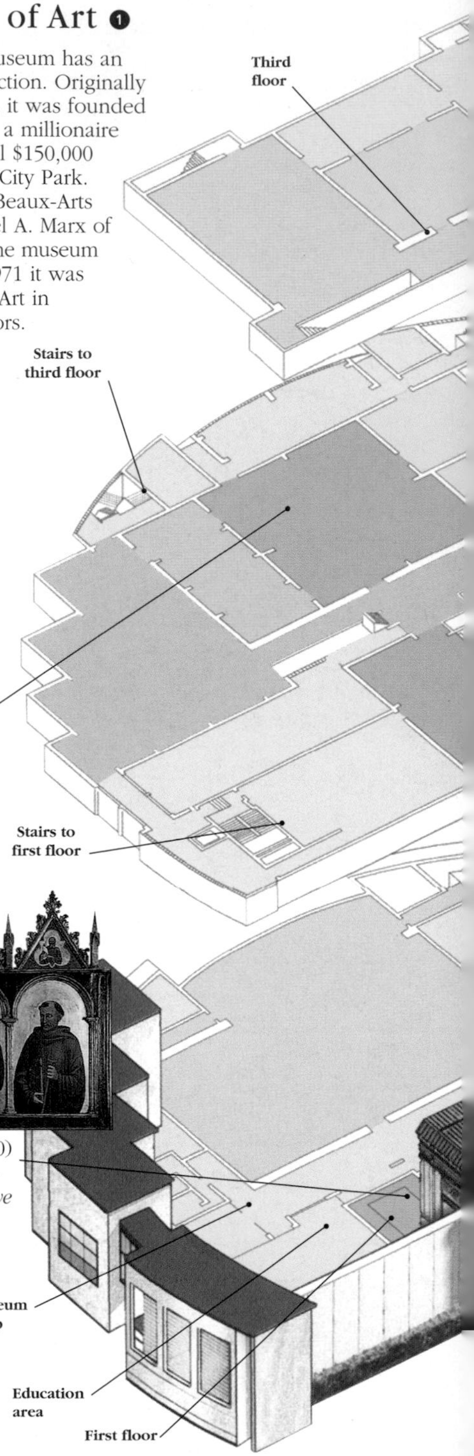

Third floor

Stairs to third floor

★ Woman in an Armchair (1960)
Showing the sitter's face in profile and from a frontal view, this Picasso reveals a style derived from his earlier analytical Cubism.

Stairs to first floor

★ Madonna and Child with Saints (1340)
Attributed to a close follower of Bernardo Daddi, this is an example of the decorative linear elegance of Sienese painting.

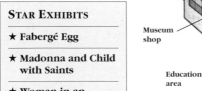

Museum shop

Education area

First floor

STAR EXHIBITS

★ Fabergé Egg

★ Madonna and Child with Saints

★ Woman in an Armchair

Melanesian Ancestor Figure
This carved-wood figure from the Abelan peoples in Papua New Guinea is one of the finest representations of the religious art of Melanesia.

VISITORS' CHECKLIST

1 Collins Diboll Circle, City Park.
Map 2 A2. 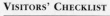 488-2631.
45, 87. 10am–5pm
Tue–Sun. Public hols.
 W www.noma.org

Lousiana Indians Walking Along the Bayou (1847)
Alfred Boisseau portrayed the Choctaw indians engaged in everyday activities.

Japanese Suit of Armor
This 18th-century Domaru-style one-piece body armor manifests the moral and spiritual traditions of the Samurai warriors.

Stairs to third floor

Second floor

GALLERY GUIDE
The main entrance leads to three European art collections. The second floor houses the American Art, the Fabergé, and three further European collections. The third floor offers African, Oceanic, and Native American exhibits.

Stairs to second floor

Main entrance

★ Fabergé Egg (1896)
This beautifully detailed egg was made by Peter Carl Fabergé for the Russian Empress Alexandra Feodorovna.

KEY TO FLOOR PLAN

☐	African and Oceanic Art
☐	American Art
☐	Asian Art
☐	Contemporary Art
☐	Decorative Arts
☐	European Art
☐	Prehispanic/Native American Art
☐	Photography and Graphics
☐	Temporary exhibition space
☐	Non-exhibition space

Exploring the New Orleans Museum of Art

THE MAJOR COLLECTIONS displayed in the museum's 46 galleries include a vast selection of European art, from 12th-century Italian Florentine to 20th-century French and Spanish works. There are specialized collections of Latin American and Prehispanic art; Native and modern American works; arts of Africa and Asia; photography; and decorative arts. The planned Besthoff Sculpture Garden allows space for 60 sculptures by major 20th-century artists.

AFRICAN AND OCEANIC ART

Yoruba mounted warrior

THIS IS ONE OF the finest African art collections in the country. Established in 1953, it now represents Sub-Saharan Africa's five major art-producing regions, including works by the Baman and Dogon peoples of Mali and the Benin, the Yoruba, the Ibo, and the Ekoi peoples of Nigeria, Cameroon, and the Ivory Coast. Among the highlights is a rare palace veranda post carved in the shape of an equestrian warrior figure by Yoruba artist Olowe of Ise. Another gem is a terra-cotta head from the Nok culture dating from around 500 BC–AD 200. *The Head of an Oba* (late 18th century) is a striking bronze funerary portrait, which might have been placed on an altar in the Benin royal palace to commemorate the deceased.

The Oceania gallery includes wooden figures from Papua New Guinea; nephrite (a hard green jade-like stone) weapons, tools, and ornaments from the Maoris; and a standing Malanggan figure, also from New Zealand.

AMERICAN ART

THIS COLLECTION includes some fine examples of early American artists such as John Singleton Copley, Gilbert Stuart, Charles Willson Peale, Benjamin West, and John Singer Sargent. An entire gallery is devoted to a collection of Louisiana paintings, including *Louisiana Indians Walking Along the Bayou (see p121)* by Alfred Boisseau, *Back of Algiers* (1870–73) by Richard Clague, and *Blue Crab and Terrapins* (1880) by Achille Perelli. The *Portrait of Mme. René de Gas, née Estelle Musson*, painted in 1872–3 by Edgar Degas during a visit to New Orleans, is also displayed.

ASIAN ART

ONE OF THE FINEST collections of Edo (1600–1868) Japanese paintings can be seen in these galleries. All the major Japanese schools are represented, and it is particularly strong on the Nanga, Zenga, and Maruyama-Shijo schools. The collection also includes a wide variety of ceramics, lacquer, textiles, prints, photographs, and armor.

Portrait of a Bijin (courtesan), Yamaguchi Soken (1800)

The Chinese collection has ceramics from the Neolithic to the modern era. There are stone, wood, and bronze sculptures, plus miniatures, and religious art from India.

CONTEMPORARY ART

A GREAT VARIETY of sculpture, paintings, and mixed-media works, such as Joseph Cornell's intricate small-scale shadow boxes, are included in the Contemporary Art collection, which is divided into Contemporary European Art and the American Art exhibits. The European collection features works from such artists as Miró and Picasso. The American exhibit ranges from Georgia O'Keefe's *My Back Yard* (1937) and Hans Hofmann's *Abstraction with Chair and Miró* (1943), to Jackson Pollock's *Composition (White, Black, Blue, and Red on White)* (1948) and Roger Brown's *California Hillside* (1988).

Portrait of a Young Girl, Joan Miró (1935)

DECORATIVE ARTS

THE MUSEUM has a fabulous glass collection consisting of more than 6,000 items. The collection is particularly strong in ancient glass, and later European and American traditions such as Tiffany vases. In pottery, the American art collection is centered on a large group of pieces from New Orleans' own Newcomb Pottery. The silver collection contains some lustrous pieces by English silversmith Paul Storr. There is also a rare collection of "Old Paris" porcelain, plus examples of Sevres, Nidervillier, and Limoges. The main part of the exhibition lies on the second floor.

EUROPEAN ART

SUPERB GEMS such as Picasso's *Woman with Tambourine* (1938), Miró's *Lady Strolling on the Rambla in Barcelona* (1925), Degas' *Dancer in Green* (1878), Rodin's *The Age of Bronze* (1876), and works by other European masters are highlights of this excellent display.

The Kress Collection includes sublime Italian Old Master paintings from the 13th to the 18th centuries. Because of New Orleans'

Morning Glory Tiffany vase

history, French art is well represented, with works from the 17th to the 20th centuries. The Hyams Gallery features lesser-known 19th-century Salon and Barbizon painters, in contrast to the more familiar Impressionist and Post-Impressionist painters represented in the adjacent Forgotston Gallery.

Two small but world-famous galleries contain exquisite collections of works by Peter Carl Fabergé and portrait miniatures by European painters. The Fabergé exhibit, the largest collection of these works in the South, holds three Imperial Easter Eggs, a jeweled *Imperial Lilies of the Valley Basket* crafted for the Empress Alexandra Feodorovna, and a jade rabbit with ruby eyes. The other small gallery on this floor displays Dutch and Flemish portraits and other works from the 16th and 17th centuries.

PREHISPANIC/NATIVE AMERICAN ART

THESE GALLERIES ARE particularly strong in material from the Maya culture, displaying some impressive sculptures and ceramics. Other Central American and Mexican cultures represented include

Native American sculptures representing a family (1958)

Olmec and Mixtec along with the later Aztec civilization.

The Native American collections include Kachina dolls from the Hopi and Zuni, pottery from the Acoma Santo Domingo and San Ildefonso pueblos, Apache and Pima baskets, and Percé beadwork and textiles from the northwest coast.

The museum also has a special collection of Latin American colonial art, much of it from Cuzco, Peru. It includes such works as an early 18th-century portrait of an archangel with a musket and a refined 17th-century polychrome-on-wood statue of the Archangel Michael.

PHOTOGRAPHY AND GRAPHICS

THIS COLLECTION of more than 7,000 vintage photographs is one of the finest of its kind in the southeast. It includes works by all the known masters, such as William Henry Fox Talbot's *View of the Paris Boulevards* (1843), André Kertész's *Théâtre Odeon* (1926), Man Ray's *Portrait of Berenice Abbott in front of Man Ray Composition* (1922), and Diane Arbus's *A Young Brooklyn Family Going on a Sunday Outing* (1966). In his 1946 *Elegy for the Old South (No. 6)*, Clarence John Laughlin captures the nostalgia of the old South in surrealistic images of decay. His photographs of abandoned plantation homes and of the South in the early 20th century are justly famous.

The Cardinal's Friendly Chat, Jehan Georges Vibert (1880)

Miniature train passing through the oaks at City Park ▷

Some of the city's most poignant tombs at St. Louis Cemetery #3

St. Louis Cemetery #3 **8**

3421 Esplanade Ave. **Map** 2 B1.
[482-5065. 🚌 45, 87.
⭕ 8am–4:30pm Mon–Sat,
8am–4pm Sun. ● Mardi Gras.

THIS PRISTINE cemetery, with its beautiful wrought-iron gates, opened in 1856. Among the notables buried here is Antoine Michoud, the original owner of a plantation which is now the site of the NASA plant where the Saturn rockets were built in the 1960s. There is also a memorial to architect James Gallier, Sr. *(see p95)* and his wife, who are buried in Metairie Cemetery. Both were killed when the steamer *Evening Star* sank en route from New York to New Orleans in October 1866.

Other famous New Orleans figures here include Father Rouquette, missionary to the Choctaw, and black philanthropist Thomy Lafon, owner of the old Orleans Ballroom,

Reproduction furniture in the dining room at Degas House

where the famous "quadroon balls" were held. Lafon also sponsored an orphanage for African American children.

Fair Grounds **9**

1751 Gentilly Blvd. **Map** 2 C1.
[944-5515. 🚌 45, 87. 🖼 ♿

IN THE MID-19TH century, New Orleans was the leading center for horse racing, the "sport of kings," with four tracks operating. The Creole Racecourse operated during the 19th century on what is now the Fair Grounds. When Metairie Racecourse closed, the Louisiana Jockey Club took over and purchased the Luling Mansion on Esplanade as a clubhouse. The name change occurred when the Fair Grounds Corporation took over in 1940. Races are still run here from November to March, and in April the Fair Grounds host the ever popular New Orleans Jazz Fest *(see p41)*.

Degas House **10**

2306 Esplanade Ave. **Map** 3 D3.
[821-5009. 🚌 45, 87. ⭕ 9am–6pm daily. 🖼 🗷

CALLING HIMSELF "almost a son of Louisiana," Impressionist painter Edgar Degas (1834–1917) visited his uncle, Michel Musson *(see p107)*, at this house from October 1872

until March 1873. Degas was charmed with America and especially New Orleans. Several important paintings evolved from his sojourn here, despite the fact that he did not venture far from the house for fear of the intense New Orleans sun affecting his eyesight. *The Cotton Buyer's Office* (1873) shows his uncle with several members of his family, including the artist's own brothers René and Achille, who both worked in the cotton business.

The Esplanade house, which dates from 1854, has Greek Revival details and cast-iron balconies. The house is beautifully maintained throughout and offers bed and breakfast accommodations *(see p162)*, as well as welcoming visitors during the day. Many reproductions of Degas' work are on display.

Cypress Grove Cemetery **11**

120 City Park Ave. **Map** 1 C2.
[482-3232. 🚌 45, 87.
⭕ 8am–4:15pm daily. ♿

THIS CEMETERY, established by the Firemen's Charitable Association, was laid out in 1841. The impressive Egyptian-style gate leads into a graveyard filled with handsome memorials. Many of the tombs are dedicated to individual firefighters, such as Irad Ferry, who lost their lives in the line of duty. Ferry's tomb, which features a broken column, was designed by

Marble statue at Cypress Grove

the famous architect J. N. B. de Pouilly *(see p83)*.

The cemetery also contains a large number of rich protestants, who were buried here after Girod Cemetery began to deteriorate. Many of the tombs have remarkable ironwork, like the weeping cupid gate which is crowned with lovebirds and set between inverted torches.

An extension to Cypress Grove was built right across the street to fulfil a need for space after the yellow fever epidemic of 1853. Known as Greenwood Cemetery, it was the first in New Orleans to be built without a boundary wall. It is the site of the city's first Civil War Memorial.

Metairie Cemetery ⑫

5100 Pontchartrain Blvd. **Map** 1 B1.
⚏ 486-6331. ⛟ 45, 87.
◷ 7:30am–5pm daily. ♿

THIS IS THE MOST attractively landscaped cemetery in New Orleans, and the final resting place of many of its bluebloods. In the 19th century, the city was the premier venue for horseracing, and the Metairie Racetrack was the most famous. After the Civil War, mismanagement afforded Charles T. Howard the opportunity to take revenge on the racetrack members who had refused him admission. He purchased it in 1872 and converted it into a cemetery. The oval racecourse became the cemetery's main drive.

Many magnificent tombs are located here, and near the entrance stands the massive 85-ft (26-m) high Moriarty monument, which required the laying of a special railroad to bring it into the cemetery. Daniel

Egan Family tomb, modeled after the ruins of an Irish chapel

Moriarty was an Irish immigrant and saloonkeeper who had succeeded financially but was scorned socially. He was determined to avenge his wife, Mary, and designed this tomb so that in death she could look down on all those who had snubbed her.

The tomb of legendary madame Josie Arlington bears a bas-relief of a young girl knocking on a door. Orphaned at the age of four, Josie went into business for herself as a teenager. She became a notorious whore and brawler, and once bit off half an ear and the lower lip of a fellow prostitute.

A large bell from his boat *America* marks the grave of

Captain Cooley, who ran several steamboats until his death in 1931. Other denizens include P. B. S. Pinchback, a free man of color who became Louisiana's only black governor in 1872–3, and William C. C. Claiborne *(see p17)*, first governor of Louisiana. David C. Hennessy, the police chief who was assassinated in 1891, also has an impressive tomb.

Longue Vue House and Gardens ⑬

7 Bamboo Road. **Map** 1 A2.
⚏ 488-5488. ⛟ 45, 87.
◷ 10am–4pm Mon–Sat, 1pm–5pm Sun. ● Public hols. ♿

COTTON BROKER Edgar Stern and his wife Edith Rosenwald, heiress to the Sears fortune, established this estate between 1939 and 1942. The interiors are exquisitely decorated with antiques, Oriental carpets, and fine art, including works by Jean Arp, Pablo Picasso, and Barbara Hepworth. The gardens, which contain 23 fountains created by Ellen Biddle, are exceptional examples of landscape design. The estate's largest garden is modeled on Spain's 14th-century Alhambra gardens; others are inspired by French and English designs.

One of Ellen Biddle's fountains gracing the gardens of Longue Vue House

BEYOND
NEW ORLEANS

BEYOND NEW ORLEANS

THE COUNTRYSIDE *around New Orleans is a land full of history and tradition. The beautiful plantations of the Mississippi River, Baton Rouge (the capital of Louisiana), and the famous Cajun Country are full of cultural and entertainment interest. Venturing beyond New Orleans allows you to experience the unique mixture of Louisiana's cultures in all their various accents.*

The lifeblood of New Orleans was, and still is, the Mississippi River. In the 18th and 19th centuries the river banks were lined with large, wealthy plantations producing all kinds of commodities, including sugar, tobacco, indigo, and cotton, which were shipped around the world via New Orleans. Today only a handful of these plantation homes survives along the River Road, but many of these are open to visitors.

Baton Rouge is the state capital, a major port, and an oil-refining center with a population of about 600,000. It has several attractions associated with its role in state government, including the State Capitol, the Old State Capitol, and the Governor's Mansion. Other sights in Baton Rouge include the Rural Life Museum, the

Sculpture at the Louisiana State Capitol

World War II destroyer the USS *Kidd*, and the Louisiana State University. To the west of Baton Rouge lie the massive Atchafayala Swamp and Cajun Country. The latter is famous for its Francophone culture, Cajun, and zydeco music, and its robust, spicy cuisine. Visitors can explore Cajun culture in a number of towns in this area – Eunice, Lafayette, and Opelousas – as well as along the bayous of New Iberia, and Avery Island. To get a feel for life on the bayous, you can attend a *fais do-do* (dance), feast on the excellent local cuisine, or even tour the McIlhenny Tabasco Sauce Factory. Visitors can also drift among 1,500-year-old cypress trees in the swamps, and visit museums and historic villages, all of which provide insights into the Cajun way of life.

Original Cajun house in the Acadian Village near Lafayette

◁ St. John the Evangelist cathedral in Lafayette

Exploring Beyond New Orleans

An excursion to the bayous and small towns a few hours away from New Orleans will show visitors just how different the city is from its Louisiana surroundings. Upriver, the Cajun heritage is evident in the architectural styles, the food, and even the language, since French is spoken almost everywhere. Only a few hours' drive from New Orleans, it is possible to visit more than a dozen Creole and American plantations along the Mississippi River and to get a taste of life as it used to be. The city of Baton Rouge, the state capital, makes an interesting modern counterpoint.

Vermilionville
This restored 19th-century Cajun-Creole settlement is peopled by costumed staff. Traditional ways of life are enacted.

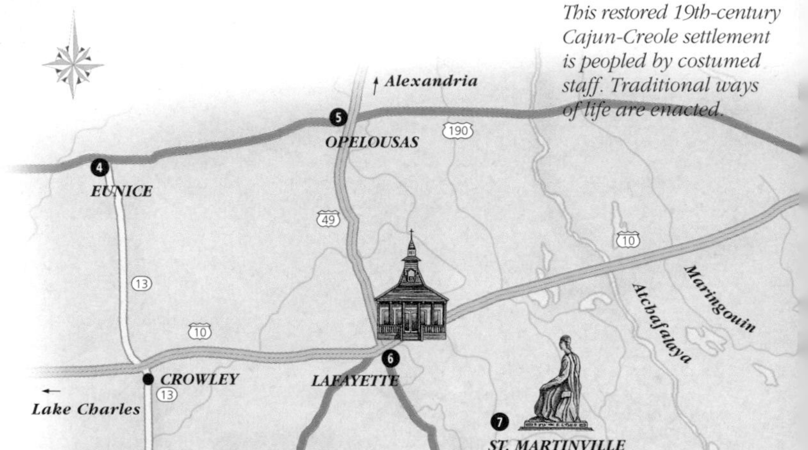
Alexandria
5
OPELOUSAS
190
4
EUNICE
49
10
13
10
Maringouin
Atchafalaya
6
CROWLEY
13
LAFAYETTE
Lake Charles
7
ST. MARTINVILLE
167
8
NEW IBERIA &
AVERY ISLAND
Lake
Fausse
Pointe
14
90
Houma

The Acadian Village, Lafayette
This is a fully reassembled Cajun bayou community, with houses boasting traditional Cajun furnishings.

CAJUN MUSIC HALL OF FAME AND MUSEUM

Cajun Music Hall of Fame, Eunice
A country store dating from the 1930s now houses a museum of local music.

Getting Around

All of the sights can be reached easily by road from New Orleans. Interstate 10 (I-10) connects the city directly to Baton Rouge. Some exits from route I-10 also lead to the River Road Plantations and to Cajun Country. From New Orleans, several guided tours to the bayous are available *(see p213)*, which offer a convenient way to explore life on the bayous.

Nottoway
Built in 1859, Neo-Classical Nottoway Plantation has 64 rooms. Today it operates as a bed and breakfast and has a fine restaurant.

Old State Capitol, Baton Rouge
This Gothic Revival castle, built in 1847, was burned by the Union Army and repaired in 1882. Today it houses a museum of local history.

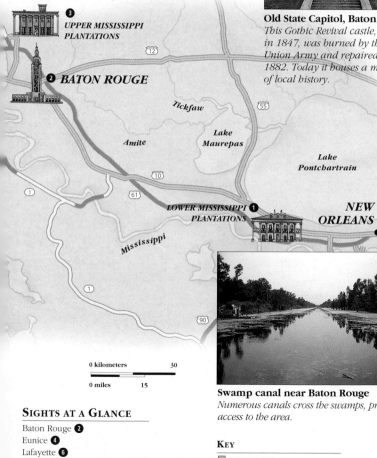

❸ UPPER MISSISSIPPI PLANTATIONS

12

❷ BATON ROUGE

Tickfaw 55

Lake Maurepas

Amite

Lake Pontchartrain

10

61

1

LOWER MISSISSIPPI PLANTATIONS ❶

NEW ORLEANS 10

61

Mississippi

1

90

0 kilometers   30
0 miles   15

Swamp canal near Baton Rouge
Numerous canals cross the swamps, providing access to the area.

SIGHTS AT A GLANCE

Baton Rouge ❷
Eunice ❹
Lafayette ❻
Lower Mississippi Plantations ❶
New Iberia and Avery Island ❽
Opelousas ❺
St. Martinville ❼
Upper Mississippi Plantations ❸

KEY

▨ Interstate highway
▨ State highway
▢ State road
▨ River

Lower Mississippi Plantations ➊

Old plantation water pump

Tᴏ ᴛʜᴇ ʀɪᴠᴇʀ ʀᴏᴀᴅ meanders along both banks of the Mississippi River, changing route numbers as it goes. It runs behind the levee, past petrochemical plants, towering live oaks draped with Spanish moss, and magnificent plantation homes. Creole families once owned and operated the plantations located between New Orleans and Baton Rouge. Some of the old plantation residences have been given a new lease of life as small museums.

Restored Plantations
Many plantations are carefully restored and are open to the public as bed and breakfast hotels.

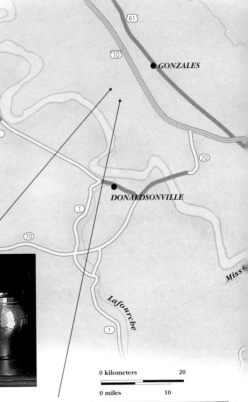

Nottoway
The largest plantation in the area, Nottoway boasts an impressive 65 rooms.

Houmas House
The country's largest sugar plantation in the 19th century, this grand house now displays a fine antiques collection.

Tezcuco
This raised cottage and its surrounding buildings contain some fine Mallard and Seignouret furniture as well as Newcomb pottery.

Oak Alley
*Two glorious rows of oaks, each of 14 live trees,
line the drive to this mansion, built in 1836.*

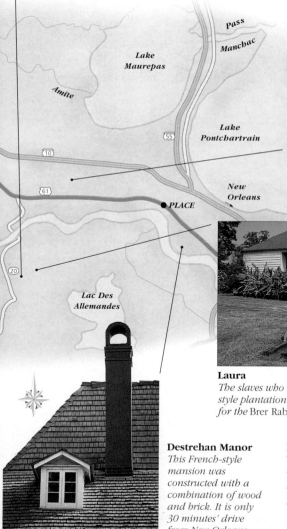

Pass

Manchac

**Lake
Maurepas**

Amite

**Lake
Pontchartrain**

55

**New
Orleans**

10

61

PLACE

20

**Lac Des
Allemandes**

San Francisco
*"Steamboat Gothic" style is
displayed in all its glory
at this plantation.*

Laura
*The slaves who worked this typical Creole-
style plantation are thought to be the source
for the* Brer Rabbit *folktales.*

Destrehan Manor
*This French-style
mansion was
constructed with a
combination of wood
and brick. It is only
30 minutes' drive
from New Orleans.*

KEY

▦	Freeway
▦	Major road
☐	Minor road

Exploring Lower Mississippi Plantations

BY 1850, TWO-THIRDS OF AMERICA'S MILLIONAIRES lived on plantations located along the Great River Road. The economic relationship between the plantations' production and the trade from New Orleans to the rest of the world made it one of the wealthiest regions of the nation. The treasures of this glory are displayed in homes from New Orleans to Baton Rouge, with colorful French and Spanish Creole architecture and beautiful natural surroundings.

Destrehan plantation

🏛 Destrehan

13034 River Rd, Destrehan. 📞 *(504) 764-9315.* 🕐 *9am–4pm daily.* ⬤ *Major holidays.* 📷 📹 ♿

Charles Pacquet, a free man of color, built this home for Robert de Logny in 1787. The original Creole cottage was modified in 1810 and 1840. Union troops housed freed slaves here during the Civil War *(see pp18–19).*

🏛 San Francisco

Hwy 44, River Rd, Garyville. 📞 *(504) 535-2341.* 🕐 *10:30am–4:30pm daily.* ⬤ *Dec 25, Jan 1, Mardi Gras, and Thanksgiving.* 📷

The term "Steamboat Gothic" has been applied to this ornate plantation home built for Edmond Bozonier Marmillion in 1856. Originally it was painted in flamboyant purples, blues, and greens, and the structure was decorated with plenty of ornate grillwork and gingerbread trim. The interiors feature some splendid ceiling paintings completed by Dominique Canova (cousin of the famous sculptor) featuring cherubs, trailing vines, flying parrots, and exquisite faux marbling and graining. Commissioned by Edmond's son, Valsin, and his daughter-in-law during major renovations in 1860, they were so expensive that Valsin named the house Saint Frusquin, from the French *sans fruscins,* meaning "without a penny." The name eventually became corrupted to "San Francisco." Valsin died before he could enjoy the house he had imagined, and shortly after the Civil War his widow sold it to a Colonel Bougere. The grounds of the original plantation have been reduced by several levee setbacks over the years, and so today it stands very close to the road.

🏚 Laura

2247 Hwy 18, Vacherie. 📞 *(225) 265-7690.* 🕐 *9am–5pm daily.* ⬤ *Major holidays.* 📹

Laura is named after the last owner of this classic Creole plantation, Laura Locoul Gore. The memoir she wrote about life on the plantation until 1891 has been used to produce an engaging historical tour of the property. Guillaume DuParc built the home in 1805 and his wife, Elizabeth, managed the property for 47 years. Later Laura reluctantly took over.

Scholars believe folklorist Alcée Fortier first recorded the Senegalese stories about Brer Rabbit from the slaves on this plantation. Joel Chandler Harris made the stories famous when he wrote his *Uncle Remus and Brer Rabbit* tales in 1906.

🏚 Oak Alley

3645 Hwy 18, Vacherie. 📞 *(225) 265-2151.* 🕐 *Mar– Oct: 9am–5:30pm, Nov–Feb: 9am–5pm.* ⬤ *Dec 25, Thanksgiving.* 📷 📹 ♿

Oak Alley's name comes from the 28 magnificent live oaks that line the entrance to this plantation home. They were planted about 300 years ago, even before the house was built for Jacques Telesphore Roman III in 1837. The house and grounds are so striking that it has been used as a location for several movies,

San Francisco plantation, the ultimate in "Steamboat Gothic" style

The Great White Ballroom at Nottoway plantation

latter features exhibits about famous African Americans, the role that many blacks played in the Civil War, and the contribution African Americans have made to the music of the Mississippi Delta.

🏛 Houmas House
40136 Hwy 942, River Rd, Burnsville. 📞 *(225) 473-7841.* ⏱ *Feb–Oct: 10am–5pm, Nov–Jan: 10am–4pm.* ● *Thanksgiving, Dec 25.* 📷
Antique lovers will appreciate the fine early Louisiana furniture collection assembled by scholar-collector Dr. Crozat, whose family still occupies this home, which he purchased in 1940. There are two interconnected houses on the property. The oldest dates to the late 1700s and was built by Alexandre Latil on land purchased from the Houmas Indians in 1776.

In 1840, John Smith Preston and his wife, the daughter of Revolutionary War general Wade Hampton, built the second Greek Revival home. In 1858 they sold the house plus 10,000 acres to John Burnside for $1 million dollars. A wealthy Irish merchant, Burnside amassed a 20,000-acre sugar plantation with four sugar mills. His property survived the Civil War, because he claimed immunity as a British subject. At the end of the 19th century this plantation was producing as much as 20 million pounds (9 million kg) of sugar each year.

Embroidery stand

including *The Long Hot Summer* (1985) and *Interview with the Vampire* (1994). A slave gardener developed the first commercial variety of pecan nut, the "Paper Shell," on the property.

🏛 Nottoway
30970 Hwy 405, White Castle. 📞 *(225) 545-2730.* ⏱ *9am–5pm daily.* ● *Dec 25.* 📷
This is the largest plantation on this stretch of the Mississippi. It was designed by architect Henry Howard to accommodate John Hampden Randolph, his wife, and a family of 11 children, and completed in 1859. Randolph was a wealthy sugar planter who moved south from his native Virginia. The mansion occupies 53,000 sq ft (18,000 sq m), featuring 64 rooms, 16 fireplaces, 200 windows, and 165 doors. At the time it was built, it incorporated some innovative conveniences such as indoor plumbing, gas lighting, and coal fireplaces. In the Great White Ballroom, which is 65 ft (22 m) long, seven of Randolph's daughters celebrated their weddings. It is the largest and most impressive room in the house. During the 19th century, this plantation was surrounded by 7,000 sugar-producing acres. It survived the Civil War because of the intervention of a Union gunboat officer, who

Antique clock at Nottoway

asked that it be spared because he had once been a guest of the Randolphs. Nottoway resembles an enormous white castle, and the little town of White Castle grew up around it.

🏛 Tezcuco
3138 Hwy 44, River Rd, Darrow. 📞 *(225) 562-3929.* ⏱ *9:30am–4:30pm daily.* ● *Thanksgiving, Dec 25.* 📷
The house was built in 1855–61 by Benjamin Tureaud, a veteran of the Mexican War (1846–48). The name "Tezcuco" means "resting place" in Aztec. He was the son of Elizabeth Bringier, who was from a prominent Louisiana family. Two museums at this plantation provide some context to the region's history and plantation economy – the Civil War Museum and the Afro-American History Museum. The

Houmas House, a fine example of Greek Revival style

Baton Rouge ❷

I N 1719, THE FRENCH ESTABLISHED Baton Rouge as a fort designed to control access to the Mississippi and the interior. It was so named by Jean Baptiste Le Moyne, Sieur de Iberville *(see p15)*, after he observed the spikes (red sticks) hung with bloody fish heads that were arranged along the river bluffs. In 1762, the French ceded it to the British. During the American Revolution, the Spanish took the opportunity to seize the garrison, which remained under their control until 1810. After that, the local American population took the fort and proclaimed the Republic of West Florida. The area was claimed for the United States and it was incorporated into the Union in 1817. It has been the state capital since 1849.

Lantern at LSU

The graceful interior of Louisiana Old State Capitol

👭 Louisiana Old State Capitol

100 North Blvd. 📞 *(225) 342-0500.* 🕙 *10am–4pm Tue–Sat, 12pm–4pm Sun.* ⬤ *Public hols.* ♿ ⛔
James Harrison Dakin designed this striking castle-like building in 1847. William Freret conceived the soaring iron spiral staircase, installed during a renovation in 1882, which winds from the foyer toward the stained-glass dome. It was here, in the House Chamber, that Louisiana's state representatives voted in 1861 to secede from the Union. Seven decades later, in 1929, impeachment proceedings were begun here against Huey "Kingfish" Long. Today, this magnificent building serves as the state's Center for Political and Government History. Visitors can view and listen to many of the state's colorful political orators expressing their views.

👭 Louisiana State University

Nicholson Drive btw. Highland Rd. and W. Chimes St. 📞 *(225) 388-3202.*
With its 31,000 students, this is the state's flagship university. The tree-shaded campus is attractively landscaped and boasts some unique features. In the northwest corner, for example, two mounds rise some 20 ft (6 m) high. Archeologists believe that they are 5,000-year-old Native American mounds built before the first Egyptian pyramids.

The university's sports teams are some of the hottest tickets in college sports. In baseball, the Tigers have won national titles for several consecutive years, and the enthusiasm generated by the football team is legendary.

The university also has two cutting edge research facilities; the Pennington Biomedical Research Center, devoted to nutritional medicine, and the Center for Microstructures and Devices. The collections at the Museum of Natural Science in Foster Hall (225-388-2855) are also worth seeing. The visitor information center is at Dalrymple Drive and Highland Road.

🏛 Magnolia Mound Plantation

2161 Nicholson Dr. 📞 *(225) 343-4955.* 🕙 *10am–4pm Tue–Sat, 1pm–4pm Sun.* ⬤ *Public hols.* ♿
John Joyce built this plantation home in 1791. In the 19th century it stood at the center of a 900-acre farm, producing indigo, cotton, perique tobacco, and sugarcane. The building has been carefully restored to reflect the antebellum era.

👭 Old Governor's Mansion

502 North Blvd. 📞 *(225) 387-2464.* 🕙 *10am–4pm Tue–Fri.* ⬤ *Public hols.* ♿ ⛔
Governor Huey Long had this mansion built in 1930. He modeled it on the White House, even down to the office, which is a smaller version of the Oval Office. The building has been carefully restored, and the rooms have even been repainted in their original colors, some of which are outlandish; Huey Long apparently loved hot pinks, purples, and greens, which appear in several bathrooms. Many of the furnishings in the library and the master bedroom are original to the house. There is also memorabilia from other governors, including the singing governor, Jimmie Davis, who wrote *You Are my Sunshine.*

Façade of the Greek Revival Old Governor's Mansion

The House Chamber, State Capitol

⊞ State Capitol

State Capitol Dr. ☎ (225) 342-7317.
◯ 8am–4:30pm daily. Observation
deck closes at 4pm. ● Thanksgiving,
Dec 25, Jan 1, Easter Sunday. 🖼 ♿
Huey Long worked hard to
persuade the legislators to
approve the $5 million fund-
ing for this Modernist 34-story
building, erected in 1932. It is
the tallest capitol in the
United States. Both the House
and Senate chambers are
impressive, as are the murals
in Memorial Hall. Visitors can
still see the bullet holes in the
marble walls of the first-floor
executive corridor, where
Long was assassinated on
September 8, 1935, by Dr.
Carl A. Weiss, the son-in-law
of a political enemy, Judge
Benjamin Pavy. The grounds
contain Long's grave in a
sunken memorial garden.
There are excellent views of

the Mississippi and the
city from the 27th-floor
observation deck.

🏛 USS *Kidd*

305 S River Rd. ☎ (225)
342-1942. ◯ 9am–5pm
daily. ● Thanksgiving, Dec
25. 🖼 ♿
Commissioned in
1943, this World War II
destroyer saw action
in the Pacific, where
she suffered a kami-
kaze attack on April 11, 1945,
and 38 of the crew were
killed. She also served in the
Korean War and other mis-
sions until 1964, when she
was decommissioned. Visitors
can see the anti-aircraft guns
and other equipment on the
ship, and tour the
cramped quarters
shared by the 330-
man crew below
decks.

**Old tractor at the Rural
Life Museum**

🏛 Rural Life Museum and Windrush Gardens

Essen Lane at I-10.
☎ (225) 765-2437. ◯ 8:30am–5pm
daily. ● Thanksgiving, Dec 24, Dec
25, Jan 1, Easter Sunday. 🖼 ♿
Ione Burden and her brother,
Steele, who landscaped
Louisiana State University,
assembled this collection of
buildings and 19th-century

VISITORS' CHECKLIST

56 km (35 miles) NW of New
Orleans. ⋔ 576,330. ✈ 9430
Jackie Cochran Drive, (225) 356-
9592. 🚌 Greyhound Bus Lines,
1253 Florida Blvd, (225) 383-3811.
ℹ 730 North Blvd, (800) 517-
0843. 🚩 Greater Baton Rouge
State Fair (for 10 days, mid-Oct).

tools and artifacts. Each building is filled with fascinating
objects – a washing machine
dating from 1900, pirogues
(a type of boat used on the
bayous), cockfighting spurs,
and a tobacco press, to name
a few. Steele Burden's paintings and ceramic figures are
also displayed, along with
other collectibles.
In the time
before it was
fashionable to
preserve African
American culture,
Steele also rescued
all the buildings
from nearby Welham
Plantation and re-erected
them in a typical plantation
layout. Today, visitors can
gain some insight into how
such a plantation functioned
as a self-contained community.
Crape myrtle, azaleas, and
other plantings fill the
adjacent gardens.

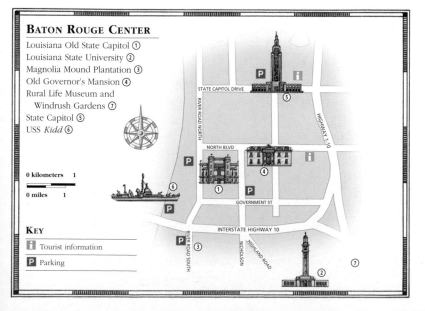

BATON ROUGE CENTER

0 kilometers   1

0 miles   1

KEY

ℹ Tourist information

P Parking

STATE CAPITOL DRIVE

RIVER ROAD NORTH

NORTH BLVD

GOVERNMENT ST

INTERSTATE HIGHWAY 10

RIVER ROAD SOUTH

NICHOLSON

HIGHLAND ROAD

HIGHWAY I-10

Upper Mississippi Plantations ❸

Weather vane

THE WEST FELICIANA PARISHES, to the north of Baton Rouge, were not included in the Louisiana Purchase (*see p17*) and remained part of the Spanish domain until 1810. The plantations in this area differ from the southern Creole-style plantations. They were established by British immigrants or by Americans from North Carolina and Virginia, who made their fortunes here and brought their own culture and architectural styles. These beautiful plantations, with exceptional surrounding gardens, are well worth visiting.

Living Traditions
Many of the original work-shops and tools have been reconstructed and are in use.

Greenwood Plantation
One of the largest and most beautiful plantation houses in the area, Greenwood was built in 1830 by William Ruffin Barrow in classic Greek style.

Butler Greenwood
Built in 1790, this house is thoroughly Victorian, both in its architecture and furniture.

Mississippi

← Alexandria

66

10

NEW ROAD

1

The Myrtles
Built in 1895, The Myrtles plantation is exceptionally well preserved. Its 120-ft (40-m)-long cast-iron gallery is its most extravagant exterior feature.

Cottage Plantation
Cottage Plantation, with its original 14-karat gold wallpaper in the parlor, offers one of the best stays in the area. Andrew Jackson stayed here after the Battle of New Orleans (see p17).

LOCATOR MAP

0 kilometers   5

0 miles   3

NEW ORLEANS

↗ **Natchez**

10

956

ST FRANCISVILLE

61

↘ **Baton Rouge**

Catalpa
This little Victorian cottage is surrounded by 30 acres of splendid gardens. Tours of the interior reveal numerous interesting historic family heirlooms.

Oakley House
Naturalist John James Audubon (see p111) tutored James Pirrie's daughter, Eliza, at this plantation. Many of Audubon's original prints are on display. Fascinating nature trails are also available.

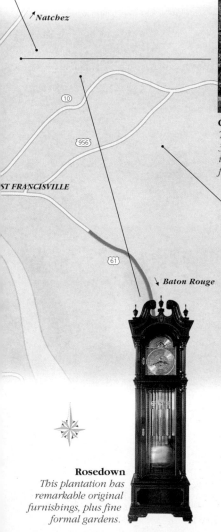

Rosedown
This plantation has remarkable original furnishings, plus fine formal gardens.

KEY

■ Major road

☐ Minor road

Exploring the Upper Mississippi Plantations

THE FRENCH ESTABLISHED BATON ROUGE in 1719 when they built a fort to control access to the Mississippi River and the interior (see pp138–9). After being controlled by the Spanish and the British, this city was finally incorporated into the United States in 1817, and became the state capital in 1849. North of Baton Rouge the plantations were established by British or Americans, who held on to their Anglo-Saxon heritage. A different architecture with Greek Revival influences is dominant in this area. Many of these plantations have been restored and are now charming B&Bs.

Butler Greenwood, surrounded by beautiful gardens

🏛 Butler Greenwood

8345 Hwy 61, St. Francisville.
📞 (225) 635-6312.
🕙 9am–5pm Mon-Sat, 1–5pm Sun.
⬤ Major holidays. 🈺 🗹

Pennsylvania Quaker physician Samuel Flower founded this plantation in 1796. His daughter, Harriet, ran it for most of the 19th century as a cotton-producing plantation. Today it is still a working plantation operated by the eighth generation of the family, which makes this visit particularly interesting. Family portraits hang throughout the house, which contains many of the original 19th-century furnishings, including a fine 12-piece parlor set made of rosewood and upholstered in the original scarlet-colored fabric.

Exhibit at Butler Greenwood

🏛 Catalpa

9508 Hwy 61, St. Francisville.
📞 (225) 635 3372. 🕙 1–4pm daily.
⬤ Dec 25, Jan 1. 🈺 🗹

The current building is a reconstruction of the original, which was destroyed in a fire in 1885. Carolinian William J. Fort established the plantation in the early 1800s. He was famous for his hospitality and for the many parties he gave in the gardens, which were landscaped with a pond complete with an island for picnics, a deer park, and several summer houses. He also maintained greenhouses filled with exotic tropical plants including banana, guava, and mandarin.

🏛 Cottage Plantation

10528 Cottage Lane, St. Francisville.
📞 (225) 635-3674.
🕙 9:30am–4:30pm daily.
⬤ Major holidays. 🈺 🗹

The land on which this house stands was granted to John Allen and Patrick Holland in 1795. Judge Thomas Butler purchased the original cottage and property in 1810. He was the son of Colonel Thomas Butler, one of the five fighting Butlers who served under General Washington during the American Revolution (1775–83). He extended the house to accommodate his family. The interiors are lavishly decorated with 14-karat gold-leaf wallpaper and plenty of *faux*

Old slave cabin at Cottage Plantation

bois. The property includes several outbuildings, one of which has been converted into a restaurant.

🍴 Greenwood Plantation

6838 Highland Rd, St. Francisville.
📞 (225) 655-4475. 🕙 Nov-Feb: 10am–4pm; Mar-Oct: 9am–5pm.
⬤ Easter Sunday, Thanksgiving, and Dec 25. 🈺 🗹 ♿

In 1830, James Hammon Coulter designed this majestic Greek Revival home for William Ruffin Barrow, who had migrated from the Carolinas. It stood on 12,000 acres, which were worked by 750 slaves. Some 40 outbuildings housed workshops that made the plantation completely self-sufficient. The Barrows became one of the most prominent families in the area, but anticipating the Civil War they sold the plantation to the Reed family. It survived the war serving as a hospital, but afterward it deteriorated rapidly. In 1906 Mr. and Mrs. Frank

Greenwood Plantation, furnished with impressive antebellum pieces

Percy restored it, salvaging the marble mantels and silver hinges and door-knobs. Tragically, in 1960 lightning destroyed the entire structure, except for the 28 massive Doric columns that supported the building. It has since been restored, and visitors can once again see the splendor of the 70-ft (21-m)-long central hall and the rest of the interior.

Greenwood Plantation, one of the largest American-style plantations

🏛 The Myrtles

7747 Hwy 61, St. Francisville.
📞 *(225) 635-6277.* ⏱ *9am–5pm daily.* ⬤ *Dec 25.* 📷 🅿 ♿

A leader of the Whiskey Rebellion (1794) in Pennsylvania, Judge David Bradford fled south and established this plantation in 1796. He built the north wing of the house. In the early 19th century, his daughter and her husband, Judge Clark Woodruff, added the 107-ft (36-m)-long gallery, decorated with iron grillwork. Ruffin Gray Stirling bought the house in 1834, and added the south wing. Local legend says that several murders were committed at the house after the Civil War *(see pp18–19)*, giving it a reputation for being haunted.

The handsome cast-iron veranda surrounding The Myrtles

🏛 Rosedown Plantation

12501 Hwy 10, St Francisville.
📞 *(225) 635-3332.* ⏱ *9am–5pm daily.* ⬤ *Jan 1, Thanksgiving, and Dec 25.* 📷 🅿

Rosedown is one of the largest and most complete of the plantations along the river. The gabled central structure, built of cedar and

cypress, has a double gallery supported by Doric columns. Other sections of the house feature Georgian details.

The Turnbull family owned and operated the plantation from 1835 to 1955. Practically all of the contents of the house are original, including rosewood furniture by Mallard and Seignoret, portraits by Thomas Sully, brocade draperies, and marble mantels. Daniel and Martha Turnbull, who established the plantation in 1835, purchased most of the furnishings on their initial Grand Tour of Europe in 1834 and on subsequent trips abroad. The grounds contain a kitchen building, the doctor's office, a barn, and a gardener's tool house. The 28 acres of French-style gardens are exquisite too. Martha Turnbull was a well-known horticulturist, who introduced the first azaleas and camellias to the region.

In 2000 the state of Louisiana purchased the plantation from a private owner, who had unfortunately sold some of the original furnishings. The estate has been renovated and now offers a fascinating 45-minute tour of the house and grounds.

⚜ Oakley House and Audubon State Historic Site

Hwy. 965, St. Francisville. 📞 *(225) 635-3739.* ⏱ *9am–5pm daily.* ⬤ *Thanksgiving, Dec 25.* 📷 🅿

Wealthy Scott James Pirrie built this house between 1808 and 1810, and it is a splendid example of the way colonial

architecture was adapted to the Louisiana climate. Since then, it has been surrounded by a bosky paradise inhabited by numerous species of birds.

In 1821, naturalist John James Audubon *(see p111)* and his assistant arrived to teach daughter Eliza Pirrie dancing, music, drawing, and math. He and his assistant received room and board and $60 a month. The arrangement did not last, and he left after only four months, having quarreled with his employer. Still, in that brief time he began at least 32 bird portraits, which later appeared in *The Birds of America.* Today, visitors can see the room Audubon stayed in and wander the trails around the property. Magnolias, beeches, and poplars still shelter abundant bird life in the state park surrounding the house.

Study used by John James Audubon in Oakley House

The Liberty Theater, home of the *Rendez-Vouz des Cajuns* radio show

Eunice ④

Cajun Country. 🏛 *18,000*.
🚌 *1238 W Landry St.* ℹ *941 East
Vine Street (318) 948-6263*.

Every weekend there is a
Cajun music celebration in
this picturesque Louisiana
town, where most of the
main attractions are in the
downtown area. The town
was founded by C. C. Duson
in 1893, who named it in
honor of his wife. **The
Liberty Theater** is the
keeper of the flame of Cajun
music – the Grand Ole Opry
of Cajun music. It opened in
the 1920s as a movie and
vaudeville theater. Every
Saturday from 6 to 8pm the
theater hosts a live broadcast
of the *Rendez-Vous des Cajuns*
radio show. It is filled with
Cajun and zydeco music and
plenty of good Cajun humor.
The master of ceremonies
makes introductions in both
English and French.

Visitors to **The Acadian
Cultural Center**, located just
behind the theater, can
observe musical instruments
and other items being made
in the craft room. Other
displays focus on aspects of
Acadian culture, including the
Courir. Literally "the race,"
this is the Cajun, and distinc-
tly medieval, version of Mardi
Gras. Participants wear a
capuchon (a tall, cone-
shaped hat, which covers the
face as well as the head) and
ride on horseback from farm
to farm begging for the
ingredients for a community
gumbo, which will be eaten

at the end of the day. The
key ingredient, a chicken, has
to be chased down and
caught live.

Located nearby are two
other cultural
centers. **The Cajun
Music Hall of Fame
& Museum**, which
opened in 1997,
honors the ori-
ginators of Cajun
music and the
artists who have
kept the tradition
alive. It displays
memorabilia, ins-
truments such as
accordions and
violins, photographs, and
biographies
of the 40 inductees.

Cajun music is a blend of
several traditions – German,
Scottish, Irish, Spanish, Afro-
Caribbean, and Native
American – which have been
laid over a base of French
and French-Acadian folk

tradition. Zydeco developed
from the same traditions but
incorporates much more Afro-
Caribbean rhythm and style.

The Hall of Fame features
the great names in Cajun
music, from such early
musicians as Amédé Ardoin,
Alphé Bergeron, Dennis
McGee, Joe Falcon, Amédé
Breaux, Iry Lejeune, and
Lawrence Walker, to more
recent interpreters, including
Michael Doucet, Zachary
Richard, and Wayne Toups.

Heading from Eunice to
Opelousas along Highway
190, there is **The Savoy
Music Center**, the informal
headquarters for Cajun
musicians in the area. The
store is owned by accordion-
maker-musician Marc Savoy

**Cajun accordion in The
Savoy Music Center**

and his wife, Ann. It sells
musical instruments,
CDs, and books on
Cajun culture and
music. On Saturday
mornings local
musicians assemble
in the front of the
store for a jam
session around the
upright piano. They
bring accordions,
triangles, and
fiddles, and play
together. People
can bring beer, boudin, and
other snacks. Visitors are
welcome to listen, dance, and
join the band.

🏛 **The Acadian Cultural
Center**
250 West Park Ave. 📞 *(337) 262-
6862.* 🕐 *8am–5pm daily.*
⬤ *25 Dec.* ♿

Mardi Gras costume and memorabilia at The Acadian Cultural Center

Opelousas Museum and Interpretive Center

🏛 **The Cajun Music Hall of Fame & Museum**
240 South CC Duson Dr. 【 (337) 457-6534. ⏰ Summer: 9am–5pm Tue–Sat; Winter 8:30am–4:30pm Tue–Sat. ● Major hols. ♿

🎵 **The Liberty Theater**
300 S. Second St. 【 (337) 457-6577. ⏰ Sat 4pm. 📷 ♿

🎵 **The Savoy Music Center**
Hwy 190 East, Savoy. 【 (337) 457-9563. ⏰ 9am–5pm Tue–Fri, 9am–noon Sat. ● Major hols. ♿

Opelousas ❺

Cajun Country. 👥 11000. 🏛 200 West Park Ave (318) 457-7389.

THIS CITY, the capital of Confederate Louisiana during the Civil War (see pp18–19), was named after the Native American tribe that lived in this area before the Europeans arrived. It was founded as a French trading post settlement during the 1700s, and today it is one of the liveliest towns in this district, thanks to its excellent cuisine and music.

The major collections of the **Opelousas Museum** focus on the local culture and history of the town. The two main exhibit areas are devoted to the prehistory of the area, its agricultural and commercial development, and to the people of different races and religions who developed the region and contributed to its culture. One room is devoted to memorabilia from the Civil War, while another houses a fascinating collection of more than 400 dolls.

The **Opelousas Museum of Art** stands in the oldest part of the city, in a historic Federal-style brick building, built originally as a one-story tavern. The second story was added in 1828. Today, the museum mounts several shows each year featuring art on loan from major museums and private collections. Recent shows have focused on paintings by Louisiana's African American folk painter, Clementine Hunter, jazz photographs taken by William P. Gottlieb, and the wood engravings made by Winslow Homer for *Harper's Weekly*.

The name **Tony Chachere** is one of the those heard most often in Louisiana kitchens. He was an Opelousas boy, who enjoyed two successful careers as pharmacist and insurance salesman before attaining fame in 1972 when he wrote his *Cajun Country Cookbook*. Many of the recipes use a special seasoning he developed, and soon after publication the "Ole Master," as he was called, was making and selling his Original Seasoning. He added several other products, ranging from jambalaya and other seasoning blends, to gumbo and rice and beans. Today, the company manufactures 25 different, but essentially Cajun, products. Visitors can tour the factory, where more than 6.5 million pounds (3 million kg) of raw ingredients are combined annually to produce the miraculous mixtures. No one interested in Cajun cuisine should miss this opportunity.

Cajun specialty foods on sale at the Tony Chachere factory

🏛 **Opelousas Museum**
329 N. Main St. 【 (337) 948-2589. ⏰ 9am–5pm Mon–Sat. ● Major hols. 📷 ♿

🏛 **Opelousas Museum of Art**
100 North Union St. 【 (337) 942-4991. ⏰ 1–5pm Tue–Sun. ● Major hols. ♿ 📷

🏠 **Tony Chachere**
519 N. Lombard St. 【 (337) 948-4691. ⏰ 9am–11am and 1–3pm Mon–Fri. ♿

Main façade of the Opelousas Museum of Art

Lafayette ●

WHEN THE FIRST ACADIANS arrived in 1764, they settled along the bayous and in the prairie lands west of New Orleans. Being rural people, they worked as farmers and made a living from the swamps. Lafayette was the first city they founded, and it has remained at the heart of the Cajun culture, because of their family traditions, as well as their cultural heritage. Community centers, restaurants, several detailed reconstructions of Cajun villages, and its own local architectural style imprint this city with a unique atmosphere and the distinctive feeling of being in the Cajun Country.

Harp on display at the Alexandre Mouton House

🏛 Acadian Cultural Center

501 Fisher Rd, Lafayette. **[** *(337) 232-0789.* **◯** *8am–5pm daily.* **●** *Dec 25.* **&**

A 37-minute film dramatizes the British deportation of the Acadian population from Canada's Acadie, and charts their diaspora to France and to places along the east coast of North America, before their final arrival in Louisiana. In an adjacent display area, informative exhibits, featuring photographs and artifacts, focus on every aspect of Acadian culture, including language, music, architecture, religion, cuisine, the *Courir* festival *(see p144)*, and all kinds of handcrafts.

Old-fashioned Cajun plough

🏛 Vermilionville

1600 Surrey St, Lafayette. **[** *(337) 233-4077.* **◯** *10am–5pm daily.* **●** *Thanksgiving, Dec 25, Jan 1.* **&**

This fascinating living-history museum features a collection of buildings dating from 1790 to 1890 assembled into a typical Cajun village on 23 acres. Its name, Vermilionville, was the original name for the city of Lafayette. Costumed artisans demonstrate the skills that were needed to survive in 18th- and 19th-century Louisiana; woodworking, blacksmithing, spinning, weaving, and cooking. It is pleasant to wander from building to building imagining what traditional Cajun life was like. A performance hall, where Cajun bands regularly entertain, is open in the afternoon.

♛ Lafayette Museum/ Alexandre Mouton House

1122 Lafayette St, Lafayette. **[** *(337) 234-2208.* **◯** *9am–5pm Tue–Sat, 3–5pm Sun.* **●** *Major hols.* 🖼 **&**

Jean Mouton, founder of Lafayette, built the original house around 1800. He and his wife Marie and their 12 children used it only on Sundays when they came from their plantation in Carencro to attend church and socialize. In 1825 the sixth son, Alexandre, moved his family and law practice into the house. He later became a United States senator and governor of Louisiana – a notable example of Cajun success. The house contains furnishings, paintings, maps, and documents relating to the city's history, plus some glittering Mardi Gras costumes and regalia.

🏛 University Art Museum

101 Girard Park Drive, Lafayette. **[** *(337) 482-5326.* **◯** *Mon–Fri, 1–4pm.* **●** *Major hols.* **&**

This small art museum is located on the campus of the University of Louisiana at Lafayette, an institution with

Original Acadian chapel in Vermilionville

The University Art Museum, housed in an old cotton plantation, on the ULL campus

17,000 students, which has an excellent Computer Science department and is also home to both the National Wetlands Research Center and the Center for Louisiana Studies. The Art Museum was founded in 1968 to collect, preserve, exhibit, and interpret works of art unique to the cultural heritage of southwestern Louisiana. It occupies two locations; 101 Girard Park Drive, which holds the permanent collection, and Joel Fletcher Hall. The permanent collection consists of more than 1,000 outstanding works of art, including European and American art from the 18th, 19th, and 20th centuries, and a wide assortment of 2nd century BC Egyptian artifacts. This permanent exhibition also includes an excellent collection of African American folk art. Diverse architectural drawings, as well as student works, are displayed along with temporary exhibits all year long.

🏛 **The Acadian Village**
200 Greenleaf Dr, Lafayette. 📞 (337) 981-2364. ⏱ 10am–5pm daily. ⬤ Mardi Gras, Thanksgiving, Dec 25, Jan 1. 📷 ♿
At this version of a recreated 19th-century village, most of the buildings are original, although they have been moved here from other locations. The houses are furnished with typical Cajun furniture and tools, and are tended by costumed guides who demonstrate such skills as spinning, weaving, and blacksmithing. One of the residences was the birthplace of state senator, Dudley LeBlanc, the creator of a cure-all tonic called Hadacol, which was still in use as recently as the 1950s.

THE ACADIANS

Driven by the British from Acadia, in Nova Scotia, Canada, the Acadians (or "Cajuns") settled along the bayous of Louisiana in 1764, working as farmers. For generations they were disparaged, and in the 20th century their culture came under threat, first when compulsory education was introduced in 1916 and the French language was forbidden, and later in the 1930s when Huey Long (see p138) built roads across the swamps, opening their communities to a wider world. When oil was discovered, the transformation intensified; outsiders flooded in and the Francophone culture was endangered. The culture survived largely because Cajuns have a strong sense of family and attachment to place. Today Cajun Country is the largest French-speaking community in the United States. In the 1960s, Cajun pride was restored when the teaching of French returned to the classrooms. At the same time, Cajun and zydeco music started growing in popularity among a broader audience, and Cajun cuisine, promoted by chef Paul Prudhomme (see p173), spread across the country.

Traditional Acadian dress

Dentist's chair at the Acadian Village's infirmary

The Acadian Memorial in St. Martinville

St. Martinville **7**

Cajun Country. *8000.* **i** *215 Evangeline Blvd (318) 394-2233.*

THIS SMALL PICTURESQUE TOWN on a natural levee of the Bayou Teche, was founded in 1761 as a refuge for French noblemen who escaped from the French Revolution. As a result, for many years the town was known as "Petit Paris" (little Paris).
Located in the main square of this town is the **Acadian Memorial**, which houses the mural painted by Robert Dafford, *The Arrival of the Acadians in Louisiana,* which portrays some 40 people, who arrived in Louisiana between 1764 and 1788. The painter went so far as to model some of the portraits on contemporary descendants. Opposite the painting, the Wall of Names lists about 3,000 early Acadians. Behind the museum, an eternal flame burns in a small courtyard garden overlooking Bayou Teche.

Acadian Memorial

Nearby stands the **Evangeline Oak**, marking the spot where the two famous Acadian lovers, Gabriel and Evangeline, supposedly encountered each other. Gabriel confessed that after three years in exile he had despaired of ever seeing her again and married another. She went mad and died soon after. Longfellow's poem changes the ending, placing her as a nurse at his bedside as he lay dying.
St. Martin de Tours Church is the focal point of St. Martinville. Established in 1765 by French missionaries, it was the first church to serve the Acadian community. Fairly plain inside, it contains a baptismal font, which was a gift from Louis XVI, and a replica of the grotto at Lourdes. The grave of Evangeline Labiche (mythologized as Longfellow's Evangeline) and a bronze statue of her are located in the garden behind the church. The monument was donated by actress Dolores del Río, who played the role of Evangeline in the silent movie filmed here in 1929. Also on the church square there is the **Petit Paris Museum and Gift Shop**, which houses the historical records of the most important events in the town's life. The **Longfellow-Evangeline**

St. Martin de Tours church at the center of St. Martinville

State Commemorative Area is a 180-acre state park that stretches along Bayou Teche. It offers pleasant picnicking and walking trails among 300-year-old oaks. At the center of the park stands a reconstruction of a typical Acadian cabin representative of the 1790s. This can be contrasted with the Olivier House, a plantation home built in 1815. The cypress and brick structure has 14-inch (36-cm) thick walls. There is also a museum, which focuses on Acadian history and culture.

m Acadian Memorial
121 South New Market St. **(** *(318) 394-7334.* ○ *10am–4pm daily.*
● *Major hols.* & 🖼

m Petit Paris Museum and Gift Shop
103 S. Main St. **(** *(318) 394-2258.* ○ *9:30am–4pm daily.*
● *Major hols.* & 🖼

† St. Martin de Tours Church
201 Evangeline Blvd. **(** *(318) 394-6021.* ○ *8am–6pm daily.* ● *Fri mornings until noon.* &

m The Longfellow-Evangeline State Commemorative Area
1200 N Main St. **(** *(318) 394-3754.*
○ *9am–5pm daily.* ● *Thanksgiving, Dec 25, Jan 1.* & 🗺

New Iberia and Avery Island **8**

Cajun Country. *32000.*
🚍 *1103 E Main St.* **i** *2704 Highway 14, (888) 942-3742.*

NEW IBERIA is notable for its many sugar cane plantations. The area also owes its wealth to oil drilling and salt mining. In fact, the so-called "islands" in the region, such as Avery and Jefferson, are not actually surrounded by water: rather they are domes located atop salt mines.
At the plantation home known as **Shadows on the Teche**, 40 trunks were found in the attic, filled with 17,000 letters, photographs, receipts, and papers relating to the family who lived here. This documentation is used as background for the fascinating tour of the house.

A native of Maryland, David Weeks, built the plantation home in 1831. He died shortly thereafter, leaving his wife, Mary Clara, to run it. During the Civil War *(see pp18–19)*, when Union General Nathaniel P. Banks seized it and made it his headquarters, Mary Clara retired to the attic where she died in 1863. The last owner, Weeks Hall, was a well-known artist and scholar, who restored the house and entertained many famous visitors in it, including director Cecil B. DeMille and writer Henry Miller. Their names are inscribed in the foyer.

Moss-draped oaks and spring-flowering plants in the Jungle Gardens

On Avery Island the **McIlhenny Company Tabasco Factory and Jungle Gardens** is the source of the famous hot sauce, which is an essential ingredient in Bloody Marys and in local cuisine. Approximately 75 acres of pepper plants blaze their bright red color from August to November. A brief film explains the process in which the red chili peppers are crushed and combined with salt and vinegar to make the zesty sauce. Visitors can also tour the bottling factory.

The founder considered himself a botanist-naturalist and the Jungle Gardens that he assembled are spectacular. In addition to abundant camellias and azalea, there are such exotica as Latin American papaya. The gardens also shelter a diverse population of egrets, herons, peacocks, as well as the beaver-like nutria. In winter, ducks and wild fowl stop here too.

The **Rip Van Winkle House** is located on the salt dome called Jefferson Island. It was built by the actor Joseph Jefferson in 1870 and named after the role he played 4,500 times. Architecturally, it is a hodgepodge of Moorish, Steamboat Gothic, and Victorian. The house is surrounded by 25 acres of beautiful gardens, which sweep along the banks of Lake Peigneur. Both the house and gardens are temporarily closed to the public.

After Jefferson died in 1905, J. Lyle Bayless of the Salt Island Mining Company purchased the house. Shortly afterward, oil was discovered on the property. It was soon producing up to 250,000 barrels of oil a week from 30 wells. In 1972, the Texaco Oil Company mistakenly drilled through the salt dome, causing a major explosion that set off a minor tidal wave on the lake. Miraculously, no one was killed.

🏚 **Shadows on the Teche**
317 East Main St., New Iberia.
📞 *(337) 369-6446.* ◯ *9am–4:30pm daily.* ⬤ *Thanksgiving, Dec 25, Jan 1.* 📷

🏛 **McIlhenny Company Tabasco Factory and Jungle Gardens**
Hwy 329, Avery Island. 📞 *(337) 365-8173.* ◯ *9am–4pm daily.* ⬤ *Major hols.* ♿ 📷 📹

🏚 **Rip Van Winkle House**
5505 Rip Van Winkle Rd, Jefferson Island. 📞 *(337) 365-3332.* ⬤ *Closed to the public.*

Shadows on the Teche in New Iberia

TRAVELERS' NEEDS

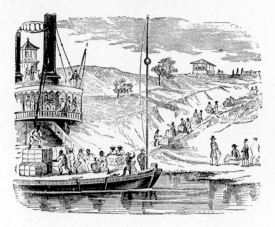

WHERE TO STAY

NEW ORLEANS is a big convention town and for that reason it has numerous representatives of big name chains – Hyatt, Hilton, Marriott, Sheraton, Wyndham, Embassy Suites, and Holiday Inns. It also has some elegant hotels, like the Windsor Court, the Ritz Carlton, Le Pavillon, and the Fairmont, but the remainder are fairly average establishments. Nevertheless, all of the city's hotels have a bit of New Orleans flavor in them. Some of the very best accommodations can be found in bed and breakfasts, like the House on Bayou Road, or in such small hotels as the Soniat House. Budget options include guest houses and the economy versions of the big chains. We have selected those hotels that best deliver the New Orleans experience.

Bellman

The Holiday Inn in the Central Business District *(see p159)*

WHERE TO LOOK

MOST HOTELS are located in the French Quarter or in the Central Business District along Canal Street, the latter being within walking distance of both the Quarter and the Convention Center. Bed and breakfasts (B&Bs) are scattered throughout the city, uptown in the Garden District, and on the fringes of the Quarter in the Faubourgs Marigny and Treme.

HOTEL PRICES AND SERVICES

NEW ORLEANS has accommodations to fit any budget, from the least expensive motel to the fabulous French Quarter hotels and guest houses. Prices vary according to the location and the level of luxury; many boutique hotels are as expensive as the splendid high rises, and if the hotel or B&B is in the French Quarter, the price will reflect this sought-after location. Discounts are rare in this city, and prices can rise more than 50 percent during Mardi Gras, Jazz Festival, and the Sugar Bowl.

All hotel accommodations, unless otherwise stated, include air-conditioning, elevators, non-smoking rooms, and full bathrooms.

During major festivals, such as Mardi Gras, many hotels require a three- or four-night minimum stay. In the off-season, special rates and vacation packages offer amazing discounts.

BED AND BREAKFAST

GUEST HOUSES and boutique hotels are usually in re-novated historic homes, and B&Bs are rooms in a private residence. All offer some meals, full breakfasts or just coffee and croissants, and often, afternoon tea or cocktails are provided. All have a limited number of rooms, so advance reservations are necessary. Some of the budget-priced guest houses and B&Bs have shared bathrooms, and facilities for disabled guests can be limited.

HIDDEN EXTRAS

TAXES will add 11 percent to the bill plus an additional $1. Valet parking will cost anywhere from $12 to $20 a day. Some motels and B&Bs have free parking, so always ask ahead. Hotel telephone charges are generally very high. It is always cheaper to use a pay phone in the lobby, particularly when calling overseas. You will also pay a premium on products in your minibar. A tip of $1 to $2 per bag is usually paid to the bellman for carrying bags. Room-service waiters expect the standard 15 percent tip. If you are staying more than one night, it is also customary to leave $1 to $2 a day for the housekeeping staff.

Lobby of the Omni Royal Orleans hotel *(see p155)*

A perfect welcome at the Hotel Monteleone *(see p155)*

FACILITIES

MOST ESTABLISHMENTS offer full facilities, such as well-appointed rooms, cable TV, phone, modems, mini-bars, and full bathrooms. Often the larger hotels have one or two fine restaurants, several bars, a fitness room, a swimming pool, and a business center. At virtually every hotel, you will find complimentary toiletries, a morning newspaper delivered to your door, 24-hour room service, and wake-up and reservation services.

Because the weather in New Orleans is semi-tropical, all accommodations are air-conditioned. B&Bs generally do not offer these amenities, but the ambience in these homes makes up for any lack.

HOW TO BOOK

IF YOU WANT to visit the city during Mardi Gras or the Jazz and Heritage Festival, you will need to book six months to a year in advance. At other times, a few months' advance booking is recommended. You can make telephone reservations using a credit card. A deposit of one night is usually required, and there are specific cancellation policies that guests should clarify at the time of booking. If you anticipate arriving after 6pm, ask for guaranteed late arrival. Most hotels have toll-free reservation numbers, and many take reservations by fax or e-mail.

SPECIAL RATES

WHEN MAKING reservations, it won't hurt to ask for special AAA, AARP, or senior citizen rates. Some agencies offer discount rates, or can contact a discount reservation service. You can reserve by using a major credit card. Package tours may also offer savings from hotel or B&B accommodations to airport/hotel transportation. Check the newspapers for specials.

A four-poster bed in one of the upscale bed and breakfasts

DISABLED TRAVELERS

SINCE 1992 all hotels have been required by law to provide wheelchair-accessible accommodations. However, older properties are exempt from this, but most have at least one room equipped for disabled guests. Call in advance to confirm suitability if you have special needs.

TRAVELING WITH CHILDREN

MOST HOTELS welcome children, although New Orleans may not be an ideal destination for the young. Children aged up to 12, 16, or 18 (depending on the place) can usually stay free in their parents' room.

YOUTH AND BUDGET ACCOMMODATIONS

NEW ORLEANS has a few hostels, like the YMCA in the Warehouse District, plus some guest houses with rooms with shared baths that are modestly priced. Many motels on the outskirts are inexpensive.

Choosing a Hotel

These hotels have been selected across a wide price range for their good value, facilities, and location; they are listed area by area, starting with the Upper French Quarter and moving on to hotels farther outside the city. All hotels in this guide have air conditioning and private baths. Map references refer to the *Street Finder* on pages 214–222.

	24-Hour Concierge	Credit Cards Accepted	Private Parking	Swimming Pool	Restaurant
UPPER FRENCH QUARTER					
A Creole House W www.big-easy.org $$$ 1013 St. Ann St. **Map** 4 C1. (504) 524-8076; (888) 251-0197. FAX 581-3277. This hotel is located off the main drag in a restored 1850 Creole home, decorated with period furnishings. Continental breakfast is served. TV Rooms: 31		●			
Bienville House W www.bienvillehouse.com $$$$ 320 Decatur St. **Map** 4 C3. (504) 529-2345; (800) 535-7836. FAX 525-6079. Bienville House offers European charm in the heart of the French Quarter and one of the best locations overlooking the Mississippi. Newly renovated rooms are provided, plus a very good restaurant. TV Rooms: 83		●	■	●	■
Bourbon Orleans Hotel W www.wyndham.com $$$$ 717 Orleans St. **Map** 4 C2. (504) 523-2222. FAX 571-4651. Located in the exact heart of the French Quarter, in what was once the Quadroon Ballroom, this hotel was built in 1815. Everything worth seeing is just a short walk away. TV Rooms: 261		●		●	■
Chateau Le Moyne-New Orleans Holiday Inn $$$$$ 301 Dauphine St. **Map** 4 C2. (504) 581-1303; (800) 447-2830. FAX 532-5709. Occupying an historical building in the heart of the French Quarter, this hotel has a beautiful courtyard. The exterior is lovely, but inside it is like most other Holiday Inns. TV Rooms: 171		●	■	●	■
Chateau Sonesta Hotel W www.chateausonesta.com $$$$ 800 Iberville St. **Map** 4 C3. (800) 766-3782; (800) 766-3782. FAX 586-1987. Originally the site of an old-line department store, Chateau Sonesta is one of the Quarter's newest hotels. Each guest room is spacious and individually designed. TV Rooms: 251		●	■	●	■
Cornstalk Hotel W www.travelguides.com/bb/cornstalk $$$$ 915 Royal St. **Map** 5 D2. (504) 523-1515. FAX 522-5558. This hotel with its famous fence is a great place to stay in Victorian splendor and comfort. The second-floor gallery is a perfect place for morning coffee and people-watching. TV Rooms: 14		●			
Dauphine Orleans W www.dauphineorleans.com $$$$$ 415 Dauphine St. **Map** 4 C2. (504) 586-1827; (800) 521-7111. FAX 586-1409. This hotel has a colorful history; in the 1850s it was a famous brothel, complete with ghosts. Secluded courtyards, Continental breakfast, afternoon tea, and all amenities are provided. TV Rooms: 111		●	■	●	
Grenoble House W www.grenoblehouse.com $$$$ 329 Dauphine St. **Map** 4 C2. (504) 522-1331; (800) 722-1834. FAX 524-4968. The personal, attentive service is unequaled in this restored 1834 Creole townhouse. Every suite is a complete apartment, and there is a small pool for guests. TV Rooms: 17		●		●	
Historic French Market Inn W www.neworleansfinehotels.com $$$$$ 501 Decatur St. **Map** 4 C3. (504) 561-5621; (888) 538-5651. FAX 569-0619. This small hotel with a brick courtyard and swimming pool overlooks the Mississippi River. There is a free Continental breakfast and a complimentary cocktail hour. TV Rooms: 118		●	■	●	
Hotel Maison de Ville and the Audubon Cottages $$$$$ 727 Toulouse St. **Map** 4 C2. (504) 561-5858; (800) 634-1600. At this little hotel, the high-ceilinged rooms in the main house are furnished with antiques, four-poster beds, and period paintings. The historic Audubon Cottages have private courtyards, rare antiques, and John James Audubon prints. A free Continental breakfast is served, and cocktails are available in the afternoon. TV Units: 23		●	■		■

Price categories for a standard double room per night in the tourist season, including tax and service:
[$] under $50
[$][$] $50–100
[$][$][$] $100–150
[$][$][$][$] $150–200
[$][$][$][$][$] over $200

CREDIT CARDS ACCEPTED
One or more of the following credit cards are accepted: American Express, Diners Club, MasterCard, or VISA.

PRIVATE PARKING
The hotel has its own parking lot or parking spaces. These may not be on the same premises and are not necessarily locked.

SWIMMING POOL
The pool is outdoors unless otherwise stated in the text.

RESTAURANT
The restaurant or dining room is open to the public. See Restaurant section for additional information.

Hotel	24-Hour Concierge	Credit Cards Accepted	Private Parking	Swimming Pool	Restaurant
IBERVILLE SUITES [W] *www.ibervillesuites.com* [$][$][$] 910 Iberville St. **Map** 4 C3. ☎ *(504) 523-2400.* [FAX] *524-1321.* In this sector of the Ritz Carlton the rooms have marble bathrooms, and each is provided with a refrigerator and coffeemaker. For business travelers, two-room suites have an office and a bedroom. [TV] ❄ 🏋 ♿ 🧒 **Rooms:** 230	■	●	■	●	■
INN ON BOURBON STREET [W] *www.innonbourbon.com* [$][$][$][$] 541 Bourbon St. **Map** 4 C2. ☎ *(504) 524-7611; (800) 535-7891.* [FAX] *568-9427.* This comfortable hotel offers Old South decor and all amenities, and the rooms are quiet, despite the bustle of the street. The site originally held the French Opera House (1858). [TV] ❄ 🏋 ♿ **Rooms:** 186		●	■	●	
MAISON DUPUY [W] *www.maisondupuy.com* [$][$][$][$][$] 1001 Toulouse St. **Map** 4 C2. ☎ *(504) 586-8000; (800) 535-9177.* [FAX] *525-5334.* This hotel has one of the largest and most decorative courtyards in the city. It is also close to many sights and has an excellent restaurant. [TV] ❄ 🏋 **Rooms:** 200	■	●	■	●	■
MONTELEONE [W] *www.hotelmonteleone.com* [$][$][$][$][$] 214 Royal St. **Map** 5 D2. ☎ *(504) 523-3341; (800) 535-9595.* [FAX] *528-1019.* The oldest, largest, and most charming hotel in New Orleans has superb facilities. The Carousel Bar in the lobby is world famous. [TV] ❄ 🏋 🛗 **Rooms:** 597		●	■	●	■
OMNI ROYAL ORLEANS [W] *www.omnihotels.com* [$][$][$][$][$] 621 St. Louis St. **Map** 4 C2. ☎ *(504) 529-5333; (800) 843-6664.* [FAX] *529-7037.* Located in the heart of the French Quarter, between Royal and Bourbon streets, this hotel is a reconstruction of the 1836 St. Louis Exchange Hotel. The exterior has wrought-iron balconies, and the rooms are truly elegant. The 4-star Rib Room is a local favorite, but call in advance for reservations. [TV] ❄ 🏋 ♿ 🧒 🏛 💻 **Rooms:** 351		●	■	●	■
PLACE D'ARMES HOTEL [W] *www.frenchquarter.com* [$][$][$] 625 St. Ann St. **Map** 4 C1. ☎ *(504) 524-4531; (800) 366-2743.* [FAX] *571-2803.* The Place d'Armes is the perfect place for families and honeymooners, with Jackson Square, St. Louis Cathedral, Café du Monde, and the Mississippi just steps away. ♿ 🧒 🏛 💻 **Rooms:** 80	■	●	■	●	
PRINCE CONTI HOTEL [W] *www.frenchquarter.com* [$][$][$] 830 Conti St. **Map** 4 C2. ☎ *(504) 529-4172; (800) 366-2743.* [FAX] *581-3802.* Located just off Bourbon Street, this small and friendly hotel is perfect for the first-time visitor to the Big Easy. [TV] ❄ 🧒 **Rooms:** 60	■	●	■		■
RITZ CARLTON [W] *www.ritzcarlton.com* [$][$][$][$][$] 921 Canal St. **Map** 4 C3. ☎ *(504) 524-1331; (800) 241-3333.* [FAX] *524-7233.* Two of the Crescent City's restored architectural landmarks – the Maison Blanche and the Kress Building – house this luxurious hotel. Many of the original turn-of-the-century design elements have been preserved. [TV] 🏋 ♿ 🧒 **Rooms:** 452	■	●	■		■
ROYAL SONESTA [W] *www.royalsonestano.com* [$][$][$][$][$] 300 Bourbon St. **Map** 4 C2. ☎ *(504) 586-0300; (800) 766-3782.* [FAX] *586-0335.* Royal Sonesta is timelessly elegant and luxurious. Pink marble and beveled glass doors highlight the lobby, and two great restaurants, a good jazz bar, and every conceivable amenity can be found inside. It is probably the most expensive hotel in the city, but it is worth every penny. [TV] ❄ 🏋 🛗 🧒 🏛 💻 **Rooms:** 500	■	●	■	●	■
ST. ANN/MARIE ANTOINETTE [W] *www.stannmarieantoinette.com* [$][$][$][$] 717 Rue Conti. **Map** 4 C2. ☎ *(504) 525-2300; (888) 508-3980.* [FAX] *524-8925.* The St. Ann/Marie Antionette hotel offers the privacy and comfort of a gentle Southern lifestyle. A restaurant, lounge, and courtyard are provided. [TV] ♿ 🧒 🏛 **Rooms:** 66	■	●	■	●	■

For key to symbols see back flap

Price categories for a standard double room per night in the tourist season, including tax and service:
- ⓢ under $50
- ⓢⓢ $50–100
- ⓢⓢⓢ $100–150
- ⓢⓢⓢⓢ $150–200
- ⓢⓢⓢⓢⓢ over $200

CREDIT CARDS ACCEPTED
One or more of the following credit cards are accepted: American Express, Diners Club, MasterCard, or VISA.

PRIVATE PARKING
The hotel has its own parking lot or parking spaces. These may not be on the same premises and are not necessarily locked.

SWIMMING POOL
The pool is outdoors unless otherwise stated in the text.

RESTAURANT
The restaurant or dining room is open to the public. See Restaurant section for additional information.

	24-HOUR CONCIERGE	CREDIT CARDS ACCEPTED	PRIVATE PARKING	SWIMMING POOL	RESTAURANT
STE. HÉLÈNE W www.stehelene.com ⓢⓢⓢ 508 Chartres St. **Map** 4 C3. ☎ *(504) 522-5014; (800) 348-3888.* **FAX** *523-7140.* This is a very romantic and special place, and the location can't be beaten. Front rooms have balconies, and almost every room has a courtyard view. Continental breakfasts and complimentary cocktails. TV ♿ **Rooms:** 26	■	●	■	●	
ST. LOUIS W www.stlouishotel.com ⓢⓢⓢ 730 Bienville St. **Map** 4 C3. ☎ *(504) 581-7300; (800) 537-8483.* **FAX** *524-8995.* This small, centrally located hotel has just about everything you could want. The 4-star, elegant, Louis XVI restaurant is one of the best in the city. TV ▦ ♿ ♻ **Rooms:** 81	■	●			■
STE. MARIE W www.frenchquarter.com ⓢⓢⓢⓢ 827 Toulouse St. **Map** 4 C2. ☎ *(504) 561-8951; (800) 366-2743.* **FAX** *571-2802.* Most rooms have private balconies, some overlooking the romantic courtyard. It is located close enough to Bourbon Street to be convenient, but far enough away to be quiet. TV **Rooms:** 100	■	●	■	●	■
W NEW ORLEANS FRENCH QUARTER W www.whotels.com ⓢⓢⓢⓢⓢ 316 Chartres St. **Map** 4 C3. ☎ *(504) 581-1200.* **FAX** *523-2910.* This glitzy new boutique hotel may seem more Los Angeles than New Orleans, but it is luxurious, and the restaurant, Bacco, is owned and operated by a branch of the Brennan family *(see p172).* TV ♿ **Rooms:** 98	■	●	■	●	■
WYNDHAM NEW ORLEANS AT CANAL PLACE W www.wyndham.com ⓢⓢⓢⓢ 100 Iberville St. **Map** 4 C3. ☎ *(504) 566-7006; (877) 999-3223.* This modern hotel at upscale Canal Place Mall is within walking distance of Canal Street and the Quarter. Business travelers can take advantage of the Guest Office program. TV ▦ ♻ ♿ **Rooms:** 437		●	■	●	■

LOWER FRENCH QUARTER AND MARIGNY

	24-HOUR CONCIERGE	CREDIT CARDS ACCEPTED	PRIVATE PARKING	SWIMMING POOL	RESTAURANT
A QUARTER ESPLANADE W www.quarteresplanade.com ⓢⓢⓢ 719 Esplanade Ave. **Map** 5 D1. ☎ *(504) 948-9328; (800) 546-0076.* A reasonable alternative to the noisier Bourbon Street guest houses, this restored grand mansion offers privacy, a great location, and free breakfasts. TV ♻ ▦ **Rooms:** 8	■	●			
B&W COURTYARDS BED & BREAKFAST W www.bandwcourtyards.com ⓢⓢⓢ 2425 Chartres St. **Map** 5 E1. ☎ *(504) 945-9418; (800) 585-5731.* B and W (Boyd and Wu) run this delightful, small inn, right on the edge of the Quarter. No two rooms are alike, and there are two beautiful courtyards. The owners pamper each guest as if they were family. TV ▦ **Rooms:** 5		■	●		
BISCUIT PALACE W www.biscuit-palace.com ⓢⓢⓢ 730 Dumaine St. **Map** 5 D2. ☎ *(504) 525-9949.* **FAX** *940-6190.* The Biscuit Palace has large rooms in the main house, smaller ones in the restored slave quarters, and a beautiful courtyard with a fountain. Across the street stands the Clover Grill restaurant, offering good food and lots of fun round the clock. TV ▦ **Rooms:** 8					
BOURGOYNE GUEST HOUSE ⓢⓢⓢⓢ 839 Bourbon St. **Map** 4 C2. ☎ *(504) 524-3983.* This guest house, with only three studios and two suites, offers Old World charm and a quiet neighborhood. It is a good alternative to the expensive hotels. The local Clover Grill restaurant is a good place to eat breakfast at any hour. ▦ **Rooms:** 5			●	■	
CHATEAU HOTEL W www.chateauhotel.com ⓢⓢ 1001 Chartres St. **Map** 4 C3. ☎ *(504) 524-9636.* **FAX** *525-2989.* The rooms here overlook the courtyard and the streets of the French Quarter. Enjoy a Continental breakfast as you read the complimentary morning paper. Free parking. TV ▦ ▢ **Rooms:** 45	■	●	■	●	

FRENCH QUARTER SUITES [W] *www.frenchquartersuites.com* $$$$
1119 N. Rampart St. **Map** 4 C1. [C] *(504) 524-7725; (800) 457-2253.* FAX *522-9716.*
Located near Armstrong Park and the Mahalia Jackson Theater of the
Performing Arts, all suites include a large living room, a dining area, and a
private bath. Continental breakfast is served. [TV] **Rooms:** 38

FRENCHMEN HOTEL [W] *www.french-quarter.org* $$$$
417 Frenchmen St. **Map** 5 D2. [C] *(504) 948-2166; (888) 365-2877.* FAX *948-2258.*
Located in Faubourg Marigny, just a block away from the Quarter,
this was once two grand, old homes. Every member of staff is
exceptionally friendly and helpful.
[TV] [≈] **Rooms:** 27

GARLANDS GUEST HOUSE [W] *www.garlandsguesthouse.com* $$$
1129 St. Philip St. **Map** 4 D2. [C] *(800) 523-1060.* FAX *(504) 523-1372.*
These delightful Creole cottages are just a four-minute walk from Bourbon
Street. Each has a private entrance and a bath. A sumptuous breakfast and
a limo service from the airport are provided. [TV] [≈] [🚗] **Rooms:** 12

HOTEL PROVINCIAL [W] *www.hotelprovincial.com* $$$$
1024 Chartres St. **Map** 4 D2. [C] *(504) 581-4995; (800) 535-7922.*
Situated in a series of 1800s French Quarter buildings, including the Old
Royal Military Hospital and a feedstore, this hotel is unusual in having
plenty of parking space. The service is also outstanding, it has its own
restaurant (Nu Nu's), and five lovely courtyards. [TV] [≈] [🍴] **Rooms:** 94

HOTEL ROYAL [W] *www.melrosegroup.com* $$$
1006 Royal St. **Map** 5 D1. [C] *(504) 524-3900; (800) 776-3901.* FAX *558-0566*
This 1830s building has extra-large rooms, some with traditional balconies
overlooking Royal Street. The hotel offers a complimentary Continental
breakfast, and free local telephone calls. [TV] **Rooms:** 37

HOTEL ST. PIERRE [W] *www.historicinnsneworleans.com* $$$$
911 Burgundy St. **Map** 5 D2. [C] *(504) 524-4401; (800) 225-4040.* FAX *524-6800.*
The Hotel St. Pierre is a compound of French-style cottages offering a
Continental breakfast served in your room or by the pool. [TV] [&] **Rooms:** 74

HOTEL VILLA CONVENTO [W] *www.villaconvento.com* $$$$
616 Ursulines St. **Map** 5 D1. [C] *(504) 522-1793; (800) 887-2817.* FAX *524-1902.*
Experience the charm of an 1830s Creole townhouse, rumored to be
the "House of the Rising Sun." Try this place for a modest-cost getaway,
with balconies, courtyards, and Continental breakfast.
[TV] [≈] [🚗] **Rooms:** 25

LAMOTHE HOUSE [W] *www.new-orleans.org* $$$$$
621 Esplanade Ave. **Map** 5 D1. [C] *(504) 947-1161; (800) 367-5858.*
This 150-year-old double townhouse with antique furniture is situated
beneath moss-draped oaks on Esplanade Avenue at the edge of the
Quarter. Its vintage character takes you back to Victorian times.
[TV] [≈] [🚗] **Rooms:** 20

LA MAISON FAUBOURG GUEST HOUSE $$$
608 Kerlerec St. **Map** 5 D1. [C] *(504) 271-0228*
This house on a little-known street, just three blocks from Jackson Square, was
built in 1805 by Bernard de Marigny. All suites have a private bath, bed-
room, and parlor. Watch out for incognito famous guests. [TV] [🚗] **Suites:** 7

LANDMARK FRENCH QUARTER [W] *www.nolahotels.com* $$$$
920 Rampart St. **Map** 4 C1. [C] *(504) 524-3333; (877) 791-1312*
Despite the chain hotel name, this intimate hotel has a beautiful courtyard,
and the restaurant is open for breakfast and deli foods until midnight. It is
located close to the historic St. Louis Cemetery #1. [TV] **Rooms:** 102

LE RICHELIEU [W] *www.lerichelieuhotel.com* $$$$
1234 Chartres St. **Map** 5 D1. [C] *(504) 529-2492; (800) 535-9653.*
The guest rooms and suites here are individually and traditionally
decorated. Enjoy a cup of coffee at the terrace café, or a relaxing drink by
the pool or in the courtyard. [TV] [🚗] **Rooms:** 86

NEW ORLEANS GUEST HOUSE [W] *www.neworleans.com/nogh* $$$
1310 Esplanade Ave. **Map** 5 D1. [C] *(504) 832-4131; (800) 562-1177.*
A bit off the beaten path, but a bargain in expensive New Orleans, this
1840s Creole cottage offers simple, clean rooms, complimentary breakfast,
delightful hosts, and resident cats. [TV] **Rooms:** 14

For key to symbols see back flap

Price categories for a standard double room per night in the tourist season, including tax and service:
- Ⓢ under $50
- ⓈⓈ $50–100
- ⓈⓈⓈ $100–150
- ⓈⓈⓈⓈ $150–200
- ⓈⓈⓈⓈⓈ over $200

CREDIT CARDS ACCEPTED
One or more of the following credit cards are accepted: American Express, Diners Club, MasterCard, or VISA.

PRIVATE PARKING
The hotel has its own parking lot or parking spaces. These may not be on the same premises and are not necessarily locked.

SWIMMING POOL
The pool is outdoors unless otherwise stated in the text.

RESTAURANT
The restaurant or dining room is open to the public. See Restaurant section for additional information.

	24-HOUR CONCIERGE	CREDIT CARDS ACCEPTED	PRIVATE PARKING	SWIMMING POOL	RESTAURANT
OLDE VICTORIAN INN Ⓦ www.oldevictorianinn.com ⓈⓈⓈ 914 N. Rampart St. **Map** 4 C1. 🄲 *(504) 522-2446; (800) 725-2446.* A restored 1840s home three blocks away from Bourbon Street offers six period rooms, some with balconies, and most with fireplaces. An astounding breakfast is included. 🛏 **Rooms:** 6		●	▩		
PECAN TREE INN OF NEW ORLEANS Ⓦ www.pecantreeinn.com ⓈⓈⓈⓈ 2525 N. Rampart St. **Map** 4 C2. 🄲 *(504) 943-6195; (800) 460-3667.* This charming hotel is really just three Victorian homes. Each suite/house offers private living and dining rooms, a kitchen, two bedrooms, a courtyard, and fireplaces. 📺 **Rooms:** 8		●			
SONIAT HOUSE Ⓦ www.soniathouse.com ⓈⓈⓈⓈⓈ 1133 Chartres St. **Map** 5 D1. 🄲 *(504) 522-0570; (800) 544-8808.* Two classic early 19th-century buildings are hidden in the quiet residential section of the Quarter. It is expensive but has everything you could ask for. The Southern special breakfast is extra but worth it. 🛏 **Rooms:** 33	▩	●	▩		
SUN AND MOON B&B Ⓦ www.sunandmoonbnb.com ⓈⓈⓈ 1037 N. Rampart St. **Map** 4 B3. 🄲 *(504) 529-4652; (800) 638-9169.* This hotel has only four rooms, but two are full apartments; the others are large rooms with full bath. Southwestern decor. 📺 **Rooms:** 4		●	▩		
WAREHOUSE AND CENTRAL BUSINESS DISTRICTS					
AMBASSADOR HOTEL Ⓦ www.neworleans.com/ambassador ⓈⓈⓈⓈ 535 Tchoupitoulas St. **Map** 4 C4. 🄲 *(504) 527- 5271; (888) 527-5271.* This 19th-century coffee warehouse was converted into a modern New Orleans-style hotel. It has hardwood floors, huge rooms, four-poster beds, and is close to everything. 📺 🄱 **Rooms:** 165	▩	●	▩		▩
BEST WESTERN PARC ST. CHARLES ⓈⓈⓈⓈⓈ 500 St. Charles Ave. **Map** 4 B4. 🄲 *(504) 539-9000; (888) 856-4489.* Situated five blocks from the French Quarter and adjacent to Lafayette Square, this chain hotel offers executive services and facilities for conventions. 📺 📱 🄱 🄴 **Rooms:** 120	▩	●	▩	●	▩
COMFORT SUITES DOWNTOWN Ⓦ www.comfortinn.com/hotel/la071 ⓈⓈⓈ 346 Baronne St. **Map** 4 B4. 🄲 *(504) 524-1140; (800) 524-1140.* **FAX** 523-4444. Only four blocks from the French Quarter, this 100-year-old building was renovated in 1994. Close to the St. Charles streetcar route and handy for the Superdome. Continental breakfast. 📺 🄴 🚻 **Rooms:** 103		●	▩		
DEPOT HOUSE AT MADAME JULIA'S ⓈⓈ 7048 O'Keefe St. **Map** 4 B3. 🄲 *(504) 529-2952.* **FAX** 529-1908. Just around the block from the arty section of the CBD, this small guest house offers the budget-conscious traveler a great alternative to the pricier hotels in the area. All rooms have shared baths. 📺 **Rooms:** 15		●			
DOUBLETREE HOTEL Ⓦ www.doubletreeneworleans.com ⓈⓈⓈⓈⓈ 300 Canal St. **Map** 4 C3. 🄲 *(504) 581-1300; (866) 874-9074.* **FAX** 522-4100. Near the French Quarter, the Aquarium, the St. Charles Avenue streetcar, and right across Canal Street from Harrah's Casino, this chain hotel offers the usual amenities, plus complimentary chocolate chip cookies. The Art Deco rooms are striking. 📺 📱 🄱 🄴 **Rooms:** 363	▩	●	▩	●	▩
EMBASSY SUITES HOTEL Ⓦ www.embassyneworleans.com ⓈⓈⓈⓈⓈ 315 Julia St. **Map** 4 C5. 🄲 *(504) 525-1993; (800) 362-2779.* This hotel is situated in the CBD, right in the middle of the new Warehouse neighborhood. The early 20th-century architecture combines marble and brick, making the atmosphere one of the most interesting in the city. 📺 📱 **Rooms:** 372		●	▩	●	▩

FAIRMONT HOTEL W www.fairmont.com $$$$$
123 Baronne St. **Map** 4 B3. C (504) 529-7111; (800) 441-1414. FAX 529-4764.
This used to be the famous Roosevelt Hotel. The Sazerac Bar and the
extravagant lobby still speak of the 1930s. Every conceivable luxury is
here, including in-room computer hook-ups. TV ♦ ♦ ♦ ♦ **Rooms:** 700

HILTON NEW ORLEANS RIVERSIDE W www.neworleans.hilton.com $$$$$
2 Poydras St. **Map** 4 C5. C (504) 561-0500; (800) 445-8667
Here you get an excellent view of the Mississippi River and the Riverwalk,
and Harrah's Casino is accessible through the lobby. Otherwise it is a
fairly standard place. Pete Fountain's Jazz Club moved here from Bourbon Street.
TV ♦ ♦ ♦ ♦ ♦ **Rooms:** 1,600

HOLIDAY INN SELECT W www.holiday-inn.com $$$$
881 Convention Center Blvd. **Map** 4 C5. C (504) 524-1881.
Situated steps away from the Convention Center and close to the
Riverwalk, this hotel has a good restaurant and a spectacular central
atrium. TV ♦ **Rooms:** 170

HOTEL INTER-CONTINENTAL W www.interconti.com $$$$$
444 St. Charles Ave. **Map** 4 B4. C (504) 525-5566; (800) 445-6563.
The hotel is a five-minute walk from the Quarter. It is quiet, big,
comfortable, and popular with celebrities. The spacious rooms are modern
and luxuriously well-equipped. TV ♦ ♦ ♦ **Rooms:** 482

HOTEL MONACO NEW ORLEANS W www.monaco-neworleans.com $$$$
333 St. Charles St. **Map** 4 C3. C (504) 561-0010; (888)685-8359.
This highly evolved boutique hotel is the latest in the Hotel Monaco series.
Located in a former Masonic temple building, the decor is Moorish-on-the-
bayou. The restaurant is Susan Spicer's hugely popular Cobalt. The bar
attracts a very hip crowd. Pets are welcome. TV ♦ ♦ ♦ **Rooms:** 250

HYATT REGENCY W www.hyatt.com $$$$$
500 Poydras Plaza. **Map** 4 B3. C (504) 561-1234; (800) 233-1234.
One of the best big hotels in the city, the Hyatt Regency is just a short
walk from the Louisiana Superdome, so it is very popular with sports fans.
Enjoy the views of the city from the revolving rooftop restaurant. Free
transportation to the French Quarter is provided. ♦ ♦ ♦ **Rooms:** 1184

LA QUINTA INN & SUITES W www.laquinta.com $$$$
301 Camp St. **Map** 4 C3. C (504) 598-9977.
Three blocks away from the French Quarter, this hotel offers all amenities
and is convenient to all parts of the city. TV ♦ ♦ **Rooms:** 166

LA SALLE HOTEL W www.lasallehotelneworleans.com $$$
1113 Canal St. **Map** 4 B2. C (504) 523-5831.
Offering moderate prices and carefully detailed Old New Orleans-style
decoration, the La Salle is situated a block from the French Quarter. It is
popular with European and budget-minded visitors. TV ♦ ♦ **Rooms:** 57

LAFAYETTE HOTEL W www.thelafayettehotel.com $$$
600 St. Charles Ave. **Map** 4 B4. C (504) 524-4441.
The arty Warehouse District is home to this small European-style hotel. Lots
of charm, from the marble baths to wrought-iron balconies, make staying
away from the noise of the Quarter worth it. TV ♦ **Rooms:** 44

LE MERIDIEN HOTEL W www.lemeridien.com $$$$$
614 Canal St. **Map** 4 C3. C (504) 525-6500; (800) 543-4300.
This is the best place to stay if you want a bird's-eye view of the Mardi
Gras parades. Expensive and luxurious, every amenity you could ever want
is here. Try the Midi Restaurant for a quiet, romantic dinner.
TV ♦ ♦ ♦ **Rooms:** 494

LE PAVILLON HOTEL W www.lepavillion.com $$$$
833 Poydras St. **Map** 4 B3. C (504) 581-3111; (800) 535-9095. FAX 529-4415.
Built in 1907, this historic hotel has the most spectacular lobby in New
Orleans. It is reasonably priced for the area, and you'll get location, a very
decent restaurant, and upscale amenities. TV ♦ ♦ ♦ **Rooms:** 226

NEW ORLEANS MARRIOTT W www.marriott.com $$$$$
555 Canal St. **Map** 4 C3. C (504) 581-1000; (800) 228-9290. FAX 523-6755.
This modern hotel on the edge of the French Quarter welcomes you
with jazz in the lobby. There is rooftop dining at the Riverview restaurant.
Ask for weekend-special prices. TV ♦ ♦ ♦ ♦ ♦ **Rooms:** 1,310

For key to symbols see back flap

	24-Hour Concierge	Credit Cards Accepted	Private Parking	Swimming Pool	Restaurant

Price categories for a standard double room per night in the tourist season, including tax and service:
$ under $50
$$ $50–100
$$$ $100–150
$$$$ $150–200
$$$$$ over $200

CREDIT CARDS ACCEPTED
One or more of the following credit cards are accepted: American Express, Diners Club, MasterCard, or VISA.

PRIVATE PARKING
The hotel has its own parking lot or parking spaces. These may not be on the same premises and are not necessarily locked.

SWIMMING POOL
The pool is outdoors unless otherwise stated in the text.

RESTAURANT
The restaurant or dining room is open to the public. See Restaurant section for additional information.

OMNI ROYAL CRESCENT HOTEL [W] www.omnihotels.com $$$$
535 Gravier St. **Map** 4 C3. 【 (504) 527-0006; (800) 843-6664.
One of the most modern hotels in the Central Business District, this is a good choice for conventioneers and business travelers. Though not as large as most downtown hotels, it offers every amenity. [TV] [↑] [&] **Rooms:** 98

Amenities: 24-Hour Concierge, Credit Cards Accepted, Private Parking, Restaurant

THE PELHAM HOTEL [W] www.decaturhotel.com $$$$$
444 Common St. **Map** 4 C3. 【 (504) 522-4444, (888) 856-4486.
Part of a complex of new boutique hotels in New Orleans, the Pelham offers a pleasant location, good amenities, and a cozy ambience. Room service is available during restaurant hours. [TV] [↑] [&] [↑] **Rooms:** 60

Amenities: 24-Hour Concierge, Credit Cards Accepted, Restaurant

QUEEN & CRESCENT HOTEL [W] www.queenandcrescent.com $$$
344 Camp St. **Map** 4 C3. 【 (504) 587-9700; (800) 975-6652.
This centrally located, European-style boutique hotel offers small but nicely decorated rooms, each with handmade furniture and unique art.
[TV] [↑] [&] [↑] **Rooms:** 196

Amenities: 24-Hour Concierge, Credit Cards Accepted, Private Parking

RADISSON HOTEL [W] www.radisson.com/neworleansla $$$
1500 Canal St. **Map** 4 B2. 【 (504) 522-4500; (800) 333-3333.
Popular with middle-sized conventions, this hotel has easy access to the CBD. From the rooftop pool, you can enjoy spectacular views of the French Quarter and the CBD. [TV] [≈] [↑] [&] **Rooms:** 759

Amenities: 24-Hour Concierge, Credit Cards Accepted, Private Parking, Swimming Pool, Restaurant

SHERATON NEW ORLEANS HOTEL [W] www.sheraton.com $$$$
500 Canal St. **Map** 4 C3. 【 (504) 525-2500; (800) 396-6364.
This is just what you expect from one of the best hoteliers in the country. There is a price for every budget, from basic to top-level business-class, and every amenity is provided, including an excellent restaurant.
[TV] [≈] [↑] [&] [↑] **Rooms:** 1110

Amenities: Credit Cards Accepted, Private Parking, Swimming Pool, Restaurant

WINDSOR COURT HOTEL [W] www.windsorcourthotel.com $$$$$
300 Gravier St. **Map** 4 C3. 【 (504) 523-6000; (800) 262-2662.
This may be the best hotel in New Orleans in terms of class, chic, and amenities. The corridors in the lobby level display original Renaissance and Baroque art, and the staff is exceptionally attentive.
[TV] [↑] [&] **Rooms:** 324

Amenities: 24-Hour Concierge, Credit Cards Accepted, Private Parking, Swimming Pool, Restaurant

WYNDHAM RIVERFRONT HOTEL [W] www.wyndham.com $$$$
701 Convention Center Blvd. **Map** 4 C5. 【 (504) 524-8200; (800) 996-3426.
An excellent place to stay, whether you are on business or on vacation. The restaurant specializes in Creole cooking, and the lobby lounge is pleasant. [TV] [↑] [&] **Rooms:** 202

Amenities: 24-Hour Concierge, Credit Cards Accepted, Private Parking

GARDEN DISTRICT AND UPTOWN

1891 CASTLE INN [W] www.castleinnofneworleans.com $$$$
1539 4th St. **Map** 7 F3. 【 (504) 897-0540; (888) 826-0540.
The rooms in this large, converted Garden District house boast ornate mirrors and carved wooden furniture, including some fantastic four-poster beds. [TV] **Rooms:** 9

Amenities: Credit Cards Accepted

AVENUE PLAZA HOTEL & PRO SPA [W] www.avenueplazahotel.com $$$$
2111 St. Charles Ave. **Map** 8 A3. 【 (504) 566-1212; (800) 525-6899.
Located right on historic St. Charles Avenue, this suite-style hotel offers a full-service restaurant and the best spa/fitness club in the city. Its location is very convenient to all sights. [TV] [↑] **Rooms:** 256

Amenities: Credit Cards Accepted, Private Parking, Swimming Pool, Restaurant

THE CHIMES B&B [W] www.historiclodging.com $$$
1146 Constantinople St. **Map** 7 E4. 【 (504) 488-4640; (800) 729-4640.
The rooms in this hotel surround a private courtyard behind the owner's home. The area is quiet, and you are only two blocks from St. Charles Avenue. Continental breakfast is served in the main house. [TV] **Rooms:** 5

Amenities: Credit Cards Accepted, Private Parking

CLARION GRAND BOUTIQUE HOTEL W www.nolahotels.com $$$$
2001 St. Charles Ave. **Map 8 A3.** C (504) 558-9966; (877) 427-8332. FAX 571-6464.
This is an historic building right on the St. Charles Avenue streetcar line. All
rooms are "junior suites," which include microwaves, fridges, sitting rooms,
and business facilities. TV **Rooms:** 44

COLUMNS HOTEL W www.thecolumns.com $$$
3811 St. Charles Ave. **Map 7 E4.** C (504) 899-9308; (800) 445-9308.
Built in 1883, this Victorian hotel featured in the movie *Pretty Baby*. The
rooms still have many of their original details, and the beautiful columns in
its façade are a landmark. TV ⬛ **Rooms:** 20

FAIRCHILD HOUSE BED & BREAKFAST W www.fairchildhouse.com $$
1518 Prytania St. **Map 8 A2.** C (504) 524-0154; (800) 256-8096. FAX 568-0063.
Open since a detailed renovation in 1991, the three houses that form this
bed and breakfast are some of New Orleans' 19th-century architectural
treasures. TV ⬛ **Rooms:** 20

GRAND VICTORIAN BED & BREAKFAST W www.gvbb.com $$$$$
2727 St. Charles Ave. **Map 7 E4.** C (504) 525-5566; (800) 977-0008.
This corner-located Victorian mansion is the perfect place to watch Mardi
Gras parades, if you can get a reservation. Commander's Palace is just a
block away for that special dinner. TV ⬛ ⬛ ⬛ **Rooms:** 8

HAMPTON INN W www.hamptoninn.com $$$
3626 St. Charles Ave. **Map 7 E4.** C (504) 899-9990; (800) 426 7866. FAX 899-9908.
This Garden District chain hotel is located right on the streetcar line. The
rooms strike a balance between the elegance of Old New Orleans and the
comfort of modern facilities. TV ⬛ ⬛ **Rooms:** 100

JOSEPHINE GUEST HOUSE W www.bbonline/la/josephine $$$
1450 Josephine St. **Map 8 A3.** C (504) 524-6361; (800) 779-6361.
Small, intimate, and reasonably priced, Josephine offers knowledgeable
hosts and a good Creole breakfast. There are rooms in the main house and
in the garçonnier behind the courtyard. TV **Rooms:** 5

THE McKENDRICK-BREAUX HOUSE W www.mckendrick-breaux.com $$$$
1474 Magazine St. **Map 8 B3.** C (504) 586-1700; (888) 579-1700.
Treat yourself to at least one night at this hospitable, spacious, and very
comfortable B&B in the Lower Garden District. Owner Eddie Breaux
pampers every guest. TV **Rooms:** 9

MAISON ST. CHARLES QUALITY INN W www.maisonstcharles.com $$$
1319 St. Charles Ave. **Map 8 A3.** C (504) 522-0187; (800) 831-1783. FAX 529-4379.
This six-building complex offers rooms and suites. It is convenient to
everything, and offers a free shuttle service. La Madeleine Bakery is on the
grounds for your morning croissant.
TV ⬛ ⬛ **Rooms:** 130

PARK VIEW GUEST HOUSE W www.parkviewguesthouse.com $$$
7004 St. Charles Ave. **Map 6 B2.** C (504) 861-7564; (888) 533-0746.
The building is an architectural treasure, and its decor incorporates some
beautiful antiques. Some of the rooms have balconies with views of
Audubon Park or St. Charles Avenue. TV **Rooms:** 22

PONTCHARTRAIN HOTEL W www.pontchartrainhotel.com $$$$
2031 St. Charles Ave. **Map 7 E4.** C (504) 524-0581; (800) 777-6193.
A New Orleans landmark, this Garden District hotel offers a step back into
a more elegant time. Locals rely on the Bayou Bar for after-work ambience,
and no one should miss the Café Pontchartrain's Mile-High Pie.
TV ⬛ **Rooms:** 104

PRYTANIA PARK HOTEL W www.prytaniaparkhotel.com $$$
1525 Prytania St. **Map 8 A2.** C (504) 524-0427; (800) 862-1984.
A sister hotel of the Queen Anne Inn a block away, this comfortable com-
pound of buildings offers good rates and unique touches, such as rooms
with lofts. Free shuttle to the Quarter and CBD.
TV ⬛ ⬛ ⬛ **Rooms:** 74

QUEEN ANNE INN W www.thequeenanne.com $$$
1625 Prytania St. **Map 8 A2.** C (504) 524-0427; (888) 498-7591. FAX 522-2977.
The epitome of a New Orleans B&B, the Queen Anne has large rooms,
large baths, and most rooms have kitchenettes. The check-in desk is at the
Prytania Park Hotel down the street. TV **Rooms:** 12

For key to symbols see back flap

Price categories for a standard double room per night in the tourist season, including tax and service:
$ under $50
$$ $50–100
$$$ $100–150
$$$$ $150–200
$$$$$ over $200

Credit Cards Accepted
One or more of the following credit cards are accepted: American Express, Diners Club, MasterCard, or VISA.

Private Parking
The hotel has its own parking lot or parking spaces. These may not be on the same premises and are not necessarily locked.

Swimming Pool
The pool is outdoors unless otherwise stated in the text.

Restaurant
The restaurant or dining room is open to the public. See Restaurant section for additional information.

St. Charles Inn [W] *www.stcharlesinn.com* $$
3636 St. Charles Ave. **Map** 7 E4. ☎ *(504) 899-8888; (800) 489-9908.* [FAX] *899-8892.*
This is nothing fancy, but it is located in the heart of the Garden District, and is close to Audubon Park, the universities, and the St. Charles Avenue streetcar. Continental breakfast is served in your room, and the morning *Times-Picayune* newspaper is complimentary. [TV] **Rooms:** 40

Sully Mansion [W] *www.sullymansion.com* $$$
2631 Prytania St. **Map** 8 A2. ☎ *(504) 891-0457; (800) 364-2414.*
A luxurious and intimate bed and breakfast in a house designed in 1890 by architect Thomas Sully, this mansion offers Caswell Massey toiletries, Continental breakfast, and every amenity you could want. [TV] **Rooms:** 7

Terrell House [W] *www.lacajun.com/terrellhouse.html* $$$
1441 Magazine St. **Map** 8 D3. ☎ *(504) 524-9859; (800) 878-9859.* [FAX] *566-1518.*
This pleasant antebellum mansion in the Lower Garden District is a delightful change from the average hotel in New Orleans. Cable TV, hot tubs, antique furniture, and a giant courtyard are all provided, as are full breakfast and complimentary cocktails. [TV] **Rooms:** 10

Mid-City and Suburbs

Best Western New Orleans Airport [W] *www.bestwestern.com* $$$
1021 Airline Drive, Kenner. **Map** 1 B3. ☎ *(504) 464-1644; (800) 780-7234.*
This is the closest hotel to New Orleans International airport, so it is convenient for business travelers. Shuttles to downtown, the Quarter, and the Convention Center are available. [TV] ❄ 🏋 🚸 💻 **Rooms:** 166

Degas House [W] *www.degashouse.com* $$$$
2306 Esplanade Ave. **Map** 3 D3. ☎ *(504) 821-5009; (800) 755-6730.*
Wide Esplanade Avenue in Mid-City is the site of this historic three-story home where artist Edgar Degas lived with relatives. Tasty Creole breakfasts are provided on weekends, and you can pretend you're a Parisian artist by staying in the attic room. [TV] **Rooms:** 6

Doubletree Hotel Lakeside New Orleans $$
3838 N. Causeway Blvd, Metairie. ☎ *(504) 836-5253.* [FAX] *846-4562.*
This hotel is located on the scenic shores of Lake Pontchartrain, on the north side of New Orleans. It offers beautiful views of the lake and the New Orleans skyline, and it is reasonably priced. [TV] ❄ 🏋 🍸 🚸 **Rooms:** 210

Hilton New Orleans Airport [W] *www.neworleansairporthilton.com* $$$$
901 Airline Dr, Kenner. ☎ *(504) 469-5000; (800) 445-8667.* [FAX] *524-1059.*
This is probably the best place to stay if you are a business traveler. There are all kinds of extras, like a lighted tennis court and a putting green, in addition to the usual Hilton style. [TV] 🏋 🍸 🚸 **Rooms:** 317

Holiday Inn New Orleans–Airport $$$
2929 Williams Blvd, Kenner. ☎ *(504) 833-8201; (800) 887-7371.* [FAX] *838-7781.*
An alternative to the higher-priced airport hotels, this place offers most amenities, plus shuttles to the city center. [TV] ❄ 🏋 🍸 🚸 **Rooms:** 303

House on Bayou Road [W] *www.houseonbayouroad.com* $$$$
2275 Bayou Rd. **Map** 3 D3. ☎ *(504) 945-0992; (800) 882-2968.* [FAX] *822-2328.*
This plantation, located on 2 lush acres, offers a unique experience away from the noise and bustle of the Quarter. Breakfast is served on the patio overlooking the pool. [TV] **Rooms:** 8

Marriott Courtyard $$$
2 Galleria Blvd, Metairie. ☎ *(504) 838-3800; (800) 654-3990.* [FAX] *838-7050.*
The Marriott Courtyard is located in Metairie, close enough to the airport for business travelers. Freshly baked cookies and coffee are served in the afternoons. The fitness center never closes. [TV] 🏋 💻 **Rooms:** 120

Hotel	24-Hour Concierge	Credit Cards Accepted	Private Parking	Swimming Pool	Restaurant
St. Charles Inn	■	●	■		
Sully Mansion		●			
Terrell House		●	■		
Best Western New Orleans Airport	■	●	■	●	■
Degas House		●	■		
Doubletree Hotel Lakeside New Orleans	■	●	■	●	■
Hilton New Orleans Airport	■	●	■	●	■
Holiday Inn New Orleans–Airport	■	●	■	●	■
House on Bayou Road		●	■	●	
Marriott Courtyard	■	●	■	●	

ROSE MANOR B&B W www.rosemanor.com $$
7214 Pontchartrain Blvd. C (504) 282-8200; (877) 886-7634. FAX 282-7283.
Overlooking beautiful Lake Pontchartrain, this inn has nice, cozy rooms,
Continental breakfast, and a convenient bus direct to Canal Street.
Rooms: 9

BEYOND NEW ORLEANS

BEST WESTERN OF OPELOUSAS $$
5791 I-49 Service Road South, Opelousas. C (337) 942-5540; (800) 780-7234.
FAX 942-5540. Offering practical accommodation in the center of Opelousas,
the zydeco capital of the world, this hotel is close to the Acadian
Tourist Center. TV 🛗 🔥 Rooms: 46

BIENVENUE HOUSE W www.bienvenuehouse.com $$$
421 N Main St, St. Martinville. C (337) 394-9100; (888) 394-9100.
This antebellum house has porch swings, gardens, and Foti's is just across
the square for the best food in Louisiana. One of the loveliest towns in
South Louisiana, St. Martinville was once called "Petit Paris." Rooms: 4

BOIS DES CHENES INN $$$
338 N. Sterling Ave, Lafayette. C FAX (377) 233-7816.
A gem in Cajun Country, this former 1820s sugar and cattle plantation has
suites with antique furniture and ambience galore. The owner will arrange
trips through the Atchafalaya Swamp for nature lovers. Reservations are
essential. TV Rooms: 5

COMFORT SUITES NEW IBERIA W www.comfortsuites.com $$
2817 Highway 14, New Iberia. C (337) 367-0855.
Catering mostly to business travelers, this hotel offers large suites and a
central location. Jefferson Island, Avery Island and Jungle Gardens, and a
very good restaurant, the Little River Inn, are close at hand. TV 🛗 🔥 🔥
Rooms: 78

COURTYARD ACADIAN CENTER W www.marriott.com/btrch $$$
2421 S Acadian Thwy, Baton Rouge. C (225) 924-6400; (800) 321-2211.
Close to downtown Baton Rouge, this chain hotel is comfortable,
convenient, and hosts lots of business travelers. TV 🛗 🔥 🔥 Rooms: 149

COURTYARD LAFAYETTE AIRPORT W www.courtyard.com/LFTCY/ $$
214 E Kaliste Saloom Rd, Lafayette. C (337) 232-5005; (800) 321-2211. FAX 235-1386.
Close to Acadian Mall, restaurants, the university, and dance halls, the
Courtyard offers spacious rooms. TV 🛗 🔥 🔥 ⬜ Rooms: 90

L'ACADIE INN $$
259 Tasso Loop, Eunice. C (337) 457-5211. FAX 550-7655.
You are right on the prairie at this Cajun-owned-and-operated motel. Be
sure to make reservations at least a year in advance for Cajun Mardi Gras
and the Folklore Festival. At other times, it is a bargain. TV 🔥 🔥
Rooms: 20

LAFAYETTE HILTON AND TOWERS $$$$
1521 W Pinhook Rd, Lafayette. C (337) 235-6111.
Close to all of Lafayette's attractions, restaurants, and museums, the
Lafayette Hilton has a beautiful view of Bayou Vermilion. TV 🛗 🔥
Rooms: 327

RADISSON HOTEL AND CONFERENCE CENTER W www.radisson.com $$$
4728 Constitution Ave, Baton Rouge. C (225) 925-2244. FAX 930-0140.
This comfortable high-rise hotel is conveniently situated near Louisiana
State University, casinos, and the Government Center. TV 🔥 🔥 Rooms: 294

ST. FRANCISVILLE INN W www.stfrancisvilleinn.com $$$$
5720 Commerce St, St. Francisville. C (225) 635-6502; (800) 488-6502.
Only a half-hour's drive from Baton Rouge, this historic inn is an
experience in South Louisiana hospitality. A gourmet breakfast buffet
is offered. 🔥 Rooms: 10

T'FRERE'S HOUSE W www.tfreres.com $$$
1905 Verot School Rd, Lafayette. C (337) 984-9347; (800) 984-9347.
One of the best B&Bs in this part of the world, this hotel has succulent
breakfasts on weekends, and delightful hosts who know the area. It is
situated close to the dance halls and the many restaurants of Lafayette.
Rooms: 5

For key to symbols see back flap

RESTAURANTS, CAFÉS, AND BARS

EVEN WHEN OTHER MAJOR CITIES in the US were living in a culinary wasteland, New Orleans had a reputation for fine, flavorful Creole cuisine. Today the reputation is still intact, but it has been enhanced by the development of "modern" Creole cuisine, Cajun cuisine, and some fine ethnic dining as well. In this city, food matters; locals

New Orleans waiter

argue about who sells the best oysters, where to secure the finest turtle soup or gumbo, who makes the best po'boy (sandwich), bread pudding, and so on. The same is true for drinks. A pharmacist in the city invented the cocktail, and bartenders here are adept at making Sazeracs, a range of mint juleps, and such hazardous concoctions as the Obituary Cocktail *(see p170)*.

Diners at the Acme Oyster House *(see p172)*

PLACES TO EAT

TOP-FLIGHT restaurants are found throughout the city, particularly in the French Quarter, the Warehouse District, and Uptown. Currently such chefs as Susan Spicer, Emeril LeGasse, Frank Brigtsen, Paul Prudhomme, and others who are updating the traditional cuisine are generating the most

Commander's Palace *(see p177)*, one of the city's finest restaurants

excitement. There are plenty of good quality restaurants that are producing traditional Creole and Cajun dishes – gumbo, oysters Rockefeller, jambalaya, crawfish étouffée, barbecue shrimp, and other zesty dishes *(see pp168–9)*.

In addition, there are Italian, Mexican, and other ethnic restaurants, plus plenty of places for cheap, good food, serving po'boys, New Orleans own *muffuletta* (a special local sandwich), pizza, and the ubiquitous dish of red beans and rice with sausage. New Orleans residents also care passionately about coffee, and the city has many good coffee and pastry shops.

OTHER PLACES TO EAT

NEW ORLEANS offers a broad range of venues other than

restaurants in which to eat good food. Many hotels have excellent dining rooms open to the public, and there are various Italian delicatessens; these are mainly at the French Market, where you can buy a salad or a sandwich. At night time, there are plenty of Cajun-style hot dog stands on the corners in the French Quarter.

HOURS AND PRICES

BREAKFAST is available between 7am and 2pm and can be inexpensive or super-expensive – the price often depends on where it is served. Jazz brunches, which are a New Orleans tradition, are given around town on weekends and can cost anywhere betwen $20 and $35.

At lunchtime, you can buy a light meal for about $7 or $10, usually between 11am and 2:30pm. In the better restaurants, prices are lower at lunchtime than at dinner. Dinner is generally served from 5 to 10pm. At a moderately priced place, main dishes might range from $14 to $24. In the very best restaurants, like Commander's Palace or Emeril's, you can enjoy a seven-course meal for $75, plus wine. A few places are open all night.

DINING ON A BUDGET

DO NOT EAT BREAKFAST at your hotel unless it is complimentary. Seek out a coffee shop or deli and feast on delicious croissants and strong coffee.

At lunch, you can pop into a corner grocery and order a po'boy or *muffuletta*, and picnic somewhere. If you do sit down in a restaurant, you will find prices are lower than at dinner, as many establishments offer discounted menus early in the day. Otherwise, you can save money by ordering one course only (which is usually enough) and drinking less wine. Depending on the hour, some restaurants offer fixed-price menus that are usually cheaper.

TAXES AND TIPPING

A SALES TAX of 9 percent is added to meal and beverages checks in all restaurants. In general, you should tip 15 percent of the check for service; 20 percent if the service is superb. When the service is very bad you need not tip at all, but the server or maitre d' may request an explanation.

RESERVATIONS

A T THE VERY BEST restaurants you will need to make reservations considerably in advance. Some restaurants, however, do not take reservations, and you will have to stand in line or enjoy a cocktail in the bar while you wait.

DRESS CODE

N EW ORLEANS is a relaxed city and most places will allow you to wear the standard

Non-smoking area at the Upperline restaurant *(see p178)*

attire of jeans and T-shirt. Several of the more upscale restaurants require a jacket, and can also lend you one; ties are rarely required. Just to be on the safe side, dress smart-casual.

CHILDREN

C HILDREN ARE WELCOME at any restaurant, and special facilities, such as booster seats or highchairs, are usually available. Some restaurants offer special menus for children. The legal drinking age is 21, and children are not allowed in bars.

WHEELCHAIR ACCESS

A LTHOUGH SINCE 1992 all restaurants have been required by law to be wheelchair accessible, it is best to call ahead to determine

precisely how accessible a particular establishment is – whether there are steps outside or inside, for example, or whether the bathrooms are downstairs or upstairs.

The Grill Room at the Windsor Court Hotel *(see p177)*

SMOKING

I N NEW ORLEANS, restaurants that seat more than 50 persons are required to offer a large non-smoking section, although some offer a special smoking section at their bar.

VEGETARIAN FOOD

A S IN THE REST of the United States, there is plenty of scope for vegetarians to eat well in New Orleans. Although much Creole and Cajun food is meat-based, most restaurants have vegetarian dishes such as salads or meat-free meals, if requested.

There are also exclusively vegetarian restaurants around town, plus Vietnamese and Thai restaurants, where vegetarian dishes are offered.

People enjoying coffee and *beignets* at Café du Monde *(see p172)*

New Orleans' Best: Restaurants

NEW ORLEANS CULTURE is well represented by the food in its many fine eateries. It is one of the few cities in the United States that has developed a cuisine of its own, one that is renowned worldwide. In addition to the finest Cajun and Creole food, New Orleans also boasts restaurants offering the best of international cuisines. In this food-oriented city, these are the top ten restaurants where excellence is presented in service, quality, atmosphere, and flavor.

0 kilometers 1

0 miles 1

Gabrielle
Gabrielle specializes in Creole cuisine. Try the slow roasted duck that melts in the mouth, or the pompano en papillotte. (See p178.)

Brigtsen's
Frank Brigtsen, a protégé of Paul Prudhomme, fuses Creole and Cajun in modern style at this uptown Creole cottage. (See p177.)

Upperline
This romantic, uptown restaurant serves a terrific range of Cajun-Creole dishes, including duck étouffée, and fried green tomatoes with shrimp remoulade. (See p178.)

GARDEN DISTRICT

Commander's Palace
The ultimate New Orleans experience is in a mansion in the Garden District. If you can't get a seat for dinner, go for the weekend jazz brunch or half-price lunch. (See p177.)

Acme Oyster House

Diners agree that this is the best place in the city for oysters on the half shell. The boiled craw-fish is great. (See p172.)

Bayona

Culinary star Susan Spicer produces superb Asian-Mediterranean-inspired, contemporary American cuisine, featuring such signature dishes as cream of garlic soup and grilled shrimp with cilantro. (See p172.)

MID-CITY

FRENCH QUARTER

Esplanade Ave

Canal Street

Tulane Avenue

Pontchartrain Expressway

Jackson Avenue

MISSISSIPPI

WAREHOUSE & CENTRAL BUSINESS DISTRICTS

Galatoire's

You can observe the haute monde *at lunch while you sample the Creole classics. The menu hasn't changed much since the restaurant opened in 1905.* (See p173.)

K-Paul's

This is the home restaurant of Paul Prudhomme, who introduced the world to Cajun cui-sine and the "blackening" technique of cooking. (See p173.)

The Grill Room

The best hotel dining room in the city provides lavish surroundings, top-class service, and superb cuisine fashioned from ultra-expensive ingredients. It is located in the Windsor Court Hotel. (See p177.)

Emeril's

The flagship of the energetic chef Emeril LaGasse offers superb, updated Creole cuisine – from the oyster dishes to the banana cream pie with caramel sauce. (See p176.)

What to Eat in New Orleans

Tʜᴇ ᴄɪᴛʏ ɪs ғᴀᴍᴏᴜs for two cuisines: Cajun and Creole. The Creole cuisine evolved as the European immigrants – French, Spanish, Germans, and Italians – adapted their cuisines to local ingredients, and incorporated Native American and African flavors. Cajun cooking arrived with the French-Canadian Acadians, who introduced their more rustic single-pot style of cooking, using the traditional blend of flour and oil as a base.

Red and green peppers

Muffuletta
This is a New Orleans Italian tradition, made with deli meats and cheeses, plus a healthy dollop of olive salad, served on round Italian bread. The best can be bought at Central Grocery (see p76).

Eggs Sardou
Poached eggs on artichoke bottoms, served with spinach and topped with hollandaise, is a classic option for brunch.

Turtle Soup
Spicy, meaty, and made from ranch-farmed turtles, this soup is a traditional New Orleans favorite.

Po'Boy
This is a massive sandwich, filled with whatever you desire, such as oysters, shrimp, ham, or roast beef.

Andouille (Acadian smoked sausage)   White rice   Boiled fresh shrimp

Oysters   Hot green pepper   Ground sassafras powder

Gumbo
This stewlike soup is made with okra, peppers, shrimp, crab, oysters, and sometimes chicken or sausage, thickened and flavored with filé powder (ground sassafras) and served on a bed of rice.

Oysters
These are prepared in many ways – fried, Rockefeller, in a stew, or raw in all their tangy, briny glory.

Crawfish (or "Mudbugs")
Boiled in a bisque, or served étouffée, crawfish dishes are nearly always on the menu.

Soft-Shell Blue Crab
These soft-shell crabs are bountiful in Louisiana waters and can be found on many menus in season.

Pompano en Papillote
The en papillote *method of cooking, which keeps the flavor inside, is perfect for this popular Gulf fish.*

Shrimp Remoulade
Shrimp served with a hot, spicy sauce, here made from cayenne, olive oil, mustard, lemon, scallions, and parsley.

Rice

Chicken

Andouille (smoked sausage)

Shellfish

Vegetables

Jambalaya
This is really the Creole version of paella. The French added jambon *(ham) to the usual Spanish mix of rice and andouille, chicken, rabbit, shellfish, and vegetables. There are numerous versions available, some using duck or alligator. A red jambalaya is made with tomatoes and tomato sauce, while brown jambalaya uses beef stock.*

Red Beans and Rice
This is a flavorsome combination of beans, rice, smoked pork, hot sauce, onions, and garlic.

Bread Pudding
Bread pudding is prepared with French bread and custard served with whiskey sauce.

Bananas Foster
A luscious dessert of bananas flambéed in rum and banana liqueur.

Beignets
Sugar-dusted, and hot, these doughnuts are served all day at Café du Monde (see p76).

Pralines
These sweet and delicious candies were originally made with almonds in France; in New Orleans, pecan nuts are used. Chocolate pralines are also popular.

What to Drink in New Orleans

A LONG TRADITION of good drinking is one of New Orleans' trademarks. There are a wide variety of cocktails served throughout the city, some of which were invented here. Delicious and easy to drink, many are extremely potent concoctions. The local beers are also worthy: New Orleans has a top-class microbrewery. The city is a coffee-drinker's delight and has its own distinctive chicory-flavored dark roast coffee – a favorite of residents and visitors alike.

Pat O'Brien's *(see p47)*, where the popular Hurricane was created

The Sazerac   **The Hurricane**   **Mint Julep**

Vieux Carré Cocktail   **Obituary Cocktail**   **Ramos Gin Fizz**

COCKTAILS

N EW ORLEANS WAS THE BIRTHPLACE of many cocktails. Local pharmacist Antoine Peychaud's store was located on the corner of Royal and St. Louis streets, and he is said to have invented the cocktail around 1830 when he combined cognac "Sazerac" mixed with his own bitters recipe, a drop of water, and a pinch of sugar. Peychaud mixed this in an egg cup *"coquetier,"* which his English-speaking customers mispronounced as "cocktail." Today, the Sazerac is one of New Orleans' most famous drinks: rye whiskey (or bourbon) is combined with bitters and sugar, and flavored with Pernod and lemon peel.

The Hurricane, served in a special glass, is very sweet and combines dark rum with passion fruit and other juices. The Mint Julep is made with bourbon, sugar, fresh mint, and crushed ice. The Vieux Carré mixes rye, cognac, vermouth, bitters, and a dash of Benedictine. For the Obituary Cocktail, a lethal drink created at Lafitte's *(see p78)*, add half a jigger of Pernod to a gin Martini. Bartender Henry Ramos shook the first Ramos Gin Fizz in 1888, combining sugar, orange flower water, citrus juice, gin, egg white, cream, and seltzer into a refreshing drink. Pousse Café is a mix of six cordials – raspberry and maraschino syrups, crème de menthe, curaçao, chartreuse, and cognac.

BEER AND WINE

N EW ORLEANS IS A BEER TOWN. Look for such local brews as Abita Springs and Dixie, plus those made by the microbrewery Crescent City. A variety of wines are also available in the city's restaurants, particularly fine French and California vintages.

Dixie and Abita Amber, local beers

Red and white California wines

COFFEE

N EW ORLEANIANS LOVE COFFEE, and it comes in all roasts and styles. Community Brand, French Market, and CDM are the three most famous Louisiana brands. The Café du Monde *(see p76)* serves "café au lait," the traditional dark roast chicory-flavored coffee with hot milk.

If you don't like the somewhat bitter taste of chicory, just ask for "pure" coffee; you'll get a tasty cup of dark or medium roast coffee. Extra-strong espresso is usually served after dinner.

Café au lait

Café espresso

Glossary of New Orleans Food

THE DISTINCTIVE CUISINE of New Orleans has its own vocabulary. Some styles and ingredients are particular to Creole and Cajun cooking; others are more common but take on that special Louisiana touch. Creole dishes often have as their base peppers, onions, and tomatoes, and can be more refined than the flavorful Cajun one-pot dishes.

Vegetables and fruit for sale in the French Market

Andouille
A hard, smoked, spicy Cajun sausage made with pork.

Bananas Foster
Bananas sprinkled with brown sugar and flambéed in rum and banana liqueur *(see p169)*.

Barbecued Shrimp
Jumbo shrimp in their shells sautéed in oil and butter, garlic, peppers, and spices.

Beignet
Deep-fried square doughnut (no hole), covered in powdered sugar *(see p169)*.

Biscuits
Flour and baking powder rolled and baked, often served with eggs at breakfast.

Boudin
Highly seasoned Cajun pork blood sausage combined with rice.

Bouillabaisse New Orleans-style
A spicier version of the French seafood dish.

Calas
Fried sweet rice cakes.

Cajun
A style of cooking that combines French methods with local Southern ingredients.

Chow Chow
A relish usually made with cucumbers, green tomatoes, and green cayenne peppers.

Courtbouillon of Redfish
A seafood stew, prepared with local fish, spices, and white wine.

Oranges and other fruits, used as ingredients in Creole food

Crawfish or "Mudbugs"
Also known as crayfish, these deliciously sweet, small crustaceans are prepared in various ways like stews, *étouffée*, or boiled *(see p168)*.

Crawfish Boil
Crawfish boiled in water seasoned with mustard, coriander, dill, cloves, allspice, bay leaves, and the main ingredient, dried chilies.

Ripe bananas, used for desserts

Dirty Rice
Rice cooked with chicken livers and gizzards, and other seasonings.

Eggs Sardou
Eggs poached on artichoke bottoms, cradled on a bed of creamed spinach, and covered with hollandaise *(see p168)*.

Etouffée
Literally "smothered," a method of cooking slowly with little liquid, in a covered pan.

Filé
Filé refers to the dried ground sassafras leaves used to thicken and flavor gumbos.

Grits
Ground, cooked corn grains served at breakfast with butter, salt, pepper, and eggs.

Gumbo
A spicy, thick soup containing shrimp, crawfish, oysters, okra, and served over rice *(see p168)*.

Shrimp Remoulade

Gumbo z'Herbes
A meatless version of gumbo, made during Lent.

Jambalaya
A mixture of rice, seafood, Tasso (ham), vegetables, and seasoned with onion, green peppers, and celery *(see p169)*.

King Cake
A round cake made during Mardi Gras. It is sprinkled with granulated and colored sugars. A tiny doll, representing the baby Jesus, is hidden inside.

Maque Choux
A Cajun dish made with a mixture of corn, tomatoes, onions, and cayenne pepper.

Mirliton
A pear-shaped vegetable with prickly ribbed skin.

Muffuletta
A sandwich combining Italian sausage, deli meats, and one or two kinds of cheese on an Italian round loaf slathered with olive salad – pickled olives, celery, carrots, cauliflower, and capers *(see p168)*.

Okra
A pod vegetable, originally from Africa, served as a side dish or used in gumbos and stews.

Pain Perdu
The local version of French toast (bread fried with eggs).

Po'Boy
A big French bread sandwich, filled with shrimp, oysters, ham, roast beef, or a combination *(see p168)*.

Pompano en Papillotte
A sweet fish common in Gulf waters, baked in an oiled paper bag to retain its flavor *(see p169)*.

Pralines
A candy patty made with brown sugar and pecans *(see p169)*.

Shrimp Remoulade
Shrimp with a mayonnaise-based sauce seasoned with mustard, anchovies, gherkins, scallions, lemon, spices, and herbs *(see p169)*.

Sweet Potato Pie
Made with sweet potatoes flavored with cinnamon, nutmeg, and ginger.

Tasso
Highly spiced smoked ham seasoned with red pepper.

Choosing a Restaurant

THE RESTAURANTS in this guide have been selected across a wide range of price categories for their exceptional food, good value, interesting location, and attractive ambience. They are listed here by region. The thumb tabs on the pages use the same color-coding as the corresponding area chapters in the main section of the guide.

	CREDIT CARDS	BAR AREA/COCKTAIL BAR	OUTDOOR EATING	CAJUN/CREOLE SPECIALTIES	GOOD WINE SELECTION

UPPER FRENCH QUARTER

ACME OYSTER HOUSE $
724 Iberville St. **Map** 4 B2. ☎ *(504) 522-5973.*
Although there are mixed opinions about the looks of the place, most maintain that the lack of decor is part of its charm, and it is still one of the best places in the city for raw oysters and crawfish.

	AE DC MC V	●		●	

ALEX PATOUT'S LOUISIANA KITCHEN $$
221 Royal St. **Map** 4 C3. ☎ *(504) 525-7788.*
This French Quarter Cajun-Creole restaurant offers good and sometimes very spicy food, as well as an award-winning wine list and understated elegance. The prices are reasonable for this area.

	AE DC MC V			●	■

ANTOINE'S $$
713 St. Louis St. **Map** 2 B3. ☎ *(504) 581-4422.*
Antoine's offers over 130 dishes on its vintage turn-of-the-century French-Creole menu. Although it is a bit faded, the classic elegance and excellent cuisine never go out of style. 🍴 🅥 ● *Sun.*

	AE DC MC V	●		●	■

ARNAUD'S $$$
813 Bienville St. **Map** 4 C2. ☎ *(504) 523-5433.*
A lovely atmosphere makes this elegant 19th-century French Quarter classic one of the great old New Orleans restaurants. The famous shrimp remoulade alone is worth the trip. 🍴 🅥 🎵

	AE DC MC V	●		●	■

BACCO $$$$
310 Chartres St. **Map** 5 D1. ☎ *(504) 522-2426.*
Even in Creole-Cajun country, Italian cuisine holds considerable sway. Bacco offers delicious wood-fired pizzas and every kind of seafood. 🅥

	AE DC MC V	●	■		■

BAYONA $$$
430 Dauphine St. **Map** 5 D1. ☎ *(504) 525-4455.*
New World is the label chef Susan Spicer applies to her cooking style. Imaginative dishes are served in an early 19th-century Creole cottage on this quiet French Quarter street. 🅥 ● *Sun.*

	AE DC MC V	●	■		■

BEGUE'S $$$
Royal Sonesta Hotel, 300 Bourbon St. **Map** 5 D1. ☎ *(504) 553-2278.*
At this elegant French Quarter hotel, the Friday lunch buffet is worth visiting, and Sunday brunch is a hidden secret. 🎵

	AE DC MC V	●	■	●	

BISTRO AT MAISON DE VILLE $$$$
Maison de Ville Hotel, 727 Toulouse St. **Map** 4 C2. ☎ *(504) 528-9206.*
A tiny French bistro serving sophisticated cuisine at one of the French Quarter's hidden treasures. Since it is always crowded, reservations are necessary. ● *Sun.*

	AE DC MC V	●	■	●	

BRENNAN'S $$$$
417 Royal St. **Map** 5 D1. ☎ *(504) 525-9711.*
Breakfast at Brennan's is a landmark New Orleans meal. It is most famous for its poached egg dishes and Bananas Foster *(see p169).* 🅥 🎵

	AE DC MC V	●	■	●	■

BROUSSARD'S $$$
819 Conti St. **Map** 4 C2. ☎ *(504) 581-3866.*
Old-fashioned elegance and the loveliest courtyard in the Quarter make this French-Creole restaurant a grand experience. Desserts are particularly elegant, and the wine list is extensive.

	AE DC MC V	●	■	●	■

CAFÉ DU MONDE $
French Market, 800 Decatur St. **Map** 5 D2. ☎ *(504) 587-0833.*
Sit and watch the world go by from this historic 24-hour, open-air coffee shop, offering mouthwatering *beignets* and *café au lait (see p76).*

			■		

Price categories include a three course meal for one, half a bottle of house wine and all unavoidable extra charges such as sales tax and service:
- $ under $25
- $$ $25–$35
- $$$ $35–$50
- $$$$ $50–$70
- $$$$$ over $70

CREDIT CARDS
Indicates which credit cards are accepted: AE American Express; DC Diners Club; MC MasterCard/Access; V Visa.

BAR AREA/COCKTAIL BAR
There is a bar area or cocktail bar within the restaurant.

OUTDOOR EATING
There are some tables on a patio or terrace.

CAJUN/CREOLE SPECIALTIES
The menu contains some Cajun and/or Creole specialties.

GOOD WINE SELECTION
Denotes a wide range of good wines.

CAFÉ MASPERO — $
601 Decatur St. **Map** 5 D1. ((504) 523-6250.
At this inexpensive and crowded seafood/sandwich shop, the *muffuletta (see p168)* and unique po'boys come in huge portions.
Cajun/Creole Specialties

THE COURT OF TWO SISTERS — $$$
613 Royal St. **Map** 5 D1. ((504) 522-7261.
There is a gorgeous bar, a great courtyard, and lovely setting at this tourist-oriented, French-Cajun-Creole old-timer; but the food needs help. However, the Sunday jazz brunch buffet offers a great variety of local specialties. **V** ♫
Credit Cards: AE DC MC V; Bar Area/Cocktail Bar; Outdoor Eating; Cajun/Creole Specialties; Good Wine Selection

FELIX'S RESTAURANT AND OYSTER BAR — $$
739 Iberville St. **Map** 4 C2. ((504) 522-4440.
The oysters, crawfish, shrimp, and crab dishes are home-style, the portions large. The stand-up oyster bar is a New Orleans tradition. **V**
Credit Cards: AE DC MC V; Bar Area/Cocktail Bar; Cajun/Creole Specialties

GALATOIRE'S — $$$$
209 Bourbon St. **Map** 5 D1. ((504) 525-2021.
This traditional restaurant epitomizes the old-style French-Creole bistro, with a lengthy menu filled with standard-setting sauces. Glistening brass chandeliers, bentwood chairs, and white-cloth tables add to its timeless atmosphere. No reservations – everyone must wait in line. **T V ●** *Mon.*
Credit Cards: AE DC MC V; Bar Area/Cocktail Bar; Cajun/Creole Specialties; Good Wine Selection

GUMBO SHOP — $$
630 St. Peter St. **Map** 4 C2. ((504) 525-1486.
This tourist-oriented Cajun-Creole restaurant is still a good place for gumbo at reasonable prices. It has a nice courtyard and decent bread pudding.
Credit Cards: AE DC MC V; Outdoor Eating

K-PAUL'S LOUISIANA KITCHEN — $$$$
416 Chartres St. **Map** 4 C3. ((504) 524-7394.
Chef Paul Prudhomme started the Cajun craze in this rustic French Quarter café. Its inventive gumbos and great seafood are superb. Prices are steep at dinner but moderate at lunch. **V ●** *Sun.*
Credit Cards: AE DC MC V; Bar Area/Cocktail Bar; Cajun/Creole Specialties; Good Wine Selection

LOUIS XVI — $$$$
St. Louis Hotel, 730 Bienville St. **Map** 4 C2. ((504) 581-7000.
Outstanding Gallic creations and classic French cream sauces dominate the menu. The predominantly French wine list is remarkable. With excellent service, its only fault is the expensive prices. **T ♫ P**
Credit Cards: AE DC MC V; Bar Area/Cocktail Bar; Good Wine Selection

MAMA ROSA'S — $
616 N. Rampart St. **Map** 4 C1. ((504) 523-5546.
Great pizza but an iffy location is the two-edged sword at this southern Italian spot on the edge of the French Quarter. Nevertheless, it is a good option if you are on a budget. **V**
Credit Cards: AE DC MC V

MIKE ANDERSON'S SEAFOOD — $$
215 Bourbon St. **Map** 5 D1. ((504) 524-3884.
This is a nice place to take visitors, although perhaps too tourist-oriented. It has good, solid seafood and a friendly atmosphere.
Credit Cards: AE DC MC V; Cajun/Creole Specialties

MR. B'S BISTRO — $$$
201 Royal St. **Map** 4 C3. ((504) 523-2078.
This pop version of Commander's Palace has remained fresh and innovative since it opened in 1979. The coconut-and-beer-battered shrimp, or any of the other items from the grill, are a real treat.
Credit Cards: AE DC MC V; Bar Area/Cocktail Bar; Cajun/Creole Specialties; Good Wine Selection

NOLA — $$$
534 St. Louis St. **Map** 2 B3. ((504) 522-6652.
Fans of chef Emeril Lagasse have this vibrant restaurant as an alternative to the original Emeril's *(see p176)*. The cedar plank-roasted fresh fish and the hickory-roasted duck are remarkable. **V**
Credit Cards: AE DC MC V; Bar Area/Cocktail Bar; Cajun/Creole Specialties; Good Wine Selection

		CREDIT CARDS	BAR AREA/COCKTAIL BAR	OUTDOOR EATING	CAJUN/CREOLE SPECIALTIES	GOOD WINE SELECTION

Price categories include a three course meal for one, half a bottle of house wine and all unavoidable extra charges such as sales tax and service:
- $ under $25
- $$ $25–$35
- $$$ $35–$50
- $$$$ $50–$70
- $$$$$ over $70

CREDIT CARDS
Indicates which credit cards are accepted: AE American Express; DC Diners Club; MC MasterCard/Access; V Visa.

BAR AREA/COCKTAIL BAR
There is a bar area or cocktail bar within the restaurant.

OUTDOOR EATING
There are some tables on a patio or terrace.

CAJUN/CREOLE SPECIALTIES
The menu contains some Cajun and/or Creole specialties.

GOOD WINE SELECTION
Denotes a wide range of good wines.

	CREDIT CARDS	BAR AREA/COCKTAIL BAR	OUTDOOR EATING	CAJUN/CREOLE SPECIALTIES	GOOD WINE SELECTION
OLD DOG, NEW TRICK CAFÉ $ 317 Frenchman St. **Map** 5 E1. ▐ *(504) 522-4569.* This hippie health-food heaven offers some of the best vegetarian dishes in the city, including delicious Cajun specialties. **V**	AE DC MC V			●	
PELICAN CLUB $$$ 312 Exchange Alley. **Map** 4 C3. ▐ *(504) 523-1504.* This restaurant hidden in a tiny French Quarter alley presents some excellent contemporary Louisiana dishes with Asian touches. **V**	AE DC MC V			●	
RALPH & KACOO'S $$ 519 Toulouse St. **Map** 4 C2. ▐ *(504) 522-5226.* This New Orleans staple offers large portions of decent fried seafood at reasonable prices. The seafood platter will knock your socks off!	AE DC MC V	●			
RED FISH GRILL $$ 115 Bourbon St. **Map** 5 D1. ▐ *(504) 598-1200.* Owned by the Brennan family, this restaurant offers a festive yet casual atmosphere, a giant-sized oyster bar, and every kind of seafood you could ever want. The desserts are spectacular, too. **V**	AE DC MC V		■	●	■
REMOULADE $$ 309 Bourbon St. **Map** 4 C3. ▐ *(504) 523-0377.* Run by the owners of the famous Arnaud's *(see p172)*, Remoulade is a more casual restaurant. You will find po' boys, burgers, pizzas, gumbos, jambalaya, and lots of seafood dishes with south Louisiana pedigrees.	AE DC MC V	●		●	
RIB ROOM $$$ Omni Royal Orleans Hotel, 621 St. Louis St. **Map** 2 B3. ▐ *(504) 529-7046.* The Rib Room is an elegant American-Continental restaurant, which serves a great prime rib and one of the best crab bisques in town. **P**	AE DC MC V	●			■
RIVERBEND GRILL $$ Westin Hotel, 100 Iberville St. **Map** 4 B2. ▐ *(504) 553-5082.* A good place to enjoy a beautiful view of the Mississippi, the Grill serves large portions of New American food with a Cajun-Creole accent. The Sunday jazz brunch is highly recommended. **V**	AE DC MC V	●	■	●	
ROYAL CAFÉ $$ 700 Royal St. **Map** 4 C3. ▐ *(504) 528-9086.* Set in a beautiful building in the Quarter, this Cajun-Creole spot is a popular destination. If you sit on the balcony, you can enjoy the street musicians below.	AE DC MC V		■	●	

LOWER FRENCH QUARTER AND MARIGNY

	CREDIT CARDS	BAR AREA/COCKTAIL BAR	OUTDOOR EATING	CAJUN/CREOLE SPECIALTIES	GOOD WINE SELECTION
BELLA LUNA $$$ 914 N. Peters St, near Decatur and Dumaine sts. **Map** 5 D2. ▐ *(504) 529-1583.* Luxurious surroundings and a great view of the Mississippi River make this an excellent place for a romantic evening. The kitchen takes an eclectic approach, although the strongest accent is Italian. **V**	AE DC MC V	●		●	
CAFÉ MARIGNY $$ 640 Frenchman St. **Map** 5 E1. ▐ *(504) 945-4472.* A new location for chef Steve Zucker, offering Creole and Cajun dishes. The food just gets better and better and the extensive wine list shines. **V**	AE DC MC V	●		●	■
CAFÉ SBISA $$ 1011 Decatur St. **Map** 5 D1. ▐ *(504) 522-5565.* This is a delightful old Creole meeting place with the most authentic Creole cuisine. It has a veranda, picturesque patio, and a balcony overlooking the historic French Market. The exposed brick walls and mural give it a festive atmosphere.	AE DC MC V		■	●	■

CROISSANT D'OR PATISSERIE ⑤
617 Ursulines St. **Map** 5 D1. ☎ *(504) 524-4663.*
A French bakery hidden deep in the Quarter offers wonderful pastries along with soups, salads, and stuffed croissants. It is one of the best bargains in the city. **V**

ELIZABETH'S ⑤
601 Gallier St (at Chartres St). **Map** 5 D2. ☎ *(504) 944-9272.*
"Eat like a native," is the motto at this breakfast and brunch bar, where lots of rich, buttery offerings and one of the biggest oyster po'boys in the city mean you won't need any lunch.
AE DC MC V

FEELINGS CAFÉ ⑤⑤
2600 Chartres St. **Map** 5 E1. ☎ *(504) 945-2222.*
Away from the bustle of the Quarter, with a beautiful patio and intimate, romantic atmosphere, this café has been noted for its updated renditions of Creole favorites like chicken Clemenceau. There is live piano music on Friday and Saturday nights. 🎵
AE DC MC V

IRENE'S CUISINE ⑤⑤
539 St. Philip St. **Map** 5 D1. ☎ *(504) 529-8811.*
Snapshots, olive jars, garlic braids, and crockery decorate this cozy Italian-Creole restaurant. Irene's rosemary chicken is worth the wait. Reservations are not accepted. **V**
AE DC MC V

JIMMY BUFFETT'S MARGARITAVILLE ⑤
1104 Decatur St. **Map** 5 D1. ☎ *(504) 592-2565.*
A place to go for the music, not the food. Conveniently located in the French Quarter, it offers non-stop live music with no cover charge – and a great variety of margaritas. 🎵
AE DC MC V

LA PENICHE ⑤
1940 Dauphine St. **Map** 5 D1. ☎ *(504) 943-1460.*
Open 24 hours, this is a great stop for breakfast regardless of the time. Although there is a huge menu, omelets are the best option. **V**
AE DC MC V

MAXIMO'S ⑤⑤
1117 Decatur St. **Map** 5 E1. ☎ *(504) 586-8883.*
This slick northern Italian restaurant in the French Quarter offers an impressive wine list. Balcony tables are very romantic, but service can be slow at peak times. **V**
AE DC MC V

PERISTYLE ⑤⑤⑤
1041 Dumaine St. **Map** 4 C1. ☎ *(504) 593-9535.*
Chef Anne Kearney's 56-seat restaurant is a treat. Her modern approach to Continental cuisine results in a small but ever-changing menu. Reservations are essential. **V** **P** ● *Sun–Mon.*
AE DC MC V

PORT OF CALL ⑤
838 Esplanade Ave. **Map** 5 D1. ☎ *(504) 523-0120.*
This small restaurant located on the far edge of the French Quarter serves fantastic charbroiled hamburgers and the best baked potatoes.
AE DC MC V

PRALINE CONNECTION ⑤
542 Frenchman St. **Map** 5 E1. ☎ *(504) 943-3934.*
Great fried chicken, collard greens, black-eyed peas, cornbread, and other dishes are the best of their kind at very reasonable prices.
AE DC MC V

SANTA FÉ ⑤⑤
801 Frenchman St. **Map** 5 E1. ☎ *(504) 944-6854.*
This is a trendy Tex-Mex place offering a great variety of strong margaritas and spicy dishes. ● *Sun–Mon.*
AE DC MC V

SIAM CAFE ⑤
435 Esplanade Ave. **Map** 5 D1. ☎ *(504) 949-1750.*
Surrounded by the sights, sounds, and aromas of Thailand, Siam offers authentic Thai food, from vegetarian dishes to such specialties as Bangkok beef in oyster sauce. **V**
AE DC MC V

TUJAGUES ⑤⑤
823 Decatur St. **Map** 5 E1. ☎ *(504) 525-8676.*
This French Quarter Creole institution is the city's second-oldest restaurant. It offers seven-course meals built around such staples as shrimp Clemenceau or a consistently superb brisket of beef. **V**
AE DC MC V

<table>
<tr><td colspan="7"></td></tr>
</table>

	CREDIT CARDS	BAR AREA/COCKTAIL BAR	OUTDOOR EATING	CAJUN/CREOLE SPECIALTIES	GOOD WINE SELECTION

Price categories include a three course meal for one, half a bottle of house wine and all unavoidable extra charges such as sales tax and service:
Ⓢ under $25
ⓈⓈ $25–$35
ⓈⓈⓈ $35–$50
ⓈⓈⓈⓈ $50–$70
ⓈⓈⓈⓈⓈ over $70

CREDIT CARDS
Indicates which credit cards are accepted: AE American Express; DC Diners Club; MC MasterCard/Access; V Visa.

BAR AREA/COCKTAIL BAR
There is a bar area or cocktail bar within the restaurant.

OUTDOOR EATING
There are some tables on a patio or terrace.

CAJUN/CREOLE SPECIALTIES
The menu contains some Cajun and/or Creole specialties.

GOOD WINE SELECTION
Denotes a wide range of good wines.

WAREHOUSE AND CENTRAL BUSINESS DISTRICTS

		Credit Cards	Bar Area	Outdoor	Cajun/Creole	Wine
BAILEY'S ⓈⓈ Fairmont Hotel, 123 Baronne St. **Map** 4 B4. ☎ *(504) 529-4834.* Location is the best thing going for this place. It is convenient for a pre- or post-symphony stop. Its only two faults are inconsistent cooking and occasional slow service.		AE DC MC V	●			
BON TON CAFÉ ⓈⓈ 401 Magazine St. **Map** 4 C4. ☎ *(504) 524-3386.* Although a bit crowded, this Creole café is a good option for lunch. The staples are great crawfish dishes, bread pudding, and *étouffées (see p171).* ● *Sun.*		AE DC MC V			●	
EMERIL'S ⓈⓈⓈⓈ 800 Tchoupitoulas St. **Map** 4 C5. ☎ *(504) 528-9393.* Chef Emeril Lagasse's fantastic contemporary Louisiana cuisine makes this avant-garde – brick-and-glass walls, gleaming wood floors, and burnished-aluminum lamps – restaurant a special treat. 🔳 🔳 ● *Sun.*		AE DC MC V	●			■
HERBSAINT ⓈⓈ 701 St. Charles Ave. **Map** 4 B4. ☎ *(504) 524-4114.* Herbsaint's contemporary French/American menu is the new star in the Warehouse District. Most diners can't pass up the Boston creme pie.		AE DC MC V			●	■
KABBY'S ⓈⓈ New Orleans Hilton, 2 Poydras St. **Map** 4 B3. ☎ *(504) 584-3880.* Ask to sit by the window at this Cajun seafood restaurant, for there is a great view of the Mississippi River. The food, though, is rather ordinary and overpriced. 🅿		AE DC MC V	●		●	
LA GAULOISE ⓈⓈ Le Meridien Hotel, 614 Canal St. **Map** 4 B3. ☎ *(504) 527-6712.* Attractive hotel-based French bistro, where the frogs' legs and the onion soup are superb. It is also an excellent choice for Sunday brunch. 🅿		AE DC MC V	●			
LEMON GRASS ⓈⓈ 217 Camp St. **Map** 4 C4. ☎ *(504) 523-1200.* Gourmet Vietnamese cuisine, for when you get tired of fried catfish. The roast chicken and the Viet bird nest (seafood in a noodle bowl) are especially good, and the wine list is extensive.		AE DC MC V	●	■		■
MICHAUL'S ON ST. CHARLES ⓈⓈ 840 St. Charles Ave. **Map** 4 B4. ☎ *(504) 522-5517.* If you want really good Cajun food, fine music, and a free dance lesson, Michaul's is the place to go. The excellent crawfish pie is only one of the excellent entrées. Try one of the curious cocktails first. 🎵 ● *Sun.*		DC MC V			●	
MOTHER'S Ⓢ 401 Poydras St. **Map** 4 B3. ☎ *(504) 523-9656.* Since 1938 locals have lined up for great po'boys, red beans and rice, and ham biscuits. Service is cafeteria-style, and you can't beat the prices. 🔳		AE DC MC V			●	
PALACE CAFÉ ⓈⓈ 605 Canal St. **Map** 4 B2. ☎ *(504) 523-1661.* Colorfully crafted from a multistory building that was once the city's oldest music store, the Palace offers imaginative contemporary Creole dishes like crab chops and rabbit ravioli in piquant sauce.		AE DC MC V	●		●	■
SAZERAC ⓈⓈⓈ Fairmont Hotel, 123 Baronne St. **Map** 4 B4. ☎ *(504) 529-4733.* This faded Continental-French restaurant with Victorian decoration and piano music remains a hotel classic, but the food can be inconsistent. 🅿		AE DC MC V	●			

THE GRILL ROOM
$$$$$ AE DC MC V
Windsor Court Hotel, 300 Gravier St. **Map** 4 C3. **☏** *(504) 522-1992.*
Set in the elegant Windsor Court Hotel, The Grill Room offers ever-changing menus of European, American, and Asian food. You certainly pay for it, but it is one of the best in town.
T V P

THE VERANDA
$$ AE DC MC V
Hotel Inter-Continental, 444 St. Charles Ave. **Map** 4 B4. **☏** *(504) 585-4383.*
With elegant Old-South settings, the Veranda offers great Nova Scotia smoked salmon, marinated shrimps, Wiener Schnitzel, and an interesting pastry buffet. The breakfasts and Sunday buffets are quite attractive. **P**

GARDEN DISTRICT AND UPTOWN

BRIGTSEN'S
$$$ AE DC MC V
723 Dante St. **☏** *(504) 861-7610.*
The ever-changing menus add up to some of the best Creole-Cajun cooking you'll find anywhere. Lucky are the customers who can get one of the two tables in an enclosed sunroom out front. ● *Sun–Mon.*

CAFÉ ATCHAFALAYA
$ AE DC MC V
901 Louisiana Ave. **Map** 7 E3. **☏** *(504) 891-5271.*
This casual Garden District shrine to down-home Southern cooking offers fried green tomatoes, grillades, and grits to die for. Great breakfast spot for socializing on a Sunday morning. ● *Mon.*

CAFÉ PONTCHARTRAIN
$ AE DC MC V
Pontchartrain Hotel, 2031 St. Charles Ave. **Map** 4 B4. **☏** *(504) 524-0581.*
Located in the Pontchartrain Hotel, the eponymous coffee shop offers powerful breakfasts and delicious blueberry muffins.

CAMELLIA GRILL
$$$$ MC V
626 S. Carrollton St. **☏** *(504) 866-9573.*
There is often a wait for one of the 29 seats, but the food is worth it. Omelets, hamburgers, and pecan pie are all close to the best.

COMMANDER'S PALACE
$$$$ AE DC MC V
1403 Washington Ave. **Map** 7 F3. **☏** *(504) 899-8221.*
No restaurant captures New Orleans' gastronomic heritage and celebratory spirit as well as this one in a stately Garden District mansion. This restaurant is considered one of the best in New Orleans.
T V ♪

FIGARO'S
$ AE DC MC V
7900 Maple St. **☏** *(504) 866-0100.*
This pizzeria offers not only Italian- and American-style pizza but also other varieties with local toppings such as crawfish *étouffée.* **V**

JAMILA'S CAFÉ
$$ AE DC MC V
7808 Maple St. **☏** *(504) 866-4366.*
Romantic restaurant in the University area, where you can coo over the couscous and other North African dishes. Among the better ethnic restaurants in New Orleans. **V** ● *Mon.*

JOEY K'S RESTAURANT
$ AE DC MC V
3001 Magazine St. **Map** 8 A4. **☏** *(504) 891-0997.*
Inexpensive family standby, a Creole place where you can taste home-made New Orleans favorites. Try the simple, not the fancy, dishes. ● *Sun.*

KELSEY'S
$$ AE DC MC V
3923 Magazine St. **Map** 8 A4. **☏** *(504) 897-6722.*
The deep south Louisiana flavors of spicy jambalaya, Cajun ham, and rabbit are some of the best Cajun and Creole dishes anywhere. ● *Mon.*

MARTINIQUE BISTRO
$$ AE DC MC V
5908 Magazine St. **Map** 8 A4. **☏** *(504) 891-8495.*
Flavor over flash is the emphasis at this French bistro, featuring a Caribbean variation on New Orleans dining and a lovely outside patio.

PASCAL'S MANALE
$$ AE DC MC V
1838 Napoleon Ave. **Map** 7 D2. **☏** *(504) 895-4877.*
The home of BBQ shrimp and a New Orleans neighborhood institution, Pascal's serves Italian-Creole cuisine. The oyster bar is excellent.

For key to symbols see back flap

<table>
<tr><td colspan="2">

Price categories include a three course meal for one, half a bottle of house wine and all unavoidable extra charges such as sales tax and service:
Ⓢ under $25
ⓈⓈ $25–$35
ⓈⓈⓈ $35–$50
ⓈⓈⓈⓈ $50–$70
ⓈⓈⓈⓈⓈ over $70

</td></tr>
</table>

CREDIT CARDS
Indicates which credit cards are accepted: AE American Express; DC Diners Club; MC MasterCard/Access; V Visa.

BAR AREA/COCKTAIL BAR
There is a bar area or cocktail bar within the restaurant.

OUTDOOR EATING
There are some tables on a patio or terrace.

CAJUN/CREOLE SPECIALTIES
The menu contains some Cajun and/or Creole specialties.

GOOD WINE SELECTION
Denotes a wide range of good wines.

	Price	CREDIT CARDS	BAR AREA/COCKTAIL BAR	OUTDOOR EATING	CAJUN/CREOLE SPECIALTIES	GOOD WINE SELECTION
UGLESICH'S 1238 Baronne St. **Map** 4 A5. ☎ (504) 523-8571. The tough neighborhood should not deter you from this unique family-owned, lunch-only Cajun-Creole seafood restaurant serving fried, grilled, or sautéed seafood at its best.	Ⓢ	AE DC MC V			●	
UPPERLINE 1431 Upperline St. **Map** 7 D5. ☎ (504) 891-9822. Nestled uptown is a charming cozy bistro, whose culinary style begins with local products and ends up as contemporary Creole with a flair. Save room for one of the outrageous desserts. **V** ● *Mon.*	ⓈⓈⓈ	AE DC MC V	●		●	■
VAQUEROS 4938 Prytania St. **Map** 7 D4. ☎ (504) 891-6441. While you're in the neighborhood, stop by Vaqueros for some Southwestern-Mexican-Fusion cuisine. The tequila bar is awesome; pair a special margarita with an oyster burrito for a sensational meal.	ⓈⓈ	AE DC MC V	●			■

MID-CITY

	Price	CREDIT CARDS	BAR AREA/COCKTAIL BAR	OUTDOOR EATING	CAJUN/CREOLE SPECIALTIES	GOOD WINE SELECTION
BANGKOK CUISINE 4137 Carrollton Ave. **Map** 1 B4. ☎ (504) 482-3606. This cozy Carrollton/Mid-City Thai next to the Rock 'n' Bowl *(see p191)* offers good, authentic daily lunch specials and overall value. **V**	ⓈⓈ	AE DC MC V				
BENNACHIN 133 N. Carrollton Ave. **Map** 2 A2. ☎ (504) 486-1313. This storefront restaurant offers a variety of authentic African cuisine of the Bassa people of Cameroon and the Mandinka of Gambia. ● *Sun.*	Ⓢ	AE DC MC V				
CAFÉ DEGAS 3127 Esplanade Ave. **Map** 2 B2. ☎ (504) 945-5635. This is a quiet, romantic French country bistro with a lovely little patio in a relaxed atmosphere. The specialties are vegetarian dishes. A good place to go after visiting the New Orleans Museum of Art *(see pp120–23)*. **V**	ⓈⓈ	AE DC MC V	●	■		■
CHRISTIAN'S 3835 Iberville St. **Map** 2 A3. ☎ (504) 482-4924. Set in an elegant, converted church, this Mid-City restaurant serves classic French-Creole dishes and softshell crab in season. ● *Sun–Mon.*	ⓈⓈⓈ	AE DC MC V			●	
DEANIE'S SEAFOOD 1713 Lake Ave. ☎ (504) 834-1225. Expect huge portions of fried seafood, barbecued shrimp, grilled chicken, and steak platters. This place is often crowded and noisy. **V**	ⓈⓈ	AE DC MC V				
DOOKY CHASE 2301 Orleans Ave. **Map** 2 C4. ☎ (504) 821-0600. Unique Creole food in a homey and artistic atmosphere. Chef Leah Chase always comes up with great traditional Creole dishes. Excellent lunch buffet served daily. It's best to take a cab in this neighborhood.	ⓈⓈ	AE DC MC V	●		●	
FELLINI'S 900 N. Carrollton Ave. **Map** 6 A1. ☎ (504) 488-2147. This old gas station, converted to a restaurant, offers Mediterranean, Italian, and Turkish dishes as well as Cajun and Creole specialties. Over-sized sandwiches, pizzas, soup, and a variety of pasta dishes, too. **V**	ⓈⓈ	AE DC Mc V	●		●	
GABRIELLE 3201 Esplanade Ave. **Map** 2 B2. ☎ (504) 948-6233. This rather small, intimate contemporary Creole place is a hit – thanks to its marvelous blends of earthy and spicy south Louisiana ingredients. Servings are generous and sauces rich. Reservations are essential. **V**	ⓈⓈⓈ	AE DC MC V			●	■

GENGHIS KHAN $$
44053 Tulane Ave. **Map** 2 B4. **C** *(504) 482-4044.*
Korean food, often accompanied by live classical music on weekends. It
has seen better days, but the whole fried fish is still excellent. Take a cab
to avoid on-street parking. **V** **♫** **●** *Mon.*
AE DC MC V

KATIE'S $
3701 Iberville St. **Map** 2 A3. **C** *(504) 488-6582.*
This family-run Mid-City lunch stop offers good Cajun-Italian home
cooking including the excellent fried catfish. Service is slow, but the wait
is worth it. **V** **●** *Sun.*
AE DC MC V

LIUZZA'S RESTAURANT AND BAR $
3636 Bienville St. **Map** 2 A3. **C** *(504) 482-9120.*
Huge frosted mugs of cold beer are always on tap at this popular Mid-
City institution serving fried seafood and Italian dishes.
V **●** *Sun.*

MANDINA'S $$
3800 Canal St. **Map** 2 A3. **C** *(504) 482-9179.*
This classic Creole seafood restaurant with an old-fashioned bar rewards
the wait with large portions of good food, especially great oyster and
shrimp po'boys *(see p168)* and wonderful trout *amandine.*

RUSSELL'S MARINA GRILL $
8555 Pontchartrain Blvd. **C** *(504) 282-9999.*
A popular lakefront family place, offering traditional American dishes
including a superb onion mum (deep fried onion). The perfect place for
Sunday brunch. **V**
AE DC MC V

RUTH'S CHRIS STEAK HOUSE $$$
711 N. Broad Ave. **Map** 2 B2. **C** *(504) 486-0810.*
This is where the Ruth's chain began – steaks are an art form here.
Every item on the menu is prepared with loving care, so order
your filet rare and enjoy. Also try the duck or the enormous
crab cakes. **P**
AE DC MC V

TAVERN ON THE PARK $$
900 City Park Ave. **Map** 2 A1. **C** *(504) 486-3333.*
This restaurant has charming old-world decor and a beautiful view of the
City Park oaks. Although the steak and seafood menu is a bit
unimaginative and expensive, it is one of the few options near City Park.
● *Sun–Mon.*
AE DC MC V

WEST END CAFÉ $
8536 Pontchartrain Blvd. **C** *(504) 288-0711.*
This is a casual and friendly old favorite serving good, home-cooked
seafood at very reasonable prices. It has a marvelous view of Lake
Pontchartrain.
AE DC MC V

BEYOND NEW ORLEANS

A LA CARTE $$
301 Heymann Blvd, Lafayette. **C** *(337) 235-8493.*
At this casual, atmospheric restaurant, Louisiana specialties such as lump
crab West Indies, shrimp remoulade, and corn and crab bisque are
offered. Live piano on Fridays. **●** *Sat–Sun.*
AE DC MC V

ALESI'S ITALIAN RESTAURANT $$
4110 Johnston St, Lafayette. **C** *(337) 984-1823.*
Lafayette's original Italian restaurant and pizza house, founded in 1957. It
is famous for its great Sicilian pasta and pizza. **V**
AE DC MC V

ANDREA'S $$$
3100 19th St at Ridgelake, Metairie. **C** *(504) 834-8583.*
Andrea's offers free transportation to and from the restaurant and some
of the best Italian food in the South. The menu will convince you that
there's more to New Orleans cuisine than Creole and French dishes. **P**
AE DC MC V

ANJO'S $$
1507 Kaliste Saloom, Lafayette. **C** *(337) 989-1977.*
A deliciously different coffee shop and bakery serving exquisite
European cakes and pastries, teas, and coffee. It is also a great option
for lunch.
AE DC MC V

Price categories include a three course meal for one, half a bottle of house wine and all unavoidable extra charges such as sales tax and service:
Ⓢ under $25
ⓈⓈ $25–$35
ⓈⓈⓈ $35–$50
ⓈⓈⓈⓈ $50–$70
ⓈⓈⓈⓈⓈ over $70

CREDIT CARDS
Indicates which credit cards are accepted: AE American Express; DC Diners Club; MC MasterCard/Access; V Visa.

BAR AREA/COCKTAIL BAR
There is a bar area or cocktail bar within the restaurant.

OUTDOOR EATING
There are some tables on a patio or terrace.

CAJUN/CREOLE SPECIALTIES
The menu contains some Cajun and/or Creole specialties.

GOOD WINE SELECTION
Denotes a wide range of good wines.

	Price	Credit Cards	Bar Area/Cocktail Bar	Outdoor Eating	Cajun/Creole Specialties	Good Wine Selection
ANTIQUE ROSEVILLE TEAROOM 2007 Freyou Rd, New Iberia. ☎ (337) 367-3000. A restaurant and tearoom, serving lunch and tea only, it has a nice antique and souvenir shop. A beautiful antebellum residence, with a 4-acre garden filled with herbs and flowering shrubs. ● Sun–Mon.	ⓈⓈ	MC V		■	●	
ANTLER'S 555 Jefferson St, Lafayette. ☎ (337) 234-8877. Great place for lunch in downtown Lafayette. The menu includes a huge selection of po'boys, salads, seafood, and Cajun specialties. ● Sun.	ⓈⓈ	AE DC MC V			●	
BARACCA'S 3502 Ambassador Caffery Pkwy, Lafayette. ☎ (337) 988-6119. An Italian restaurant with a Louisiana accent, its main dish is the Bayou Italia (fettuccini smothered in cream sauce, covered with crawfish tails), plus seafood, pizza, and pasta.	ⓈⓈ	AE DI MC V	●		●	
BAYLEY'S SEA FOOD & GRILL 5520-A Johnston St, Lafayette. ☎ (337) 988-6464. This comfortable restaurant offers a large menu of international dishes. With its relaxed atmosphere, it is perfect for a family lunch or dinner. Sunday's champagne brunch is a treat.	ⓈⓈ	AE DC MC V	●			
BAYOU BOUDIN AND CRACKLIN' 100 Mills Ave, Lafayette. ☎ (337) 332-6158. Set in an 1869 residence on Bayou Teche, this small traditional restaurant offers Cajun specialties in an authentic Cajun atmosphere. ♫	ⓈⓈ			●	●	
BIXBY'S BAGEL COMPANY 5445 Johnston St, Lafayette. ☎ (337) 989-8683. A healthy alternative, this bagel restaurant offers three varieties of soups, three of kinds of salads, bagel sandwiches, and low-fat pastries. V	ⓈⓈ	AE DC MC V				
CAFÉ VERMILIONVILLE 1316 Pinhook Rd, Lafayette. ☎ (337) 237-0100. A stately, 19th-century Acadian inn houses this casually elegant restaurant offering fine French and Cajun seafood dishes. The fried soft-shell crabs with crawfish fettuccine, the Kahlua-grilled shrimp, and the andouille gumbo are superb. ♫	ⓈⓈⓈ	AE MC V			●	■
CHALET BRANDT RESTAURANT 7655 Old Hammond Hwy, Baton Rouge. ☎ (225) 927-6040. Surrounded by pines and cypress trees, Chalet Brandt offers fine continental cuisine and an eclectic decor. ● Sun.	ⓈⓈⓈ	AE DC MC V			●	■
CHICAGO'S STEAKS, BAR, & GRILL 3723 Government St, Baton Rouge. ☎ (225) 267-5550. This steakhouse offers a good variety of grilled meat, poultry, and shellfish. It also serves salads and personalized steak cuts. ● Sun.	ⓈⓈⓈ	AE MC V				
THE CHIMES 3357 Highland Rd, Baton Rouge. ☎ (225) 383-1754. Here you can get a different lunch menu every day, plus homemade soups, sandwiches, po'boys, and fresh crawfish. You can choose between 120 different beers from all over the world.	ⓈⓈ	AE DC MC V			●	■
CLEMENTINE'S RESTAURANT 113 E Main St, New Iberia. ☎ (337) 560-1007. Classic south Louisiana and Cajun cooking offering seafood, salad bar, and a wide selection of cocktails. ♿	ⓈⓈⓈ	AE DC MC V	●		●	■

COPELAND'S OF NEW ORLEANS $$$ AE DC MC V
4957 Essen Lane, Baton Rouge. (225) 769-1800.
Tasty appetizers, plus a selection of shellfish, chicken, meats, hamburgers, salads, pasta, and desserts. Fine service for lunch and dinner. **V**

CRISPY CAJUN $$ AE DC MC V
941 E Laurel Ave, Eunice. (337) 457-9292.
Seafood is the house specialty, with a large variety of crawfish dishes.
There is a decent selection of domestic and imported wines. ● Sun.

DiNARDO'S ITALIAN RESTAURANT $$$ AE DC MC V
1881 Highland Rd, Baton Rouge. (225) 753-3458.
Italian cuisine. The menu includes meats, shellfish, seafood, and chicken.
Wide selection of fine wines and a large salad bar. ● Mon.

DON'S SEAFOOD & STEAK HOUSE $$$ AE DC MC V
6823 Airline Hwy, Baton Rouge. (225) 357-0601.
An institution since 1934, Don's main dishes are prepared with the
freshest seafood and meats. Two other locations are in Lafayette.

DRUSILLA SEAFOOD RESTAURANT $$$ AE DC MC V
3482 Drusilla Lane, Suite D, Baton Rouge. (225) 923-0896.
This restaurant's cuisine, as its name states, is based on shellfish and
seafood. It also offers meats, and a variety of salads and low-calorie
dishes. Popular for its take-out specials.

ENOLA PRUDHOMME'S CAJUN CAFÉ $$$$ AE MC V
Interstate 49, near Carencro, Lafayette. (337) 896-7964.
Country Cajun café in a little frame cottage, just north of Lafayette. The
best dishes are the pan-fried rabbit in cream sauce, and the eggplant
(aubergine) *pirogi* (ravioli-like turnovers).

FOTI'S OYSTER BAR/RESTAURANT $ AE DC MC V
108 S Main St, St. Martinville. (337) 394-3058.
Right on Main Street you'll find the very best fried seafood, boiled
crawfish, and raw or fried oysters. No frills, but this is where the locals
eat. Try the fresh-brewed Cajun coffee. ● Sun.

HUNAN CHINESE RESTAURANT $$$ AE DS MC V
4215 S. Sherwood Forest Blvd, Baton Rouge. (225) 291-6868.
A colorfully decorated place, with a very generous lunch buffet and
traditional Chinese food. Dinner portions are large and can be shared. **V**

JUBAN'S RESTAURANT $$$ AE MC
3739 Perkins Rd, Baton Rouge. (225) 346-8422.
With progressive Creole cuisine, this restaurant offers a traditional New
Orleans atmosphere. It also has a charming courtyard bar. 🎵 ● Sun.

LAGNIAPPE TOO CAFÉ $$$ AE MC V
204 E Main St, New Iberia. (337) 365-9419.
Original recipes combine classical French cooking with Cajun cuisine.
The special decor creates an intimate atmosphere. ● Sat.

RANDOL'S RESTAURANT AND DANCEHALL $ AE DC MC V
2320 Kaliste Saloom Rd, Lafayette. (337) 981-7080.
This is the best place in Lafayett for great crawfish, good music and
dancing, and the best, spiciest Bloody Mary's in Louisiana.

NEW PALACE CAFÉ $$
167 W. Landry St, Opelousas. (337) 942-2142.
Since 1927, the specialties have been Cajun and gumbo cuisines.
Reasonably priced, it offers tasty grilled catfish with crawfish *étouffée*,
meats, and the famous Pete's fried chicken salad.

PREJEAN'S $$$ AE MC V
3480 US 167N, Next to Evangeline Downs. (337) 896-3247.
This small restaurant, a favorite with locals, offers great Cajun rack of elk
and American buffalo *au poivre*, along with an authentic atmosphere and
live Cajun music every night. 🎵

VICTOR'S CAFETERIA $
109 W. Main St, New Iberia. (337) 369-9924.
A great place for local color and excellent, homestyle Cajun food.
Rodrigue prints decorate the walls, and the coffee is local and strong. **V**

Shopping in New Orleans

S HOPPING IN NEW ORLEANS is a unique experience that is much more involved than simply making a purchase. Walking from store to store through such landmark streets as Royal and Magazine provides a glimpse of the city's atmosphere and unique culture. Among the city's best buys are antiques and silverware, antiquarian

Antique porcelain jar

books, Creole and Cajun cooking spices and foodstuffs, vintage clothing and costumes, African arts and crafts, hats, masks, and CDs of local musicians. At the city's fine department stores, the latest *haute couture* and funky clothes are available. With so many shops available, there is something to suit all tastes; the following pages highlight the very best.

Jack Sutton Gallery on Royal Street

WHEN TO SHOP

G ENERALLY, stores in the Central Business District, along Magazine Street, and in the French Quarter, operate from 9am to 5pm or 10am to 6pm. Many do open on Sundays, but always call in advance. Some tourist-oriented shops in the Quarter stay open late.

HOW TO PAY

M AJOR credit cards are accepted everywhere and there are plenty of Automated Teller Machines (ATMs) from which to get cash for a small fee. Traveler's checks are also accepted.

SALES TAX REIMBURSEMENT

F OREIGN VISITORS can get reimbursement of the 9 percent sales tax on tangible goods, but you must show the vendor your passport and ask for a refund voucher. At the airport go to the Louisiana Tax Free Shopping Refund Center and show your passport, sales receipts,

refund vouchers, and round-trip air ticket (which may be up to a maximum of a 90-day trip). If you don't get reimbursed at the airport, send copies of everything, plus an explanation, to Louisiana Tax Free Shopping Refund Center, P.O. Box 20125, New Orleans, LA 70141.

MALLS AND SHOPPING CENTERS

T HERE ARE three major downtown malls. Canal Place *(see p94)* is the most upscale. Macy's anchors the New Orleans Center at Poydras and Loyola. Riverwalk Marketplace *(see p89)* is the largest, stretching several blocks along the Mississippi River between Canal and Julia streets. It features more than 140 stores.

ART AND ANTIQUES

R OYAL STREET is famous for its antiques. Browse in

any of the stores here for a vision of the magnificent objects that furnished mansions and Creole homes – rosewood bedroom suites, massive armoires, crystal chandeliers, boulle-style furnishings, silverware, china, and *objets d'art*. There are dozens of these shops, but here are some top choices. **Animal Arts** has wonderful majolica animals, terrific jardinieres, and some exquisite oyster plates. **Dixon & Dixon** is known for its tall-case clocks, while **Gerald D. Katz** has some very alluring antique jewelry. For exquisite French furnishings go to **Jack Sutton. Kiel's** has been in business since 1899, selling gorgeous 18th- and 19th-century French and English furniture. **Lucullus** specializes in antiques associated with cooking, including burnished copper pans. Whatever is displayed at **M.S. Rau** is top of the line, whether it is music boxes or Sevres. You could spend the whole day just examining antique paintings, clocks, chandeliers,

Riverwalk Marketplace shopping mall

and furniture on the five floors at **Manheim Galleries**. **Moss**, **Rothschild's**, **Royal**, **Whisnant**, and **Waldhorn & Adler** are yet more names to look out for – all are treasure troves containing countless beautiful objects to tempt you to buy.

There are plenty of galleries in the French Quarter showing a wide variety of local and international artists. Another concentration of more cutting-edge galleries like **Arthur Roger**, **Simonne Stern**, and **Marguerite Oestreicher** can be found on Julia Street in the Warehouse District. On Napoleon Street, also check out **Carol Robinson**.

BOOKS

NEW ORLEANS has several notable modern bookstores, but it is best known for its many fine antiquarian bookstores containing great stocks of regional titles, plus first editions and other specialties. In the French Quarter, look for **Dauphine Street Books**, which is filled with fine-quality titles. **Beckham's** is an interesting musty store that also sells classical LPs, CDs, and sheet music. Uptown, check out the selections at **George Herget**, which also has postcards and sheet music, and **Great Acquisitions**, which lives up to its name. **Bookstar** is a large chain store with a broad selection of books and magazines. First editions of Faulkner line the wooden shelves at **Faulkner House Books**, located in the house where William Faulkner wrote his first novel. **Maple Street Books** is another literary store where local writers are welcomed, and their books are prominently displayed. Anne Rice *(see p107)* lives right around the corner from the **Garden District Bookshop**, which has all of her titles, many of them signed.

CRAFTS

SITUATED ON the third floor of Canal Place, **Rhino Gallery** is the best place to see a broad selection of ceramics, jewelry, textiles, and glass by regional artists. On Magazine visit the **Shadyside Pottery**, where master potter Charlie Bohn creates Japanese-style bowls. Glass lovers should not miss the **New Orleans School of Glassworks**, where they can observe glassblowers at work and purchase the amazing results. **Sullivan Stained Glass** does mostly commissions, but can also craft some well-made high-quality etched and stained-glass decorations. A broad range of quality crafts can also be found at the **Ariodante Contemporary Craft Gallery**. Polished woodcrafted toys, games, sculptures, boxes, and all sorts of models fill the store at the **Idea Factory**.

African mask at the Idea Factory

FASHION

WITH SAKS FIFTH AVENUE, Macy's, and Dillards all in the center of town, New Orleans is an excellent place to find designer and casual clothes. As well as these, the city also boasts some very fine local designers who produce romantic accessories and alluring feminine fashions. It is also a costume designer's dream city.

Soft and flowing fabrics are used for the ultra-romantic range of clothes found at **The Grace Note**. If you want to indulge in silk, satin, and velvet for the boudoir then visit the **House of Lounge**. **Le Fleur de Paris** makes and sells stunning hats decorated with ribbons, feathers, fruits, and flowers, plus equally fetching dresses, blouses, and other clothes.

Uptown, **Yvonne LaFleur** designs romantic stylish hats plus stunning evening gowns; everything in the store is beautifully displayed and everything is of fine quality.

At the downriver end of Decatur there is a cluster of vintage clothing stores. Some of the finest best-preserved vintage fashions hang on the racks at **Jim Smiley**. **Funky Monkey** is the place to pick out an outrageous outfit for the club back home.

On the Other Hand, on Hampson Street, occupies several cottages and offers room after room of silk, satin, and velvet dresses and gowns decorated with sequins, feathers, and pearls. Shoes, furs, wedding dresses – whatever you want, you'll find a fine selection here.

Southerners are well known for loving hats, and **Meyer the Hatter** has been catering to their needs for more than 100 years. This store has every conceivable hat, including Stetsons, derbies, fedoras, and Kangol berets, all of which are well crafted and reasonably priced.

Fashion feathers at Funky Monkey

An array of Louisiana hot sauces

FOOD

E VERYONE WANTS to take some tasty souvenirs home, and the city is positively loaded with stores selling hot sauces and all the other appurtenances of New Orleans cuisine. Some shops are better than others and don't overcharge. **Central Grocery** *(see p76)* is an historic store, which serves the best *muffuletta (see p168)* in the city. The front of the store is jammed with mustards, sauces, pastas, and all kinds of Italian deli items. **Creole Delicacies Gourmet Shop** and the **New Orleans School of Cooking** both offer short cooking classes and also sell everything you need in the kitchen.

Want to take home some crawfish, crab, or andouille? Go to the **Big Fisherman** on Magazine, where the locals go for their fare. Many places make and sell pralines, but the best can be found at **Aunt Sally's Praline Shop** at the French Market. Here you can watch pralines being mixed and made before your eyes.

GIFTS AND SPECIALTY STORES

S INCE 1931 **Hové Parfumeur** has been sweetly perfuming residents in its lovely old-fashioned store. Maps and prints are attractive gifts at reasonable prices, and **Centuries** has thousands of them cataloged by topic – birds, botanicals, caricatures, maps, and views. If you've fallen in love with the gas lamps that flicker in the

Quarter and elsewhere in the city, then stop by **Bevolo Gas and Electric Lights** to purchase one for your own front door. There are plenty of tarot readers operating in Jackson Square, but if you want to have a private consultation go to **Bottom of the Cup Tea Room & Gifts**.

New Orleans has strong connections with the Caribbean, and there are several fine cigar-making stores in the city. At the **Cigar Factory**, visitors can watch the cigars being rolled and cut, and select their choice stogie from the humidor. **Epitome** also has all the great cigar and cigarette names: Don Diego, Monte Christo, and Dunhill.

Many visitors will want to take a Mardi Gras *(see pp24–5)* souvenir home. Masks and other regalia are available at several stores. The best place to find a flattering art mask is at the fair before Mardi Gras, but if you're not there at that time, then stop by at **Rumors**. Try the **Rodrigue**

A gifts and souvenirs stand at the popular Flea Market

Gallery for the famous Blue Dog art. **New Orleans Silversmiths** has an array of silver items that make fine gifts – salt cellars, key rings, letter openers, tea strainers, and more. **Scriptura** is the place to go for beautiful paper products, from journals and sketch books to handmade papers and calligraphy sets.

JEWELRY

T HE OLDEST PLACE to buy jewelry in New Orleans is **Adlers & Sons**, but there are several designers working here and producing some attractive handcrafted jewelry that is reasonably priced. Two such designers are **Mignon Faget**, who has three stores in the area and makes organic-looking pieces in gold and silver, and **Ruby Ann Tobar-Blanco**, who has been working for more than 25 years producing delicate, eye-catching pieces. Both local and national jewelers are represented at **Symmetry**, which has a large display of high-quality rings, necklaces, and bracelets; they will also custom-make something for you.

MUSIC

M USIC IS THE LIFEBLOOD of New Orleans. The best place to explore local music from jazz to zydeco is the **Louisiana Music Factory**, which has knowledgeable staff, plus listening stations. They stock a full range of artists, which are well cataloged. Free performances are often given on Saturday afternoons here.

Both **Tower Records** and **Virgin Megastore** are also in town. Virgin is the larger of the two, and has an appealing café. If you're a collector of vinyl, the place to browse is **Rock & Roll Collectibles**, which offers vintage LPs in all musical categories. **Werlein's** is a historic music name in New Orleans. Go to admire the trombones, cornets, banjos, drums, guitars, steel washboards, and other Cajun staples.

DIRECTORY

ART AND ANTIQUES

Animal Arts
1139 Arabella St.
Map 6 C3. 895-0518.

Arthur Roger
432 Julia St. **Map 4 C5**
522-1999.

Carol Robinson
840 Napoleon Ave.
Map 7 D4. 895-6130.

Dixon & Dixon
237 Royal St. **Map 5 D1.**
524-0282.

Gerald D. Katz
505 Royal St. **Map 5 D1.**
524-5050.

Jack Sutton
315 Royal St. **Map 5 D1.**
522-0555.

Kiel's Antiques
325 Royal St. **Map 5 D1.**
522-4552.

Lucullus
610 Chartres St.
Map 4 C2. 528-9620.

Manheim Galleries
403 Royal St. **Map 5 D1.**
568-1901.

Marguerite Oestreicher
626 Julia St. **Map 4 C5.**
581-9253

Moss Antiques
411 Royal St. **Map 5 D1.**
522-3981.

M.S. Rau
630 Royal St. **Map 5 D1.**
523-5660.

Royal Antiques
309 Royal St. **Map 5 D1.**
524-7033.

Rothschild's
241 Royal St. **Map 5 D1.**
523-5816.

Simonne Stern
518 Julia St. **Map 4 C5.**
529-1118.

Waldhorn & Adler
343 Royal St. **Map 5 D1.**
581-6379.

Whisnant Galleries
222 Chartres St.
Map 5 C2. 524-9766.

BOOKS

Beckham's
228 Decatur St.
Map 5 D1. 522-9875.

Bookstar
414 N Peters St.
Map 5 D2. 523-6411.

Dauphine Street Books
410 Dauphine St.
Map 5 D1. 529-2333.

Faulkner House Books
624 Pirate's Alley.
Map 5 D2. 524-2940.

Garden District Book Shop
2727 Prytania St.
Map 7 F4. 895-2266.

George Herget
3109 Magazine St.
Map 7 F4.
891-5595.

Great Acquisitions
8200 Hampson St,
Suite 302.
861-8707.

Maple Street Bookshop
7523 Maple St.
866-4916.

CRAFTS

Ariodante Contemporary Craft Gallery
535 Julia St. **Map 4 C5.**
524-3233.

Idea Factory
838 Chartres St. **Map 5 D1.**
524-5195.

New Orleans School of Glassworks
727 Magazine St.
Map 4 C5.
529-7277.

Rhino Gallery
Canal Place, third floor.
Map 4 C3.
523-7945.

Shadyside Pottery
3823 Magazine St.
Map 7 F4.
897-1710.

Sullivan
3827 Magazine St.
Map 7 F4.
895-6720.

FASHION

Funky Monkey
3127 Magazine St.
Map 7 F4. 899-5587.

House of Lounge
2044 Magazine St.
Map 7 F4. 671-8300.

Jim Smiley
2001 Magazine St.
Map 7 F4. 528-9449.

Le Fleur de Paris
712 Royal St. **Map 5 D1.**
525-1899.

Meyer the Hatter
120 St. Charles Ave. **Map 4 B4.** 525-1048.

On the Other Hand
8126 Hampson St.
861-0159.

The Grace Note
900 Royal St. **Map 5 D1.**
522-1513.

Yvonne LaFleur
8131 Hampson St.
Map 5 D5. 866-9666.

FOOD

Aunt Sally's Praline Shop
810 Decatur St.
Map 5 D1.
944-6090.

Creole Delicacies Gourmet Shop
1 Poydras St
Map 2 C5. 523-6425.

New Orleans School of Cooking
524 St. Louis.
Map 4 C2.
525-2665.

The Big Fisherman
3301 Magazine St.
Map 7 F4.
897-9907.

GIFTS AND SPECIALTY STORES

Bevolo Gas and Electric Lights
521 Conti St. **Map 4 C2.**
522-9485.

Bottom of the Cup Tea Rooms & Gifts
732 Royal St. **Map 5 D1.**
523-1204.

Centuries
517 St. Louis St. **Map 4 C2.** 568-9491.

Cigar Factory
415 Decatur. **Map 5 E1.**
568-1003.

Epitome
631 Royal St. **Map 5 D1.**
523-2844 .

Hové Parfumeur
824 Royal St **Map 5 D1.**
525-7827.

Rodrigue Gallery
721 Royal St. **Map 5 E1.**
581-4244.

Rumors
513 Royal St. **Map 5 D1.**
525-0292.

Scriptura
5423 Magazine St.
Map 7 F4. 897-1555.

JEWELRY

Adlers & Sons
722 Canal St. **Map 4 B3.**
523-5292.

Mignon Faget
710 Dublin St.
865-7361.

New Orleans Silversmiths
600 Chartres St. **Map 5 C2.** 522-8333.

Ruby Ann Tobar-Blanco
3005 Magazine. **Map 7 F4.** 897-0811.

Symmetry
8138 Hampson St.
861-9925.

MUSIC

Louisiana Music Factory
210 Decatur St. **Map 5 E1.** 586-1094.

Rock & Roll Collectibles
1214 Decatur St. **Map 5 E1.** 561-5683.

Tower Records
410 N Peters St **Map 5 D2.** 529-4411.

Virgin Megastore
600 Decatur St. **Map 5 E1.** 671-8100.

Werlein's
214 Decatur St. **Map 5 E1.** 883-5080.

What to Buy in New Orleans

Mardi Gras mask

NEW ORLEANS is the best place to discover original small boutiques that are owned by artists and designers of all sorts – jewelers, painters, potters, milliners, clothes designers, and many more – rather than large department stores. In addition to these, there are various tourist memorabilia and trinket stores, which sell T-shirts, rubber alligators, Mardi Gras beads, and other typical kitsch souvenirs. However, to experience the quintessential New Orleans, look out for the things that New Orleans does best – cuisine, cocktails, and music.

Mardi Gras poster

Flea market stands with Mardi Gras souvenirs

MARDI GRAS MEMORABILIA

Mardi Gras is New Orleans' biggest and longest party, and there are plenty of souvenirs that visitors can take home. Masks are the most alluring, and they can be found in shops and stalls throughout the city. Prices can range from as little as $20 to hundreds of dollars for the really gorgeous feather masks; the latter are handmade by individual artists who are often theater costume designers. Less authentic trinkets include beads, mugs, T-shirts, and other typical souvenirs.

African Art and Crafts

The heritage of New Orleans' African cultures can be found in a number of shops. Here you can buy African art and crafts, including masks, drums, sculptures, pipes, tables, and items of personal jewelry.

African wood drum

Wood–carved African sculptures

Music

Music is the lifeblood of the city, and a musical souvenir is essential. Record stores sell recordings of great artists playing traditional and modern jazz, gospel, blues, R&B, Cajun, and zydeco.

Hand-Rolled Cigars

New Orleans is close to the Caribbean, both physically and culturally, and has a strong tradition of importing Caribbean cigars. There are several stores where cigars are still hand-rolled. Even a single cigar or a rather expensive box make a perfect gift for any cigar aficionado.

Voodoo Accoutrements

New Orleans is the one place in the United States where the voodoo religion is openly practiced and celebrated (see p83). Supplies of the materials needed to perform voodoo healings and other rituals – candles, gris-gris to control the boss, ensure safe travel, or promote love, voodoo dolls, and more – can be purchased at several shops in the French Quarter. These always make colorful and unusual gifts.

Voodoo candle

Gris-gris bags

Antiques

New Orleans is famous for its tradition of dealing in fine antiques. You can find 18th-century furniture and jewelry, as well as other decorative objects, for all tastes and prices.

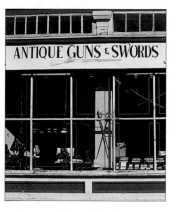

Antique shop on Royal Street

THE FLAVORS OF LOUISIANA

Louisiana is famous the world over for spicy, flavorsome cuisine *(see pp168–171)*. Most visitors want to take some of it home and duplicate those flavors in their own kitchens. In many stores, shelves are lined with hot sauces such as Tabasco, Crystal, Panola, and Cajun Chef. Strands of peppers and garlic and bottles of Cajun and Creole season-ing can be found at the French Market and numerous stores in the area. Here are some of the city's quintessential food gifts.

Roux mix for gumbos

Hats

Southerners and New Orleanians in particular love hats. There are several stores selling terrific ones for both men and women (see p183). They stock every available kind, from classic fedoras, derbies, and Stetsons to berets, French legion caps, and squashy barman hats.

Olive salad dressing

Beignet flour mix

An instant traditional dish

ENTERTAINMENT IN NEW ORLEANS

P EOPLE COME TO NEW ORLEANS to party. Twenty-four hours a day, seven days a week, drinking, eating, strolling around, and listening to music is what New Orleans is all about. Residents are relaxed and easygoing, and they operate their establishments on the same kind of basis. Two French phrases typify the Big Easy: *lagniappe*, which means "something more than expected," and the motto

Marching band tuba player

"Laissez les bons temps rouler!" or "Let the good times roll!" From the blatant Bourbon Street bars and jazz clubs to the riverfront casinos, from the languorous restaurants in the Garden District to the boiled crawfish and two-step music at a Cajun dance hall, New Orleans promises that you will have a good time. For a selectio of of New Orleans' best jazz venues, see pp192–93.

Street musicians playing jazz on Jackson Square

ENTERTAINMENT GUIDES

F OR INFORMATION on what is happening in the city, see such publications as the Friday edition of the *Times-Picayune*, *Offbeat*, and *Gambit*. The official Louisiana Tour Guide (call 800-99-GUMBO for a free copy) is a helpful booklet for where to go, eat, stay, and what to do.

Liquor laws in the city are flexible; it is fine to drink on the street, just as long as you carry a plastic "go cup", provided by almost all the bars. Some of the bars and music venues are outside the French Quarter, such as parts of Mid-City and the area north of Rampart. Stay with a group after dark, or just hop into a cab. Many jazz clubs often do not begin their sets until 10pm or later. Relax, sip out of your "go cup", and join the party atmosphere on the sidewalk. Outside, the music is just as loud, it's free, and the air is a lot fresher.

TICKETS

T HE EASIEST WAY TO BUY tickets for concerts, football games, theatrical productions, or other events is to call the relevant box office or Ticketmaster. Most of the major hotels and B&Bs have a concierge who can facilitate booking tickets. The New Orleans Metropolitan Convention and Visitors' Bureau (800-672-6124) offers free advice; also check the free entertainment guides available at kiosks and in hotel lobbies for student and senior citizen discounts.

ROCK, BLUES, AND OTHER MUSIC VENUES

A LL MUSIC VENUES charge an entry fee, but cafés and bars rarely do; on some nights of the week, however, a cover charge may be required.

A colorful crowd gathers at **Café Brasil** to listen and dance to whatever is playing

– funk, Latin, or reggae. The party usually spills out on to the street. **House of Blues** *(see p193)* is the largest and most expensive of the clubs. It features big names from out of town, plus major local entertainers, and a rousing gospel brunch on Sundays. The on-site restaurant is first rate.

Howlin' Wolf is a barebones rock music club where superstars Jackson Brown and Jimmy Paige have been know to drop in for a jamming session. You can also see emerging bands here. You can always find free musical entertainment at **Jimmy Buffett's Margaritaville Café**. **Jimmy's Music Club** is the oldest in the city and puts on an array of sounds, from Latin to hip-hop and reggae. **Tipitina's** (Uptown) was the best-known music club until the arrival of the chain House of Blues, which has lured away some of the big names.

Jazz parade and band in the streets of the French Quarter

Fire fountain in Pat O Brien's on St. Peter Street

It is still legendary as the shrine to Professor Longhair, Dr. John, the Radiators, and many other popular groups. On Sunday afternoon there is usually a *fais-do-do* (Cajun dance). A young hip crowd (with piercings and day-glo hair) rocks with two-step at the **Mermaid Lounge**.

Thursday night is the night to go out to **Vaughn's Lounge** in Bywater; Kermit Ruffins cooks up an excellent barbecue before entertaining with his band. For New Orleans charm, top DJs from around the world, and high-energy dancing try **Club 735** on Bourbon Street. **Vic's Kangaroo Café** has blues and R&B on weekends with no cover charge.

Bars

YOU CAN DRINK around the clock in New Orleans; there are many, many bars catering to the local passion for a good beer or a finely shaken cocktail. Try the historic hotel bars, such as the **Sazerac Bar** at the Fairmont, or the **Polo Club Lounge** at the Windsor Court, or the Garden District's **Pontchartrain Hotel**.

Well-made cocktails and piano music can be enjoyed at the **Carousel Bar** in the Monteleone, which is in fact a colorful revolving carousel.

Two beloved bars in the French Quarter are the **Napoleon House** *(see p59)* and **Lafitte's Blacksmith Shop** *(see p78)*. Both places offer authentic New Orleans decor – and locals frequent these places too. Head to

Pat O'Brien's to sample a Hurricane, the rum and fruit drink served in a tall glass. There's often a long line to get in, but once inside, there are three bars to choose from – a large romantic courtyard with a flaming fountain, a sing-along bar, and a sports bar.

Just outside the French Quarter in Faubourg Marigny, locals repair to the atmospheric bar and courtyard at **Feelings**, in the old slave quarters of the d'Aunoy plantation.

New Orleans has few "see and be seen" bars but there are some, including the chic, modern **Whiskey Blue Bar** in the Central Business District, the **Bombay Club** in the French Quarter, **Dos Jefes Cigar Bar** uptown, and several others in the Warehouse District.

There are plenty of bars in the city selling numerous brews on tap. The best are

Pick-up zydeco band performing on Royal Street

the **Bulldog Grill** and **Cooter Brown's Tavern**, which have anywhere from 50 to 100 beers on tap and hundreds in the bottle. If you want to keep up with your sports team, then head for **Hyttops Sports Bar** at the Hyatt Regency. There are more than 50 TV screens here, showing every kind of sport.

The Irish have contributed several good convivial bars, such as **Kerry Irish Pub**, **Ryan's**, and **Molly's at the Market** in the French Quarter. **O'Flaherty's** is the best place to hear great Irish music. It is located in an historic building in the Quarter, despite its name, and offers a Celtic-spirited bar with Guinness on tap and darts.

After grooving at Tipitina's, people often head to **F & M Patio** to play some pool. For a surreal experience, where you might even find yourself rubbing shoulders with a celebrity or two, go to the **Saturn Bar**, which doubles as an air-conditioning repair shop during the day. The latter is somewhat off the tourist track, so take a cab.

Street musician

Cajun and Zydeco Bars

FOR A UNIQUE experience, the Mid-City **Rock 'n' Bowl** *(see p192)* is the perfect place. The mixed crowd comes to dance to great Cajun/zydeco bands and to bowl during or between sets. This is classic New Orleans fun.

Even though **Mulate's Cajun Restaurant** caters to tourists, it is a fair approximation of a Cajun dance hall (the original hall is in Breaux Bridge). This is the place to learn how to two-step and to kick your heels up to stomping Cajun music. Mulate's also serves some hot and spicy food.

If you can't get enough Cajun and zydeco, attend the Jazz and Heritage Festival, or the Festival International de Louisiane in Lafayette *(see pp146–7)*; both are in April.

GAY AND LESBIAN BARS AND CLUBS

NEW ORLEANS HAS ALWAYS had a large gay community. It is concentrated at the downriver end of the French Quarter and in the Faubourg Marigny. The two most popular dance clubs are the **Bourbon Pub & Parade Disco** and **Oz**, which stand opposite each other on Bourbon Street. **Café Lafitte in Exile**, also on Bourbon, is a convivial video bar, while **Good Friends** is just that, a place for making friends.

The Superdome, one of south Louisiana's premier sports venues

THEATER, DANCE, AND CLASSICAL MUSIC

FEW PEOPLE VISIT New Orleans specifically for its opera or theater, but the city does boast some fine performance ensembles, and tickets are moderately priced.

The New Orleans Opera performs at the **Mahalia Jackson Theater of the Performing Arts** *(see p80)*, while Broadway companies appear at the **Saenger Theater**, a marvelous Italian Renaissance-style building. The universities – **Tulane** *(see p110)*, **Loyola** *(see p110)*, and the **University of New Orleans** (UNO) – all have concert programs that are worth looking into, as does the **Orpheum Theater** *(see p95)*, which is the home of the New Orleans Philharmonic Orchestra. For contemporary dance go to the **New Orleans Contemporary Arts Center** *(see p97)*, which has three stages devoted to a variety of performances.

The Orpheum Theater, home of the New Orleans Philharmonic

SPORTS AND MAJOR ARENAS

NEW ORLEANS is the home of the Sugar Bowl, the college football event played annually at the futuristic **Louisiana Superdome** *(see p95)*. Fans of the NFL team, the Saints, also gather at the Superdome to watch their team play.

The city has no major baseball or basketball team, but you can watch college baseball and basketball at the five major campuses – Tulane, UNO, Dillard University, Kayer University, and Louisiana State University in Baton Rouge *(see pp138–9)*. The women's basketball team at Tulane is the most successful of all local college teams.

A minor-league ice hockey team, called the New Orleans Brass, plays at the **New Orleans Arena** alongside the Superdome.

The city also has an historic reputation for horse racing, and you can see thoroughbreds run from November to March at the **Fair Grounds** *(see p126)*, or from mid-April to Labor Day at **Evangeline Downs Race Track** in Lafayette.

The New Orleans Arena also hosts rock and pop concerts, as does the UNO's Lakefront Arena.

TOURS

TOURS in New Orleans are a great experience, and if you are looking for adventure, try **Airboat Tours**, a ride with **Cypress Swamp Tours**, or a trip aboard an all-terrain airboat with **Cajun Encounters Swamp Tours**.

However, New Orleans is also an easy city to walk in, and there are numerous walking tours available in the French Quarter, including **Haunted History Tours**. **Friends of the Cabildo** also offers walking tours explaining New Orleans' history and architecture. The city has several cemeteries that are well worth a visit;

Greenwood Cemetery

a guided tour is advisable, since they tend to be in isolated places – **Save Our Cemeteries** offers tours of several. To experience the haunted history of the city, its voodoo traditions, and vampire stories, contact the **New Orleans Historic Voodoo Museum and Tours** *(see p77)*, which offers day and night tours through cemeteries and other supposedly haunted places.

There are several companies that offer sightseeing tours throughout New Orleans, to the plantations, and into Cajun Country, and the best of these are **New Orleans Tours Inc.** and **Tours by Isabelle**.

DIRECTORY

NEW ORLEANS' BEST JAZZ SPOTS

Donna's Bar & Grill
800 N Rampart St. **Map** 4
C1. 【 596-6914.

Fritzel's European Jazz Pub
733 Bourbon St. **Map** 4
C1. 【 561-0432.

Funky Butt at Congo Square
714 N Rampart St. **Map** 4
C1. 【 558-0872.

House of Blues
225 Decatur St. **Map** 4
C3. 【 529-2583.

Maple Leaf Bar
8316 Oak St.
【 866-9359.

Palm Court Jazz Café
1204 Decatur St. **Map** 5
D2. 【 525-0200.

Preservation Hall
726 St. Peter St. **Map** 4
C2. 【 522-2841.

Rock 'n' Bowl
4133 S. Carrollton Ave.
【 482-3133.

Snug Harbor Jazz Bistro
626 Frenchmen St. **Map** 5
E1. 【 949-0696.

ROCK, BLUES, AND OTHER MUSIC VENUES

Café Brasil
2100 Chartres St. **Map** 5
E1. 【 947-9286.

Howlin' Wolf
828 S. Peters St. **Map** 4
C2. 【 529-5844.

Jimmy Buffett's Margaritaville Café
1104 Decatur St. **Map** 5
C2. 【 592-2565.

Jimmy's Music Club
8200 Willow St.
【 861-8200.

Mermaid Lounge
1102 Constance St.
Map 8 B3. 【 524-4747.

Tipitina's (Uptown)
501 Napoleon Ave. **Map** 7
D4. 【 895-8477.

Vaughn's Lounge
4229 Dauphine St.
【 947-5562.

Vic's Kangaroo Café
636 Tchoupitoulas St.
Map 4 C5. 【 524-4329.

BARS

Bombay Club
830 Conti St. **Map** 4 C2.
【 586-0972.

Bulldog Grill
3236 Magazine St. **Map** 7
F4. 【 895-2191.

Carousel Bar
214 Royal St. **Map** 5 D1.
【 523-3341.

Cooter Brown's Tavern
509 S. Carrollton. **Map** 6
A1. 【 866-9104.

Dos Jefes Cigar Bar
5535 Tchoupitoulas St.
Map 6 B5. 【 891-8500.

F & M Patio Bar
4841 Tchoupitoulas St.
Map 6 B5. 【 895-6784.

Feelings
2600 Chartres St. **Map** 5
E1. 【 945-2222.

Hyttops Sports Bar
500 Poydras St. **Map** 4
B4. 【 561-1234.

Kerry Irish Pub
331 Decatur St. **Map** 4
C3. 【 527-5954.

Molly's at the Market
1107 Decatur St. **Map** 5
D2. 【 525-5169.

O'Flaherty's
514 Toulouse St. **Map** 4
C2. 【 529-1317.

Pat O'Brien's
718 St. Peter St. **Map** 4
C2. 【 525-4823.

Pontchartrain Hotel
2031 St. Charles Ave.
Map 8 A3. 【 524-0581.

Polo Club Lounge
300 Gravier St. **Map** 2 A4.
【 523-6000.

Ryan's
241 Decatur St. **Map** 4
C3. 【 523-3500.

Saturn Bar
3067 St. Claude Ave.
【 949-7532.

Sazerac Bar
123 Baronne St. **Map** 4
B4. 【 529-4733.

Whiskey Blue Bar
333 Poydras St. **Map** 4
B3. 【 525-9444.

CAJUN AND ZYDECO BARS

Mulate's Cajun Restaurant
201 Julia St. **Map** 4 C5.
【 522-1492.

GAY AND LESBIAN BARS AND CLUBS

Bourbon Pub & Parade Disco
801 Bourbon St. **Map** 4
C1. 【 529-2107.

Café Lafitte in Exile
901 Bourbon St. **Map** 4
C1. 【 522-8397.

Good Friends
740 Dauphine St. **Map** 5
D1. 【 566-7191.

Oz
800 Bourbon St. **Map** 4
C1. 【 593-9491.

THEATER, DANCE, AND CLASSICAL MUSIC

Saenger Theater
143 N. Rampart St. **Map** 4
C1. 【 524-2490.

University of New Orleans
2000 Lakeshore Dr.
【 (888) 514-4275.
ⓦ www.uno.edu

MAJOR SPORTS ARENAS

Evangeline Downs Race Track
1620 Northwest Evangeline
Thruway, Lafayette.
【 (337) 896-RACE.
ⓦ www.
evangelinedowns.com

New Orleans Arena
1500 Sugar Bowl Dr.
Map 4 A3. 【 587-3663.
ⓦ www.
neworleansarena.com

TOURS

Airboat Tours
4338 Hwy. 306.
【 (985) 758-5531.

Cajun Encounters Swamp Tours
1037 Breckenridge Dr.
【 236-0898.

Cypress Swamp Tours
501 Larousini St.
【 581-4501.

Friends of the Cabildo
523 St. Ann St. **Map** 5
D2. 【 524-9118.

Haunted History Tours
97 Fontainbleau Dr. NO
70125.
【 861-1444.

New Orleans Tours Inc.
【 (888) 486-8687.
ⓦ www.bigeasy.com

Save Our Cemeteries
【 (888) 721-7493.
【 (504) 525-3377.

Tours by Isabelle
【 (888) 223-2093.
ⓦ www.
toursbyisabelle.com

New Orleans' Best: Jazz Venues

NEW ORLEANS is famous as the birthplace of jazz, and the city continues to be home to some of the world's best stages for live music. On any night of the week, bars and clubs reverberate to the strains of great jazz in all its varieties from traditional Dixieland to modern, to blues and rock and roll. These clubs are a selection of some of the city's top live music venues.

Rock n' Bowl
This club combines a bowling hall, a dance hall, and a stage featuring live music, such as rock and roll, big bands, and jazz.

Funky Butt at Congo Square
Named after a dance spontaneously created by followers of Buddy Bolden, this club offers a chic downstairs lounge and good music upstairs.

MID-CITY

Carrollton Ave

Esplanade

Canal Street

Tulane Avenue

Pontchartrain Expressway

0 meters   500
0 yards   500

WAREHOUSE & CENTRAL BUSINESS DISTRICTS

Maple Leaf Bar
A real legend for rip-roaring dance parties on Wednesdays, when the Rebirth band charges up the crowd. The bar is also popular for Sunday readings, plus Cajun-zydeco, Latin, and funk music.

Jackson Avenue

GARDEN DISTRICT

Donna's Bar & Grill
Although the decor is far from plush, this is the most convenient place to listen to the city's unique brass bands.

Palm Court Jazz Café
Providing a classic jazz evening led by great bands and a hostess-owner who loves to lead a second line.

Snug Harbor Bistro
This jazz bistro is the best place to hear the very latest in contemporary jazz in attractive, comfortable surroundings.

FRENCH
QUARTER

Fritzel's European Jazz Pub
One of the few European jazz pubs left on Bourbon Street, Fritzel's is a favorite drop-in place for visiting musicians.

Preservation Hall
This place has kept jazz alive through the years. It may be musty and uncomfortable, but the music still rips. No food or drinks are allowed or served.

House of Blues
This bar offers live music every night, with a range of different bands showcasing blues, gospel, and rock.

Children's Entertainment and Outdoor Activities

Nᴇᴡ ᴏʀʟᴇᴀɴs is famous as an adult playground, but there are many places in the area designed especially for the younger generation. There is an enormous variety of attractions and entertainment, from the thrill rides in City Park and Jazzland to a ride across the mighty Mississippi on the Canal Street ferry. The city also offers numerous outdoor activities for

Storyland at
City Park

all ages, from deep-sea fishing, tennis, and golf, to swamp tours, birdwatching, biking, watersports, and horseback riding.

Roller coaster ride at Storyland
in City Park

Supermarket for children at the
Louisiana Children's Museum

MUSEUMS FOR CHILDREN

Mᴀɴʏ ᴍᴜsᴇᴜᴍs in and around New Orleans have arts and educational programs designed specifically for young audiences. In the **Contemporary Arts Center** (see p97) there is an exhibit of contemporary art and theater performances for children. **The New Orleans Museum of Art** (NOMA) (see p120–23) has a museum-on-wheels program for kids, and also offers guided tours focused on children's interests. The **Louisiana Children's Museum** (see p97) caters to kids and parents, and is specifically designed to inspire questions through hands-on exhibits.

Three museums in Kenner – the **Toy Train Museum**, the **Mardi Gras Museum**, and the adjacent **Daily Living Science Center and Planetarium** – are well worth the short trip outside the city.

ZOOS, AQUARIUMS, AND AMUSEMENT PARKS

Tᴡᴏ ᴍᴀᴊᴏʀ ᴀᴛᴛʀᴀᴄᴛɪᴏɴs for children and grown-ups alike are the **Audubon Zoo** (see p112–13) and the **Aquarium of the Americas** (see p90–91). The Zoo is home to more than 1,500 animals, many of which roam about in natural habitats. The 6.5 acre Louisiana Swamp exhibit, the Jaguar Jungle, and the touchy-feely Embraceable Zoo are all geared toward education and understanding animals. The spectacular Aquarium of the Americas houses thousands of fish, marine mammals, and water birds. An IMAX Theater shows documentaries on ocean life, and a "Touch Pool" gives kids the opportunity to touch, feel, and see such underwater denizens as sea stars and baby sharks.

The **Jazzland Theme Park**, near Lake Pontchartrain, has

more than 30 rides spread over 55 acres. The park also offers top-rate jazz, zydeco, and Cajun musicians in a re-created Cajun dance hall.

Storyland (see p118) in City Park has 26 "storybook" exhibits by the master Mardi Gras float creator, Blaine Kern (see p88). An antique, but working, carousel with 54 beautifully carved animals, bumper cars, a miniature train, and the ubiquitous Tilt-a-Whirl complete the carnival atmosphere.

FISHING

Nᴇᴡ ᴏʀʟᴇᴀɴs ɪs ꜰᴀᴍᴏᴜs for being a fishing port. Farther south toward the Gulf, shrimp boats and the larger deep-sea boats offer a glimpse of the industries that keep Louisiana rich. Anglers can fish for bass, trout, and catfish in City Park's lagoons, or a charter boat will let you try your luck at the big fish: tarpon, snapper, and marlin.

Visitors at the Audubon Zoo

Angelle's Atchafalaya Basin Swamp Tours, Capt. Nick's Wildlife Safaris, Capt. Phil Robichaux's Saltwater Guide Service, and **Louisiana Fishing Expeditions** all offer fishing tours and/or charters into the swamp, coastal waterways, and marshes.

Hotel shuttles, licenses, camera and film, and all equipment are provided by these companies.

RIVER CRUISES

A PEACEFUL BOAT RIDE is an alternative to the party atmosphere and noise of the city. Paddlewheelers offer short excursions up and down the Mississippi River from the French Quarter wharves. Swamp tours by flatboat or seaplane also abound, charter boats and houseboats are readily available, and you can splash out and book a week-long cruise on the famous **Delta Queen** *(see p213)*, which runs from Pittsburgh all the way to New Orleans.

GOLF AND TENNIS

CITY PARK'S **Bayou Oaks** is the South's largest public golf course, offering four 18-hole courses, plus a 200-tee

Lake Pontchartrain fishing area

driving range. The 18-hole course in **Audubon Park** *(see p111)* may be flat, but the beautiful surroundings make up for it. Here the trick is to keep the ball from falling into one of the scenic lagoons.

There are many country golf clubs that allow guests, and some of the best and most accessible of these are **Eastover, Belle Terre, Lakewood, Oak Harbor**, and the **Chateau Country Golf Club**. Golf is a year-round sport, but winter is the busiest season. If you play in summer, start early to avoid the heat and the late afternoon thunderstorms.

Greens fees vary from under $20 to over $75 per person, and are highest in winter.

The **City Park Tennis Center** *(see p119)* has 21 hard courts and 13 clay courts. All are well-lighted at night.

FITNESS CENTERS

I F YOU ARE LOOKING FOR a real workout, many hotels have on-site fitness centers where you can use the weights room, swim laps, relax in the sauna, or burn those extra calories on the treadmill. The **Downtown Fitness Center** welcomes guests.

SURVIVAL
GUIDE

PRACTICAL INFORMATION

NOMCVB
logo

NEW ORLEANS is known through-out the world for its lively social life and friendly atmosphere. As long as visitors take sensible precautions, they should enjoy a trouble-free stay. The Survival Guide that follows contains information that will help you plan your visit. Personal Security and Health *(pp200–201)* outlines a number of recommended precautions. Banking and Currency *(pp202–203)* answers essential financial questions, while Communications *(pp204–205)* has information on the phone and postal services.

Visitor Information Center, Greenwood

FOREIGN VISITORS

THE CONDITIONS for entering New Orleans are the same as those for entering any other part of the United States. Citizens of the UK, most western European countries, Australia, New Zealand, and Japan need to present a valid passport, but do not require a visa if their stay is for less than 90 days and they hold a return ticket. Canadian citizens require only proof of residence. Citizens of all other countries require a valid passport and a tourist visa, which can be obtained from a US consulate or embassy.

CUSTOMS ALLOWANCES

VISITORS FROM ABROAD, older than 21, have the right to carry up to 100 $US worth of cigarettes, a bottle of alcohol, and 3 lb (1.4 kg) of any kind of pipe tobacco. Fresh foods such as cheese, plants, and all kinds of meat are prohibited, as, of course, are weapons and non-prescription drugs.

TOURIST INFORMATION

THE **New Orleans Metro-politan Convention and Visitors' Bureau** (NOMCVB) is an invaluable source of information for tourists. Maps, tourist guides, and discount coupons for certain stores, restaurants, bars, and hotels are provided free of charge. It also gives help in cases of loss, theft, or accidents, offering all the pertinent information such as telephone numbers and time schedules.

OPENING HOURS

SCHEDULES at major attractions vary, but most museums open from 10am to 5pm; the Aquarium is open from 9:30am to 5pm. Most restaurants start evening service at 5pm and continue until 11pm or until the last guest leaves. Banks are open from 9am to 3pm. Souvenir stores in the French Quarter are open till late, but most other places operate from 10am to 6pm. Some bars in New Orleans stay busy all day and all night, every day of the year. Live music usually starts at 10pm, and it is a tradition not to close the place until the last guest leaves.

ADMISSION CHARGES

ADMISSION CHARGES to museums range between $5 and $10, with up to 50 percent discounts to students (with ID cards) and senior citizens. Children under 12 do not pay in some museums. Many museums do not charge entrance fees but welcome a donation, while in others it is possible to buy membership. Most museums also have guided tours, souvenir stores, publications, independent exhibitions, and other events.

ETIQUETTE

SMOKING IS PROHIBITED in many public buildings, including stores and restaurants. Check for no-smoking signs before lighting up, or smoke outside if you are unsure. The legal age for drinking alcohol is 21; people up to age 30 may be asked to show photo identification to get into bars and to buy alcohol.

No-smoking area in Tujagues restaurant, French Quarter

Tipping is expected for most services; tip 15–20 percent of the bill in restaurants, give $1 per bag to porters, and $1 to valet parking attendants. Bartenders expect 50 cents to $1 per drink. It is permissible to consume alcoholic drinks on the street in New Orleans, but they must be in plastic containers called "go cups".

ALCOHOL AND DRIVING

IN THE US, penalties for driving under the influence of alcohol are severe. You can lose your driver's license or spend a night in jail. If you drink, ask someone else to drive your car, or take a taxi home.

Parking sign

DISABLED TRAVELERS

FACILITIES for the physically impaired can be found all around the city; these include special parking spaces, and access and interior facilities, such as elevators or moving ramps in museums. Many historic buildings, though, do not have these facilities, nor do most restaurants and bars. Disabled visitors should ask about these in advance. At the airport, facilities for the disabled are strategically placed. The Riverfront streetcar route and some buses have special ramps for wheelchairs. A number of cinemas and theaters have access ramps and may also have specially equipped bathrooms. When making a hotel reservation, ask for these services and check the width of the entrance and the rooms' doors.

ELECTRICAL APPLIANCES

ELECTRICAL CURRENT flows at 110 volts AC (alternating current), and appliances require two-prong plugs. Some non-US appliances will require both a plug converter and a 110–120-volt adaptor, compatible with

the US electricity system. Most hotels have hairdryers and sockets for electrical shavers.

CONVERSION CHART

US Standard to Metric

Bear in mind that 1 US pint (0.5 liter) is a smaller measure than 1 UK pint (0.6 liter).
1 inch = 2.54 centimeters
1 foot = 30 centimeters
1 mile = 1.6 kilometers
1 ounce = 28 grams
1 pound = 454 grams
1 US quart = 0.947 liter
1 US gallon = 3.8 liters

Metric to US Standard

1 centimeter = 0.4 inch
1 meter = 3 feet 3 inches
1 kilometer = 0.6 miles
1 gram = 0.04 ounce
1 kilogram = 2.2 pounds
1 liter = 1.1 US quarts

SENIOR CITIZENS

ANYONE over the age of 65 is eligible for various discounts with proof of age, including up to 50 percent off the entry fee for museums and galleries. Contact the **American Association of Retired Persons** for details. Also, try the international senior travel organization **Elderhostel**. For car rental, you may need to show your passport, and you must have a valid driver's license.

TAX FREE SHOPPING

LOUISIANA tax-free shopping is designed to promote international tourism in Louisiana by giving a refund on sales taxes at participating merchants. It applies to those who can show a foreign passport, an international travel ticket, and who will be in the country for less than 90 days. All shops in the airport have tax-free shopping, as do several businesses throughout the city. Refunds and information can be obtained at the **Tax Free Counter**, located on the upper level of the main terminal of the International Airport.

Tax free logo

Personal Security and Health

NEW ORLEANS is a very friendly city, and you can expect people to help you if anything goes wrong. However, as in any large city, you must take some basic precautions for safety. It is important to know how to identify and locate law enforcement officers, and also to identify the less safe areas of the city. Always check with friends and hotel staff before going out in the evening. It is also important to know how to find medical help if necessary. Although weather is generally good, New Orleans experiences some extreme weather, with high humidity in the summer and occasional strong hurricanes.

LAW ENFORCEMENT

THE NEW ORLEANS Police Department has three divisions: one on foot, a second on motorcycles, and a third in patrol cars. All three patrol the city streets, especially in the most popular areas, such as the French Quarter, the Garden District, and the Central Business District. Because New Orleans has a lively nightlife, there is a strong police presence 24 hours a day.

GUIDELINES ON SAFETY

NEW ORLEANS has made great strides in reducing the high crime rates but visitors still need to be vigilant in order to deter muggers. Stay in a large group, if possible, when sightseeing out of doors and do not attempt to challenge a thief – no camera or piece of jewelry is worth the risk. Police officers regularly patrol the tourist areas, but it is still advisable to use common sense, and to stay alert. Try not to advertise the fact that you are a visitor: prepare the day's itinerary in advance, and study your map before you set off. Avoid wearing expensive jewelry, and carry your camera or camcorder securely. Only carry small amounts of cash; credit cards and traveler's checks are a more secure option. Keep these close to your body in a money belt or inside pocket.

Before you leave home, take a photocopy of important documents, including your passport and visa, and keep them with you, separate from the originals. Also make a note of your credit card numbers, in the event of their being stolen. Keep an eye on your belongings at all times, whether checking into or out of a hotel, standing at the airport, or sitting in a bar or restaurant. Keep any valuables in your hotel safe, as most hotels will not guarantee their security if they are left in your room. Also be careful not to tell strangers where you are staying or to let anyone you do not know into your room.

When parking your car, avoid dark or quiet streets, and whenever possible use well-lit public parking lots or the valet parking services of hotels and restaurants.

STAYING SAFE IN NEW ORLEANS

THE STREETS of New Orleans are safe just as long as you keep certain safety measures in mind. The police run constant watches around the French Quarter. The

Policeman   **Fireman**

Quarter's nightlife is characterized by high levels of alcohol consumption, and you can avoid trouble by steering clear of drunken revelers.

Always use a taxi in the "back of the Quarter" area, from Rampart Street to Interstate 10. Do not travel by foot alone outside of the French Quarter at night. In general, if you feel insecure, find a taxi.

LOST PROPERTY

EVEN THOUGH you have only a slim chance of retrieving stolen or lost property, it is important to report the loss to the police. Keep a copy of the police report if you are planning to make

Police vehicle

Fire engine

Walgreens, one of the city's 24-hour pharmacies

an insurance claim. Most credit card companies have toll-free numbers for reporting a loss, as do Thomas Cook and American Express for lost traveler's checks *(see p203)*. If you lose your passport, contact your embassy or consulate immediately.

Airport Operations retains items that have been lost in public areas of the terminal. The office is located on the upper level of the West Lobby, and it is open 24 hours a day. You can also contact them at (504) 464-2671 or (504) 464-2672. Items that have been turned in to Lost and Found are donated to charity after 30 days. If you lose items in the airline's exclusive areas (ticket counters, gate areas, or airplanes), check with that particular airline's baggage office located on the lower level.

TRAVEL INSURANCE

Travel insurance is highly recommended. It can help in case of loss or theft of personal goods, or if travel arrangements fall through.

Visitors from abroad should obtain insurance for emergency medical or dental care, which can be expensive in the United States.

MEDICAL TREATMENT

Even if you have medical coverage you may still have to pay for any services you use, and then claim reimbursement from your

insurance company. If you take medication, it is important to bring a back-up prescription with you.

Pharmacies close to the French Quarter are open from 9am to 7pm every day. For longer hours try a **Walgreens Drugstore** or ask your hotel for assistance. For dental emergencies, call either the New Orleans **Dental Association** or the medical center at the **Charity Hospital**, which are both open 24 hours a day.

NATURAL HAZARDS

Hurricanes are infrequent but devastating when they do strike. There are tried and tested emergency procedures, and if the worst should happen, follow the announcements on local television and radio. You can call the National Hurricane Center in Miami (305) 229-4483, which provides recorded information on impending hurricanes. In case of emergency, a hotline in Louisiana may also be established before a storm strikes. However, the most frequent climatic hazard to affect visitors is the sun. Use high-factor sunscreen lotions and try to wear a hat. Remember that heat can be as big a problem as sunlight; drink plenty of fluids.

There are several venomous snakes native to Louisiana, but unless you are alone in dense swamp or forest you are unlikely to encounter

Hospital sign

any. Biting and stinging insects, including mosquitoes, are a real nuisance between April and November, particularly in areas close to fresh water and swampland. Visits to parks and reserves can be uncomfortable if you do not wear a good insect repellent.

EMERGENCIES

To contact the emergency services, dial 911, free of charge, on any phone. The police patrol popular areas of town, and they have experience covering large events such as Mardi Gras *(see pp24–5)*. If you are arrested for any reason, you have the right to remain silent and are permitted to make one phone call.

Non-US citizens should contact their embassy or consulate for legal assistance.

DIRECTORY

SECURITY AND HEALTH

Charity Hospital
((504) 568-3414.

Child Find
((800) 426-5678.

Emergencies
(911.

Police Non-Emergency
((504) 821-2222.

Fire
((504) 581-3473.

Dental Association
((504) 834-6449.

PHARMACIES

Walgreens Drugstore
619 Decatur St.
Map 5 D2.
((504) 834-8281.
W www.walgreens.com

900 Canal St.
((504) 568-9544. **Map** 4 B3.

1615 Canal St.
((504) 524-2741. **Map** 4 A2.

Banking and Currency

Throughout new orleans there are various places to access and exchange your money. Bank branches are open during the week, and there are numerous ATMs. Foreign currency can be exchanged in comparatively few places, and exchange rates tend to be poorer than at home. The best rule is to take plenty of US dollar traveler's checks, and a credit card or two.

Automated teller machine at a local branch bank

BANKING

Banks are generally open Monday to Friday from 9am to 5pm. There are some, however, that open as early as 8:30am. Always ask if any special fees apply before you make your transaction. US dollar traveler's checks can be cashed at most banks, so long as you bring some form of identification that carries your photograph (e.g., a passport, a driver's license, or an International Student Identity Card). Foreign currency exchange is available at the main branches of large banks, many of which have separate areas or teller windows specifically for foreign exchange.

Credit unions will serve only their members, so look for banks that offer service to the general public, such as Bank One and Whitney. Numerous branches of these can be found in the French Quarter, the Central Business District, and also along St. Charles Avenue.

AUTOMATED TELLER MACHINES (ATMs)

Most banks in New Orleans have automated teller machines in their lobbies or in an external

wall. There are also ATMs in various restaurants and bars around town, mainly in the French Quarter. These machines enable you to withdraw US banknotes, usually $20 bills, from your bank or credit card account at home. Be aware that a fee will be levied on your withdrawal depending on the bank; always check the bank's policy before making a withdrawal.

Before leaving home, ask your credit card company or bank which American ATM systems or banks will accept your bankcard, and check the cost of each transaction. Make sure, too, that you have (and remember) your PIN (Personal Identification Number). The largest ATM systems are Plus and Cirrus, which accept VISA, American Express, and MasterCard, as well as a number of US bank cards.

Automated teller machines give you 24-hour access to cash, but remember to take care when using them in deserted areas, especially after dark; be vigilant of people around you.

CREDIT CARDS

Credit cards are part of everyday life in New Orleans, just as they are in other parts of the country. The most widely accepted credit cards are VISA, MasterCard, American Express, Diners Club, and Japanese Credit Bureau.

Besides being a much safer alternative to carrying a lot of cash, credit cards also offer some useful additional benefits, such as insurance on your purchases. They are

also essential if you want to reserve a hotel room or book a rental car. Credit cards can also be useful in emergencies when cash may not be readily available.

CASHING TRAVELER'S CHECKS

Traveler's checks are by far the most convenient way to carry money, both for practicality's sake and for security (lost or stolen checks can be refunded). They may even be used as cash in many places: US dollar traveler's checks are commonly accepted in shops, restaurants, bars, and hotels. Those issued by American Express, VISA, or Thomas Cook are the most widely recognized. Change will be given in cash; if your checks are in large denominations, always ask if there is enough money in the cash register before you countersign, otherwise you may waste a check needlessly.

To exchange your traveler's checks into cash directly, go to a bank, an exchange bureau, or the front desk of your hotel. Remember to inquire about commission fees before starting your transaction, as these can vary greatly. All banks can exchange dollar traveler's checks, but you will get the best rates in big banks or at private exchange offices. The latter are not common, but American Express and Thomas Cook both have branches in New Orleans, as well as in a number of other cities around the state. Both companies also have toll-free numbers for reporting lost or stolen checks.

American Express charge cards

Traveler's checks in other currencies cannot be used in shops, and only some banks and hotels will exchange them. Personal checks drawn on overseas banks, such as Eurochecks, cannot be used in New Orleans.

Coins

America's coins (actual size shown) come in 1-dollar, 50-, 25-, 10-, 5-, and 1-cent pieces. The new Golden Dollar, released on January 26, 2000, features the likeness of Sacagawea, a Shoshone Indian woman who assisted and guided the Lewis and Clark expedition across the northwest US. On the flip side is a Bald Eagle and 17 stars, indicating the 17 American states at the time of the exploration.

25-cent coin (a quarter)

10-cent coin (a dime)

5-cent coin (a nickel)

1-cent coin (a penny)

$1 coin

Bank Notes

The Golden Dollar has not replaced the dollar bill, which is still the more widely used form of this unit of currency. Paper bills were first issued in 1862 when coins were in short supply, and the Civil War needed financing. The size of the notes, the portraits, and the back designs were decided in 1929; in the 1990s the artwork for most of the bills was re-engraved.

1-dollar bill ($1)

5-dollar bill ($5)

10-dollar bill ($10)

20-dollar bill ($20)

50-dollar bill ($50)

100-dollar bill ($100)

Communications

U.S.MAIL
Postal service
logo

Because New Orleans is a major US city, the full range of telephone, fax, and Internet services is available. Public telephones can be found on many street corners, in shops, hotels, restaurants, and bars. Stamps are available not only at post offices but also at many drugstores and hotels, and additional postal services are available from private carrier firms.

Local newspapers are useful for information on events around town, and national and foreign newspapers are also available.

PUBLIC TELEPHONES

Public telephones can be found all over the city, mainly in gas stations and stores. Most public telephones take coins only, but some also accept credit cards. About $8 worth of quarters is needed to make an international call. However, there is a growing number of card-operated phones, using both credit and electronic cards. Some of these take special pre-paid cards which involve dialing a toll-free number to gain access to your required number. Alternatively, you can use your credit card on some phones: dial (800) CALLATT (225-5288): at the prompt, key in your credit card number, and wait to be connected; you will be charged at normal rates. Telephone directories provide details of the going rates and are found in most public phones.

Public telephone sign

TELEPHONE CHARGES

Toll-free numbers (prefixed by 800, 877, or 888) are common in the United States, and are well worth taking advantage of, though some hotels impose an access charge for these calls. You can also dial these numbers from abroad, but note that they are not toll-free.

When making a local call from a public telephone, 35 cents will buy you three minutes' time. For long-distance domestic calls the cheapest rate runs from 11pm to 8am on weekdays and weekends. Direct calls can also be made from hotel rooms, but they usually carry hefty surcharges. Unless you are using your own international telephone card, it is better to use the payphone in the lobby.

REACHING THE RIGHT NUMBER

- Direct-dial call outside the local area code within the United States and Canada: dial **1**.
- International direct-dial call: dial **011** followed by country code (UK: **44**; Australia: **61**; New Zealand: **64**) then the city or area code (omit the first 0), and the local number.
- International call via operator: dial **01**, then the country code, plus the city code (minus the first 0), and the local number.
- International directory inquiries: dial **00**.
- International operator assistance: dial **01**.
- An **800**, **877**, **or 888** prefix indicates a toll-free number.
- All directory assistance: dial **411**.
- Useful area codes: Cajun Country, **337**; Baton Rouge, **225**; and the north shore (across Lake Ponchartrain), 985.

USING A COIN-OPERATED PHONE

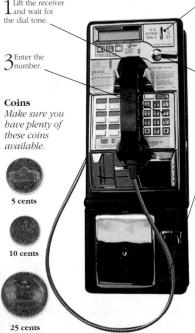

1 Lift the receiver and wait for the dial tone.

2 Insert the correct coin or coins.

3 Enter the number.

4 If you decide not to make a connection, or if the call does not get through, you can retrieve your money by pressing the coin return.

Coins
Make sure you have plenty of these coins available.

5 If the call is answered and you talk for longer than the allowed time, the operator will interrupt and ask you to deposit more coins. If you cannot complete a call the phone returns your coins.

5 cents

10 cents

25 cents

Directory assistance is free of charge by dialing 411 (local) or 00 (international). Operator assistance is available by dialing 0 (local) or 01 (international). All operator-assisted calls carry a surcharge. For emergency services only (fire, police, or ambulance) call 911.

International rates vary depending on which country you are contacting.

FAXES

PUBLIC FAX MACHINES can be found at major airports and in some stores and public buildings. Hotels accept faxes on their guests' behalf, but charge to receive and send them. Many hotels have a business center where you can send and receive faxes and also use the computer. More and more hotel rooms have dataports where you can connect your laptop.

Colorful US postage stamps

CYBERCAFÉS

KEEPING IN TOUCH via the Internet is made easy by visiting any one of the city's Internet cafés, such as the **Royal Access** Internet café. For $8 an hour you can surf the Net or send e-mails on one of their many computers.

POSTAL SERVICES

POST OFFICES are usually open from 9am to 5pm on weekdays, with some branches open on Saturday mornings. Drugstores and hotels sell stamps, and some department stores and transportation terminals have stamp vending machines; stamps bought from vending machines are often a little more expensive.

Standard US mailbox

Surface mail sent overseas from the US takes several weeks, so it is better to send letters via airmail, which takes five to ten working days.

All domestic mail goes first class and takes from one to five days (longer if you forget to include the zip code). You can pay extra for Priority Mail for a delivery of two to three days, or Express Mail, which offers next-day deliveries in the US, and within two to three days to many foreign countries. Be sure to use the right mailbox for the required service. Mailboxes are painted blue, while Express and Priority boxes are silver and blue.

Many Americans use private courier services, such as **UPS**, **DHL**, and **FedEx**, for both domestic and international mail; they offer next-day deliveries to most destinations.

TELEVISION AND RADIO

MOST HOTEL televisions have cable or satellite hookup, offering 60 channels plus the national networks (ABC, CBS, NBC, and FOX). The cable channels offer more variety: ESPN is devoted to sports, and CNN to news.

Most radio stations broadcast pop music, but if you hunt around (especially on the FM band) you can often pick up entertaining local stations. WWL (870 AM) broadcasts local news, and country music; National Public Radio WWNO (89.9 FM) broadcasts national news and classical music. The Jazz & Heritage Foundation station WWOZ (90.7 FM) is a remarkable institution, with jazz, Latin, Cajun, and zydeco programs 24 hours daily.

NEWSPAPERS

THE BEST LOCAL NEWSPAPER in New Orleans is *The Times-Picayune*, found in hotel lobbies and street dispensers throughout the city. *Gambit*, a free weekly paper distributed in cafés, shops, and hotels, is a good source of more in-depth entertainment and lifestyle news. For comprehensive national and international news, look to the *New York Times* or *USA Today*, both of which are available from coin-operated boxes all over the CBD and French Quarter. Foreign newspapers are available at good bookstores.

Local and national newspapers

NEW ORLEANS TIME

NEW ORLEANS and Louisiana are in the Central Standard Time Zone (CST), which is six hours behind Greenwich Mean Time (GMT). If you are making an international phone call from the city, add six hours for the United Kingdom, 15 hours for Australia, and 17 hours for New Zealand.

DIRECTORY

POSTAL SERVICES

UPS
(800) 742-5877.

FedEx
(504) 522-2337.

DHL
(800) 225-5345.

Main Post Office
1701 Loyola Ave.
(504) 275-8777.

CYBERCAFÉS

Royal Access
621 Royal St.
(504) 525-0401.

Travel Information

Many international airlines have direct flights to New Orleans, and charter and domestic services are numerous. Growing competition between airlines has reduced prices in low seasons, making flying an even more attractive alternative to traveling by bus or train. Amtrak trains run from major cities in the United States to the center of the city. Long-distance luxury bus services offer a less frantic and often less expensive way to travel for those arriving from other North American cities. For visitors arriving by car or bus, there can be little to beat the spectacular views of the city when driving into New Orleans by way of the River Road. If you are planning to stay in the city center, it is not necessary to rent a car; most of the sights are within easy walking distance of one another.

Passenger jet arriving in the city

Passenger jet at Armstrong International Airport

Arriving by Air

All the major US airlines, including **Continental Airlines**, **American Airlines**, **Southwest Airlines**, **United Airlines**, and **Delta Air Lines**, have scheduled services to New Orleans. Most also offer flights from abroad, but these usually entail a stop at a US airport en route. From Canada and Mexico, **Air Canada** and Continental Airlines have scheduled flights to New Orleans, while American Airlines, British Airways, Virgin, and United Airlines operate from the UK.

Air Fares

The cheapest round-trip fares to New Orleans are generally economy or APEX tickets on scheduled flights (which must be booked in advance). The competition between travel agencies and the numerous airlines serving New Orleans makes it well worth shopping around. Keep an eye out for promotional fares and package tours, which offer good deals on charter flights.

Off-season fares are cheap, and you will often get a better deal if you fly in the middle of the week. During holiday periods like December, and special events like Mardi Gras *(see pp24–5)*, seats are always in big demand, and air fares can rocket to more than double their usual price.

Travelers at a check-in desk, Armstrong International Airport

Armstrong International Airport Facilities

New Orleans International Airport is the ninth-largest arrival and departure airport in the United States. Visitors will find customs, sightseeing information, baggage claim, car-rental desks, and ground transportation into the city on the lower level of the airport. The top level, on the other hand, contains services for travelers departing from New Orleans, including foreign exchange offices, ticket and insurance counters, restaurants, bars, baggage handlers, and shops. The Louisiana tax-free refund offices can also be found on this level.

There are five Telephone Display Devices (TDD) located throughout the airport. Whitney National Bank, located in the ticket lobby, is one of the main banking facilities in the airport. ATMs (automated teller machines) are located in several places; in the East Lobby near Concourse B, in the ticket lobby next to the bank, in the West Terminal, on the Lower Level near the Southwest Airlines Baggage Claim, and on the Lower Level near the Charter Baggage Claim.

Lockers can be found on each of the four concourses

near the security checkpoint. The price for each locker is $1.00 per 30 minutes or $6.00 per day.

There is also a Traveler's Aid booth located in the East Baggage Claim. Traveler's Aid provides assistance to travelers in distress and provides tourist information.

GETTING TO AND FROM THE AIRPORT

ARMSTRONG International Airport is about 12 miles (19km) from the center of the city, about a 45-minute express bus trip. Bus and taxi stands are located outside the terminal on the first level.

There are two **Airport Shuttle Services** from the airport to the Central Business District, costing $10 per trip. To get back to the airport, call from your hotel at least two hours in advance.

The **Regional Transit Authority (RTA)** has a public bus route between the Central Business District and the airport. The trip costs $1.50 and takes about an hour. Departures for the airport are every 20 minutes from Elks Place and Tulane Avenue. The last bus leaves at 6:30pm.

Taxicabs are usually plentiful, and cost about $24 to the center of the city. In the airport there are five car-rental companies, so shop around for the best rates.

GETTING TO NEW ORLEANS BY TRAIN

TRAINS AND BUSES arrive and depart from Union Passenger Terminal, located at the edge of the Central

Long-distance Greyhound bus

Business District, a short taxi ride from the center of New Orleans. Three major **Amtrak** trains serve New Orleans: the *Crescent* (from Boston/New York/Washington, DC), the *City of New Orleans* (from Chicago), and the *Sunset Limited* (from Los Angeles). Noted for their comfort and luxury, all long-distance trains have a full complement of refreshment facilities and sleeping accommodations.

Passengers should reserve seats in advance on many services during peak periods. Amtrak offers special deals and packages, including 15- and 30-day passes that allow unlimited travel within specified zones. Ask your travel agent for details.

Visitors traveling to New Orleans by train will arrive at Amtrak's terminal in the Central Business District, near the Superdome. From here there are plenty of taxis that will take you to the main hotel areas.

GETTING TO NEW ORLEANS BY BUS

LONG-DISTANCE coach services to almost all parts of the United States are operated by **Greyhound Bus Lines**. The buses are modern, clean, and safe. Some services are "express," with few stops between major destinations, while others serve a greater number of cities. If you are planning to break your journey several times along the way, or you want to tour the country on an extended trip, there are various tour packages designed to suit

your requirements. Overseas visitors should also note that passes may be less expensive if you buy them from a Greyhound agent outside the United States.

The Greyhound buses share Union Passenger Terminal *(see p213)* with the Amtrak train operations. This terminal provides full baggage, ticketing, and package express services throughout the day and into the early hours of the morning.

DIRECTORY

AIRLINES

Air Canada
(800) 548-2814.

American Airlines
(800) 433-7300.

Continental Airlines
(800) 525-0280.

Delta Air Lines
(800) 221-1212.

Southwest Airlines
(800) 435-9792.

United Airlines
(800) 241-6522.

TRAIN INFORMATION

Amtrak
(800) 872-7245.

BUS INFORMATION

Greyhound Bus Lines
(800) 231-2222.

SHUTTLE BUSES

Airport Shuttle Services
(504) 522-3500.

Regional Transit Authority (RTA)
(504) 248-3900.

Amtrak train

Getting Around New Orleans

Bus stop sign

ALTHOUGH MOST of the city's popular tourist sights in and near the French Quarter are easily accessible on foot, New Orleans also has a useful public transportation system. Bus routes cover the city, and no visitor should miss the chance to travel on the oldest streetcar in the nation. VisiTour passes allow unlimited travel on buses and streetcars for one to three days. Riverboats also provide a pleasant way to see the sights along the basin of the Mississippi River. Taxis are affordable and convenient, and are recommended for trips after dark to areas outside the French Quarter.

St. Charles Avenue streetcar on Canal Street

RTA bus, showing route number and destination

TRAVELING BY BUS

BUS STOPS are indicated by white and yellow signs displaying the **Regional Transit Authority (RTA)** *(see p207)* logo. Route numbers of buses stopping there are usually listed at the bottom of the sign.

Buses stop only at designated bus stops which are located every two or three blocks, depending on the area of the city. On boarding, put the exact change or number of tokens in the fare box, or show your VisiTour pass to the driver. The pass can be bought through the RTA offices, at tourist information

kiosks, and in a small number of hotels. Always ask for a transfer when you pay; this will enable you to change to another bus, if necessary.

To indicate that you want to get off, pull the cord that runs along the window, or tell the driver. The "stop requested" sign above the front window will light up. Instructions about how to open the doors are posted near the exit. Make sure you look carefully for oncoming traffic when alighting from the bus. If you are unsure where to get off, ask the driver.

Smoking, drinking, eating, and playing music are all prohibited on buses. Guide dogs for the blind are the only animals allowed on RTA vehicles. Front seats are reserved for senior citizens and disabled passengers.

STREETCARS

THE RIVERFRONT LINE streetcar travels a distance of 2 miles (3 km) along the Mississippi River near the Riverfront, from Esplanade Avenue, at the far side of the French Quarter, to the New Orleans Convention Center in the

Central Business District. The streetcar runs about every 15 minutes from 6am to midnight during the week, and on weekends from 8am to midnight. Pay the streetcar driver when you board; you can exit from either the front of the car or the back, depending on how crowded the streetcar is. Remember to pull the cord if you want to stop at a certain street.

The first stop for the St. Charles streetcar is at the corner of Canal and Carondelet streets. The streetcar turns on to Canal Street, then back around again on St. Charles for the trip uptown. The car travels the length of St. Charles Avenue, turning on to Carrollton Avenue at the Riverbend. The line continues up Carrollton to Claiborne Avenue, where it terminates. The return trip is the reverse of the outbound trip up to St. Charles Avenue and Lee Circle. St. Charles Avenue becomes one-way outbound at Lee Circle, so the final leg of the inbound trip takes Carondelet Street to get back to Canal Street.

New Orleans city bus

New Orleans Taxis

Taxis, better known as cabs, are easily found at airports, bus and train stations, major hotels, and regular taxi stands. If you need to get somewhere on time, it is best to call a taxi company and arrange a pickup at a definite time and place. Most hotels have lines of taxis waiting outside for a fare. In general, all drivers are extremely knowledgeable and friendly, but it is worth establishing what the fare is going to be before getting in the cab; all fares should be metered according to the distance traveled. Some cabs accept credit cards, but always check this in advance. All taxis have a light displayed on their windshield; this indicates when they are available.

Pedestrians in Jackson Square

jaywalking. Wear comfortable shoes; the sidewalks and streets in the Quarter are very old and hard to navigate. Parts of Mid-City and the Central Business District are best avoided at night, especially if you are alone.

Taxicab

Luxury taxicab

accompanied by live jazz. The **John James Audubon**, which is not a steamboat, makes the trip from the Aquarium of the Americas to the Audubon Zoo *(see p112–13)*, taking about one hour. Finally, there is the steamboat **Natchez** *(see pp64–5)* which offers a two-hour tour in the morning, and a nighttime cruise featuring live jazz and an excellent dinner buffet. Each makes for an unforgettable trip along the Mississippi River.

Cajun Queen
Aquarium of the Americas.
📞 *(800) 445-4109.*

Creole Queen
Canal St at Riverwalk.
📞 *(800) 445-4109.*

John James Audubon
Aquarium of the Americas /
Audubon Zoo.
📞 *(504) 586-8777.*

Walking

Because the city is made up of distinct neighborhoods, it is often simplest to take public transportation to a particular neighborhood and then to explore on foot. The French Quarter is compact, and you can stroll around it in perfect safety. Only outside the Quarter do you need to watch for traffic; "Walk" and "Don't walk" signs are on major streets to prevent

Riverboats

Steamboats began plying the Mississippi River at the beginning of the 19th century, bringing new settlers down to New Orleans from the north. Today, the riverboats, as they are known, offer tours stopping at popular destinations. The **Cajun Queen** has four cruises a day, each lasting an hour, leaving from and returning to the Aquarium of the Americas *(see pp90–91)*. The **Creole Queen** has two cruises: a day trip to the Chalmette Battlefield *(see p88)* where the Battle of New Orleans took place *(see p17)*, and a night cruise on which dinner is served,

Do not cross the road

You may cross the road

Traditional paddlewheeler cruising the Mississippi River

Driving in New Orleans

DESPITE HEAVY TRAFFIC and a severe shortage of parking lots, having a car in New Orleans can be a convenience, especially if you want to visit the surrounding countryside. However, a good public transportation network and short distances between sights make driving in the city unnecessary. Driving in New Orleans takes patience, good driving skills, good humor, and the ability to read the road and the street signs quickly.

Streetcar and heavy traffic on Canal Street

RENTING A CAR

IN NEW ORLEANS you must be at least 21 years old with a valid driver's license (US or International Driver's License) to rent a car. Rates may be high for anyone under the age of 25. All agencies require a major credit card or a large cash deposit, a reservation voucher, and insurance. In the event of a breakdown, call the car-rental company first. Members of the AAA (Automobile Association of America) can also use their emergency number.

Most car rental agencies offer a range of vehicles, from "economy" to "deluxe" models. All rental cars are automatic,
have power brakes and steering, and air-conditioning. Refill the car with gas before returning it or you will pay a large service charge and inflated gas prices.

TRAFFIC REGULATIONS

IN NEW ORLEANS the traffic travels on the right side of the road. Seatbelts are compulsory for both drivers and passengers. Children under three must sit in a child seat. You can turn right on a red light unless there are signs to the contrary, but you must come to a stop first. A flashing amber light at an intersection means you must slow down, check for oncoming traffic,
and then proceed with caution. Passing (overtaking) is allowed on both sides on multi-lane roads, including Interstate highways, but it is illegal to change lanes across a double yellow line or double white solid line. If a school bus stops on a two-way road to drop off or pick up children, traffic in both directions must stop until the bus moves on. On a divided highway, only traffic traveling in the same direction as the bus needs to stop. Be aware that street signs are often missing or hard to read, especially along St. Charles Avenue.

Driving under the influence (DUI) of alcohol or drugs is illegal, and is punishable by a heavy fine, loss of your license, or a jail sentence.

TRAFFIC SIGNS

COLORFUL SIGNS and symbols point the way to the main tourist areas such as the French Quarter, Audubon and City Parks, and the Garden District. Street-name signs are posted on light posts or on telephone poles, as are directional and informational signs. Large red hexagonal stop signs are posted at intersections without traffic lights. Be absolutely sure to pay attention to parking restriction signs in the French Quarter; due to lack of parking spaces for residents, your car may be towed if you are even one minute over the time limit.

FUEL

COMPARED TO EUROPEAN prices, gas (petrol) is relatively inexpensive in the

TRAFFIC SIGNS
A range of different signs offer information and instructions for drivers. Speed limits may vary every few miles, depending on the conditions of the road and the amount of traffic. In more remote areas, drivers must watch out for wildlife that may stray on to the roads, especially alligators and armadillos.

Slippery road

Traffic flows in a single direction

| Maximum speed in mph | Right turn restriction | Left turn alowed | Stop at intersection |

US. It is sold by the US gallon, equal to 3.8 liters. Gas stations are sparse downtown, so be sure to fill up the tank before driving into remote areas. Some pumps take credit cards; in self-service stations you pay after filling the tank. Many stations have a convenience store where you can buy refreshments and pay for your gas.

PARKING

PARKING IN NEW ORLEANS can be complicated, difficult, and costly. Parking areas and garages in hotels often post their prices at the entrance. Many of the downtown businesses have designated parking lots and offer discounts or free parking for shoppers. It is almost impossible to find a curb-side parking place in the French Quarter, and many of the streets, such as Bourbon and Royal, are often closed to traffic. The streets in the French Quarter are extremely narrow; be aware that parking on the street can result not only in a towed-away car but also one that may have received some damage from passing garbage trucks, produce or other delivery trucks, or exuberant revelers. There are parking meters all over the city, but be sure to note the time limits. Rush hours in the city are Monday through Friday from 7 to 9am and from 4 to 6pm. Parking on any major street or thoroughfare in the city is

Pedestrianized Royal Street, at the heart of New Orleans

Time elapsed

Insert coins

Turn handle to register coins

A traditional parking meter

forbidden on Fridays and during Mardi Gras *(pp24–5)*.

It is best not to disregard certain parking prohibitions, such as near a fire hydrant or a crosswalk, at bus stops, in handicapped, reserved, or parade route areas, and during street cleaning. Street cleaning in the French Quarter takes place every day, early in the morning. The tow-away crew in New Orleans is very active, so be aware of all "No Parking" signs. The airport has a large long- and short-term parking area if you wish to leave your car and take a taxi into the city.

No Parking and No Stopping signs

PENALTIES

IF YOU HAVE parked on the street and cannot find your car, first call the Claiborne Auto Pound (565-7450) to find out if it has been towed away. You should know the license plate number, the make and color of the car, and where you parked it. In order to retrieve your car, you must first pay the fine, and have your driver's license, registration, or rental voucher available. If the car is not at the pound, there is a chance it has been stolen. In the latter instance, call the police department for information on how to proceed.

Traveling Outside New Orleans

T HE BEST WAY to see the areas around New Orleans is by car. Public transportation outside the city is scarce, so try an organized bus tour, or rent a vehicle. Take a day or two for a trip down to Avery Island or into Cajun Country; drive the Great River Road along the mighty Mississippi and visit the plantations; go exploring in the bayous. If hunting, fishing, or boating interests you, Louisiana is truly a "Sportsman's Paradise."

Amtrak train waiting to depart from New Orleans

TRAVELING BY TRAIN

T HE ONLY long-distance passenger train line in the United States is Amtrak. Long-distance trains have dining and sleeping cars, and in general, reservations are needed. All trains arrive and depart from New Orleans' **Union Passenger Terminal** in the Central Business District. There are always taxis outside the Terminal, and it's just a short ride away from the French Quarter, the Garden District, and the major downtown hotels. The *Crescent* train makes three trips a week to New Orleans from New York by way of Washington DC and intermediate points. The *City of New Orleans* train departs daily and goes to Chicago and points between. The *Sunset Limited* travels to and from the West Coast (Los Angeles) and also travels to and from Florida three times a week, with stops at intermediate points. The schedules for all of these trains may vary from season to season. Amtrak offers discounts for seniors, travelers with disabilities, students, and

children. There are also a number of good-value tour packages, group rates, and promotional discounts.

LONG-DISTANCE BUSES

W HETHER YOU ARE going to other parts of the country or traveling around Louisiana, Greyhound buses *(see p207)* offer the cheapest way to get around. The buses are comfortable, clean, and modern; there are also on-board toilets, a water cooler, and TV screens.

Refreshment area sign

Bus travel to the larger cities and popular tourist destinations in Louisiana is fairly frequent. Travel to the

smaller towns in Cajun Country or to off-the-beaten-path areas is not as well defined. Your best bet is to book a tour or rent a car.

Greyhound's Ameripass offers up to 60 consecutive days of unlimited travel anywhere in the US. Tickets may be less expensive if you buy them in advance, but walk-up or unrestricted fares are readily available. Ask about any discounts when you purchase your ticket. These discounts are offered to children, seniors, members of the military, students, and travelers with disabilities. Greyhound will provide assistance to disabled travelers, including priority seating and, in some cases, a personal-care assistant may travel for free. Call the ADA Assist Line for details (800-752-4841).

ROAD SIGNS

M OST ROAD SIGNS are clear and self-explanatory. Directional signs are usually green, and tourist information signs are blue.

SPEED LIMITS

S PEED LIMITS are set by individual states. There are heavy fines for going well above the limits, which in Louisiana are as follows:
• 55–70mph (89–113km/h) on highways and Interstates.
• 20–30 mph (32–48 km/h) in residential areas.
• 15 mph (24km/h) in school zones.

Speed limits vary every few miles, so keep a close eye out for the signs. On an Interstate highway it is best to drive at or slightly above the speed limit; if you are driving more slowly, stay in the right-hand lane. The left lanes are for passing only (overtaking).

Long-distance Greyhound bus

Algiers ferry crossing the Mississippi River

DAY TRIPS AND TOURS

EACH OF YOUR TRIPS outside the metropolitan New Orleans area will take at least one full day. If you set aside two or more days, you will have just enough time to savor the great diversity of Louisiana, including the bayous, spicy food, and lively music in Lafayette, Breaux Bridge, and other Cajun Country towns. The rice and sugar plantations along the Mississippi River can also be discovered, as can the spectacular wilderness of the Atchafalaya Basin.

MISSISSIPPI RIVER FERRIES AND CRUISES

THE **Canal Street Ferry** ride across the Mississippi River to Algiers Point is an experience in itself, offering excellent views between the Mississippi River and New Orleans. The passenger boarding gate is located on the upper floor of the ferry terminal at the foot of Canal Street. Passengers with cars and bicycles board on the street level of the ferry terminal.

The trip itself takes about 15 minutes. The first ferry leaves at 6am; the last departs at midnight. Remember that you may not smoke, drink alcohol, or bring food aboard the ferry. Nonetheless, the ride across the river at dawn or sunset is one of the best bargains in New Orleans (it's free), and the view of the skyline and riverfront

River cruise captain

from the other side is an experience to remember.

The **Delta Queen Steamboat Company** offers tours along the Mississippi River, from New Orleans up to Baton Rouge, Natchez, and other cities near the river. Cruises last from three to 12 days, focusing on historic sites such as plantations and old towns. There are also some cruises that travel out of the Mississippi River and into the international waters of the Gulf of Mexico; these latter are generally casino cruises, which offer dinner, cocktails, and gambling.

RULES OF THE ROAD

VEHICLES are driven on the right-hand side of the road all over the United States. A right-hand turn on a red light is permitted unless a second sign prohibits doing so. Left turns are generally not allowed at intersections.

Drivers and passengers are required by law to wear seatbelts at all times, and littering is not permitted anywhere along any road, highway, or Interstate.

Swamp tour boat moored near Baton Rouge

TRAIN INFORMATION

Union Passenger Terminal
📞 (504) 528-1610, (800) 872-7245.
🅦 www.amtrak.com

MISSISSIPPI RIVER FERRIES AND CRUISES

Canal Street Ferry
Foot of Canal St.

Delta Queen Steamboat Company
📞 (800) 543-1949.

DAY TRIP TOURS

Gray Line
📞 (504) 587-0861.

New Orleans Tours
📞 (504) 592-1991.

Tours by Isabelle
📞 (504) 391-3544.

American Acadian
📞 (504) 467-1734.

Cypress Swamp Tours
📞 (504) 581-4501.

Chacahoula Tours
📞 (504) 436-2640.

Honey Islands Swamp Tours
📞 (504) 242-5877, (985) 641-1769.

The AAA (Automobile Association of America) offers maps, emergency roadside services, and discounts at hotels and restaurants and various tourist spots. The Association is linked with numerous automobile clubs abroad, so it is worth finding out if your home club has reciprocity with the AAA. Alternatively, many rental cars offer roadside service for an extra charge.

Be aware that many roads out in Cajun Country may be under water at certain times of the year. Watch for pedestrians, cane trucks, oil tankers, and loose cattle when driving.

STREET FINDER

THE MAP REFERENCES given with all sights and venues described in this book refer to the maps in this section. A complete index of street names and all the places of interest marked on the Street Finder can be found on the pages following the maps. The key, set out below, indicates the scales of the maps and shows what other features are marked on them, including transport terminals, hospitals, post offices, emergency services, churches, and information centers. The maps include not only the sight-seeing areas (which are color-coded), but the whole of central New Orleans and all the districts important for hotels *(see pp152–163)*, restaurants *(see pp164–181)*, shopping *(see pp182–187)*, and entertainment *(see pp188–195)*. The map on the back inside cover shows the city's public transport routes.

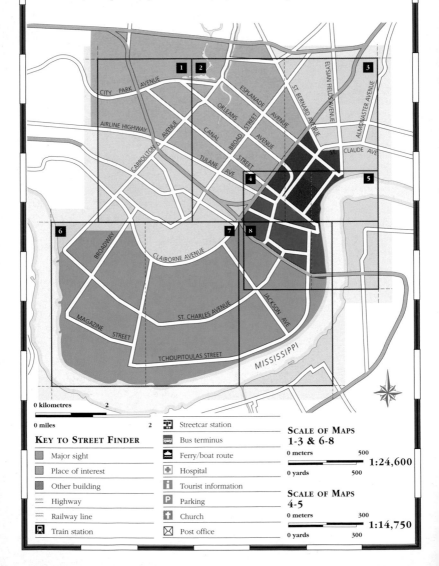

| 0 kilometres | 2 |
| 0 miles | 2 |

KEY TO STREET FINDER

- Major sight
- Place of interest
- Other building
- Highway
- Railway line
- Train station
- Streetcar station
- Bus terminus
- Ferry/boat route
- Hospital
- Tourist information
- Parking
- Church
- Post office

SCALE OF MAPS 1-3 & 6-8

| 0 meters | 500 |
| 0 yards | 500 |

1:24,600

SCALE OF MAPS 4-5

| 0 meters | 300 |
| 0 yards | 300 |

1:14,750

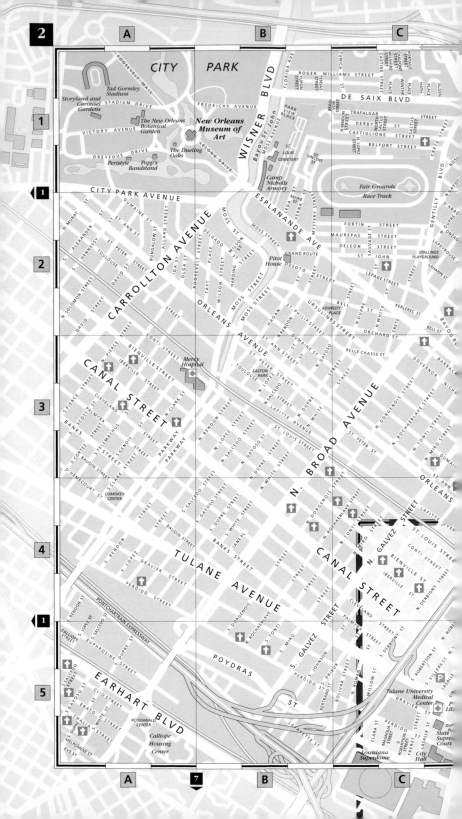

1

WASHINGTON
SQUARE

American
Aquatic
Gardens

ESPLANADE AVENUE

KERLEREC STREET

ROYAL STREET

FRENCHMAN ST.

MARIGNY STREET

MANDEVILLE STREET

SPAIN STREET

ROYAL STREET

FRANKLIN AVENUE

CHARTRES STREET

ST. FERDINAND STREET

ARCHITECT STREET

CHARTRES STREET

BURGUNDY STREET

GOVERNOR STREET

BARRACKS STREET

NICHOLLS STREET

JOSEPHINE STREET

URSULINES ST.

DAUPHINE STREET

BOURBON STREET

ROYAL STREET

CHARTRES ST.

DUMAINE ST.

ST. PHILIP STREET

ST. ANN ST.

Gauche
Villa

Latrobe
House

Lalaurie
House

Soniat House

Gallier House
Museum

Beauregard-Keyes
House

Old Ursuline Convent

Lafitte's
Blacksmith
Shop

Historic
Voodoo Museum

**St. Louis Cathedral,
Cabildo,
Presbytère**

1850
House

JACKSON
SQUARE

Café du Monde

DECATUR STREET

N. PETERS STREET

CHARTRES STREET

DECATUR STREET

US
Old Mint

P

N. PETERS STREET

P

Governor Nicholls
St Wharf

Esplanade
Avenue Wharf

Mandeville
Street Wharf

Press Street
Wharf

**FRENCH
QUARTER**

Mississippi

New Orleans
Pharmacy
Museum

**Steamboat
Natchez**

Bermuda
Street Wharf

ALGIERS

PATTERSON ROAD

WOLDENBERG
PARK

*Aquarium
of the Americas*

MORGAN STREET

BOUNTY STREET

DELARONDE

SEGUIN STREET

PELICAN AVENUE

BERMUDA STREET

LAVERGNE ST.

VERRETT STREET

DELARONDE ST.

OLIVER STREET

VALLETTE STREET

PELICAN AVENUE

ALIX STREET

ELIZA STREET

ALIX STREET

ELIZA STREET

POWDER STREET

EVELINA STREET

EVELINA STREET

OPELOUSAS AVE

VERRETT STREET

STREET

World Trade
Center

SPANISH
PLAZA

*Riverwalk
Marketplace*

BROOKLYN STREET

TECHE STREET

NUNEZ STREET

SLIDELL

HOMER

VALLETTE STREET

STREET

NEWTON STREET

DIANA STREET

TECHE STREET

NUNEZ STREET

VALLETTE STREET

BELLEVILLE STREET

Ernest
N. Morial
Convention
Center

*Louisiana
Science
Center*

DE ARMAS STREET

NUNEZ STREET

LAMARQUE STREET

VERRETT STREET

STREET

BROOKLYN STREET

SOCRATES

HERMOSA STREET

Street Finder Index

T

Street	Grid
Taft Place	2 B2
Tchoupitoulas Street	4 C4, 6 B5, 7 D5, 8 A4
Teche Street	5 F4
Tensas Street	2 B1
Terpsichore Street	7 F2, 8 B2
Thalia Street	1 C5, 2 A5, 4 A5, 7 F1, 8 A1
Toledano Street	7 E1
Toulouse Street	1 C2, 2 A2, 3 D5, 4 C2, 5 D2
Touro Street	3 E1
Trafalgar Street	2 C1
Treasure Street	3 D1
Treme Street	3 D4, 4 C1
Tulane Avenue	1 C3, 2 A4
Tunica Street	2 C1

U

Street	Grid
Ulloa Street	1 C3
Union Street	4 B3, 8 B1
Upperline Street	7 D1
Urquart Street	3 E3
Ursulines Street	2 B2, 3 E4, 5 D1, 7 C1

V

Street	Grid
Valence Street	7 D2
Vallette Street	3 F5, 5 F3
Valmont Street	6 C3
Vendome Place	1 C5
Verna Street	2 B2
Verrett Street	3 F5, 5 F3
Versailles Street	1 C5
Vicksburg Street	1 C1
Victory Avenue	2 A1
Vincennes Place	1 C5, 6 C1
Violet Street	1 A1
Virginia Court	1 C1
Virginia Street	1 C1
Vision Street	1 C1

W

Street	Grid
Walmsley Street	1 B5
Walnut Street	6 A3
Washington Avenue	1 C4, 7 E1, 8 A4
Webster Street	6 B4
Weiblen Street	1 C1
West Drive	6 A3
West End Boulevard	1 B1
W. Stadium	8 A1
Weyer Avenue	8 C5
Willow Street	2 C5, 4 A2, 6 B1, 7 F2
Wilshire Street	2 C1
Wilson Street	2 B2
Winthrall Place	2 C1
Wisner Boulevard	2 B1
Wood Avenue	1 A1
Woodland Place	1 B1

Y

Street	Grid
York Street	7 D1
Yupon Street	2 B1

Z

Street	Grid
Zimple Street	6 A1

General Index

Acknowledgments

DORLING KINDERSLEY would like to thank the many people whose help and assistance contributed to the preparation of this book.

MAIN CONTRIBUTOR
Marilyn Wood is an American travel writer who has written guidebooks to a number of cities, including New York, Toronto, Boston and London.

DESIGN AND EDITORIAL ASSISTANCE
Gadi Farfour, Christina Park, Brigitte Arora, Harriet Swift, Wendy Toole.

DORLING KINDERSLEY would like to thank the following for their kind permission to photograph at their establishments and for their assistance with photography: New Orleans Museum of Art; St. Louis Cathedral, Cabildo, Presbytere and all other churches, museums, restaurants, hotels, shops, and other sights too numerous to thank individually.

PICTURE CREDITS
t-top; tl-top left; tlc-top left centre; tc-top centre; trc-top right centre; tr-top right; cla-centre left above; ca-centre above; cra-centre right above; cl-centre left; c-centre; cr-centre right; clb-centre left below; cb-centre below; crb-centre right below; bl-bottom left; b-bottom; bc-bottom centre; bcl-bottom centre left; br-bottom right; d-detail.

Works of art have been reproduced with permission of the following copyright holders:

Portrait of a Young Girl 1935, (c) ADAGP, Paris and DACS, London 2002 - 122b; Woman in an Armchair, 1960 (c) Succession Picasso/DACS 2002 - 120cla.

The Publisher would like to thank the following individuals, companies and picture libraries for their kind permission to reproduce their photographs: Aquarium of the Americas: David Bull/Audubon Nature Institute, New Orleans 27cr; 90tr/cra/bl/br; 91tl/cra/bl.

Corbis: 129 (insert); Bettmann 34cla, 35tr/tl/crb; Philip Gould 34bl; Robert Holmes 47tl, 128-9, 193bl; Francis G. Mayer 35bl; Underwood & Underwood 34br. Corel Stock Photo Library: 22tl, 23tr/b, 199cl; 201b, 202tl, 204cr, 204clb, 206t/c/b, 212t, 207t/b. Historic New Orleans Collection: Jan Brantley 15bl, 16t, 17tr/bl, 18tr/c, 19tr/clb, 29tl, 30cla, 60-1 (except 61cl/br). IMAX Theatre: 91br.

Lousiana Office of Tourism: 198cla. McIlhenny Company: 149t. NASA: 10bl; New Orleans Metropolitan Convention and Visitors Bureau: Richard Nowitz 22cr, 26, 30br, 62-3; Ann Purcell 52tr; Carl Purcell 25tl, 27tl, 41cl, 49br, 196-7; Celeste Relle 92-3; Jeff Strout 24-5c , 25tl, 40bl, 43c.

COVER:
All special photography except Corbis: F/C bc; Image Bank/Getty Images: Harald Sund F/C cr; Richard Nowitz: B/C br; Andrea Pistolesi: F/C t; Redferns: Leon Morris F/C cl; David Redfern F/C bl; World Pictures: F/C c, spine t.

All other images © Dorling Kindersley. For further information see:
www.dkimages.com

PHRASE BOOK

SOUTH LOUISIANA has a rich heritage of blending its disparate cultures, and New Orleans is no exception. French, Spanish, Cajun French, Creole French, English, German, and even some Native American words have all been mixed together into a New Orleans patois. The following is a list of the most frequently used words and phrases, plus a guide to correct pronunciation.

WORDS AND PHRASES

armoire	(arm-wah) **cupboard or wardrobe**
arpent	**measure of 180 ft (55 m)**
au dit	(oh-dee) **ditto or "the same"**
aw-right	**accepted greeting or acclamation on meeting friends or acquaintances**
banquette	(ban-ket) **sidewalk**
baptiser	(bap-tee-zay) **to give a name to something**
bateau	**boat**
bayou	(bay-you or by'a) **a waterway or creek**
boeuf	(berf) **cow, meat, steak**
Boureé	**Cajun card game**
boursillage	(boor-sill-arge) **mixture of Spanish moss and mud, used to insulate walls**
brulé	(bru-lay) **burned, toasted (as in** *café brulé***)**
cabinette	**outhouse**
cocodrie	**alligator**
Cajun	**descendants of the Acadians who settled in South Louisiana in the 18th century**
charivari	(shi-va-ree) **noisy mock serenade to a newly married older couple**
chaudron	**a cauldron or large kettle**
cher	(share) **widespread term of endearment in Cajun French**
cold drink	**soda with ice**
coulée	(cool-ay) **ravine or gully**
Creole	**descendant of original French or Spanish settlers**
Creole of color	**descendant of French or Spanish settlers with African blood**
doubloons	**aluminum coins thrown to Mardi Gras crowds**
dressin' room	**polite term for the bathroom**
fais-do-do	(fay-doh-doh) **literally "go to sleep"; Cajun term for a community dance where parents bring their children, who often fall asleep to the music**
fourche	**the fork of a creek (as in Bayou Lafourche)**
gallery	**balcony or porch**
gris-gris	(gree-gree) **voodoo charm**
Guignolée	**New Year's Eve celebration**
jour de l'An	**New Year's Day**
krewe	**private club that sponsors a parade and a ball during Mardi Gras**
lagniappe	(lan-yap) **"something extra" at no cost**
levee	**embankment for flood control or riverside landing**
neutral ground	**the median of a large avenue or street (the St. Charles Avenue streetcar runs on the neutral ground)**
nonc	**uncle**
nutria	**South American rodent imported to Louisiana in the late 18th century. The nutria is an important part of the fur industry**
ouaouaron	(wah-wah-rohn) **bullfrog**
parish	**civil and political division in Louisiana (like a county)**
patois	(pat-wah) **dialect: different Cajun communities speak their own patois**
pirogue	(pee-row) **long, shallow canoe**
praline	(praw-LEEN) **candy made with sugar, cream, and pecans, very popular in New Orleans**
rat de bois	(rat-de-bwah) **opossum**
shotgun house	**long, narrow house**
T or Ti	**petite, junior, a nickname (T-frere = baby brother)**

Vieux Carré (voo-cah-RAY) **literally "Old Square", the French Quarter**

ward **political division of New Orleans**

where y'at? **how are you?**

STREET AND TOWN NAMES

Atchafalaya (chaf-fly) **large (800,000 acres) swampy wilderness area in South Louisiana**

Tchoupitoulas St. (chop-a-TOOL-us)

Burgundy St. (bur-GUN-dy)

Chartres St. (CHART-ers)

Euterpe St. (YOU-terp)

Melpomene Ave. (MEL-pom-meen)

Metairie (MET'ry) **suburb of New Orleans**

Terpsichore St. (TERP-si-core)

Opelousas Ave. (opp-a-LOO-sas)

Lafayette (laugh-e-YET) **unofficial capital of Cajun Country**

Plaquemine (PLACK-a-meen) **town and parish south of Baton Rouge**

Baton Rouge (bat'n ROOZH) **capital of Louisiana**

Thibodeaux (TIBB-a-doh) **common surname, also a town in Cajun Country**

Natchitoches (NACK-uh-dish) **oldest town in the Louisiana Purchase area**

Ponchatoula (ponch-a TOOL-ah) **town on the north shore of Lake Pontchartrain**

CAJUN & CREOLE COOKING

andouille **pork and garlic sausage**

beignet **square, deep-fried doughnut, dusted with powdered sugar**

boudin **spicy pork, rice, and onion sausage**

bread pudding **French bread soaked in milk and egg, baked, and served with whiskey sauce**

bouillabaisse **French seafood stew**

café au lait **dark roast coffee served with steamed milk**

chicory **coffee additive, made of roasted, ground roots**

crawfish (cray-fish) **often called "mudbugs," a delicious, small, lobster-like crustacean found in the creeks and bayous in Louisiana**

dirty rice **rice mixed with chicken gizzards and livers, green pepper, onions, and spices**

etouffée **method of cooking crawfish or shrimp, simmered with vegetables**

filé **ground sassafras leaves, used to thicken gumbo**

grillades **meat smothered with thick tomato gravy, always served with grits**

grits **ground, hulled corn, cooked and served with butter, salt, and pepper**

gumbo **spicy soup with okra, tomatoes, seafood, served over rice**

jambalaya **thick stew of rice, sausage, seafood, vegetables, and spices**

muffuletta **huge sandwich of cold cuts, cheese, and olive salad, served on Italian bread**

okra **pod vegetable, usually served in gumbo**

oysters Rockefeller **oysters on the half shell, covered with a creamy spinach sauce, and baked on a bed of salt**

po'boy **sandwich of fried seafood, roast beef, ham, or a mixture, served on French bread**

remoulade **spicy mayonnaise-based seafood sauce**

roux **mixture of butter and flour, mixed with water and seasonings; used as a base for many soups, gravies, and sauces**

shrimp Creole **shrimp cooked with tomato sauce and seasoned with onions, green pepper, celery, and garlic**

Tabasco™ **hot, red pepper sauce made only at Avery Island; often used for any brand of pepper sauce, of which there are hundreds of brands available**

tasso **local highly seasoned smoked ham**

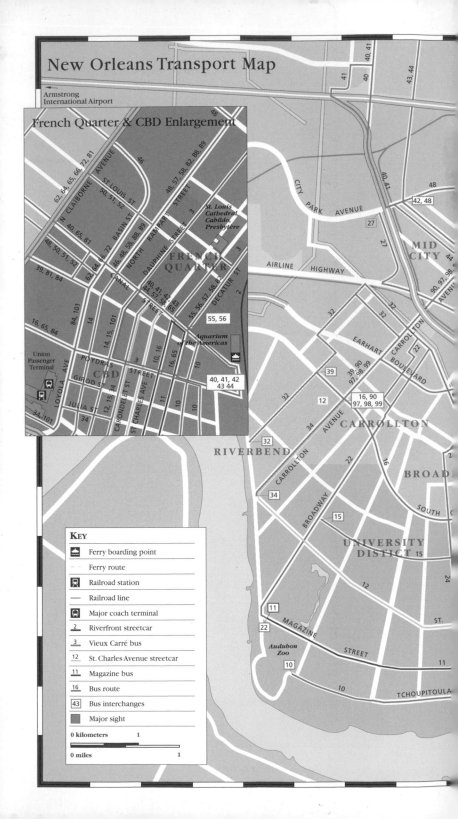